FEMINIST READINGS OF SHAKESPEARE

Literary studies have been transformed in the last twenty years by a number of new approaches which have challenged traditional assumptions and traditional ways of reading. Critics of Shakespeare and English Renaissance literature have been at the forefront of these developments, and feminist criticism has proved to be one of the most important areas of productivity and change.

'Feminist Readings of Shakespeare' is a series of five generically based books by leading feminist critics from Britain, continental Europe and North America. Each book outlines and engages with the current positions and debates within the field of feminist criticism and in addition provides an original feminist reading of the texts in question. While the authors share a commitment to feminist values, the books are not uniform in their approach but rather exemplify the richness and diversity of feminist criticism today.

ENGENDERING A NATION: A FEMINIST ACCOUNT OF
SHAKESPEARE'S ENGLISH HISTORIES
Jean E. Howard and Phyllis Rackin

ROMAN SHAKESPEARE: WARRIORS, WOUNDS, AND WOMEN
Coppélia Kahn

ENGENDERING A NATION

Engendering a Nation employs a sophisticated feminist analysis to examine the place of gender in contesting representations of nationhood in early modern England.

Taking the Shakespearean history play as their point of departure, the authors argue that the transition from dynastic kingdom to modern nation was integrally connected to shifts in cultural understandings of gender, and the social roles available to men and women. The cultural centrality of the Elizabethan theatre made it an important arena for staging the diverse and contradictory elements of this transition.

Engendering a Nation makes an original and topical contribution to the study of Shakespeare's history plays, and will be especially valuable to students and scholars with an interest in where feminist and historicist approaches to the Renaissance intersect.

Jean E. Howard is Professor of English and Comparative Literature at Columbia University. **Phyllis Rackin** is Professor of English in General Honours at the University of Pennsylvania. Both have published widely in the field of Renaissance studies.

ENGENDERING A NATION

A feminist account of
Shakespeare's English histories

*Jean E. Howard and
Phyllis Rackin*

London and New York

First published 1997
by Routledge
11 New Fetter Lane, London EC4P 4EE
29 West 35th Street, New York, NY 10001

© 1997 Jean E. Howard and Phyllis Rackin

Typeset in Garamond by
Ponting–Green Publishing Services, Chesham,
Buckinghamshire
Printed and bound in Great Britain by
Biddles Ltd, Guildford and King's Lynn

British Library Cataloguing in Publication Data
A catalogue record for this book is available from the
British Library

Library of Congress Cataloging in Publication Data
Howard, Jean E. (Jean Elizabeth)
Engendering a nation: a feminist account of
Shakespeare's English histories / Jean E. Howard and
Phyllis Rackin.
p.   cm. – (Feminist readings of Shakespeare)
Includes bibliographical references and index.
1. Shakespeare, William, 1564–1616 – Histories.
2. Shakespeare, William, 1564–1616 – Political and
social views.   3. Feminism and literature – England –
History – 16th century.   4. Women and literature –
England – History – 16th century.   5. National
characteristics, English, in literature.   6. Historical
drama, English – History and criticism.   7. Great Britain –
History 1066–1687 – Historiography.   8. Masculinity
(Psychology) in literature.   9. Nationalism in literature.
10. Sex role in literature.   I. Rackin, Phyllis.   II. Title.
III. Series.
PR2982.H67   1997   96–31661
822.3'3—dc20   CIP

ISBN   0–415–04748–X (hbk)
ISBN   0–415–04749–8 (pbk)

For Jim Baker and Donald Rackin

CONTENTS

CONTENTS

Part III Gender and nation: anticipations of modernity in the second tetralogy

PLATES

SERIES EDITOR'S PREFACE

As I write this towards the end of 1996, feminist criticism of Shakespeare has just come of age. While we will no doubt continue to rediscover and celebrate notable pre-feminist and proto-feminist precursors, it is usually acknowledged that the genre as we know it began 'officially' just 21 years ago with Juliet Dusinberre's *Shakespeare and the Nature of Women* (London: Macmillan, 1975), a book taken as the obvious starting-point by Philip C. Kolin in his *Shakespeare and Feminist Criticism: An Annotated Bibliography and Commentary* (New York and London: Garland, 1991) which lists 439 items from 1975 to its cut-off date in 1988. A glance at any publisher's catalogue will reveal that the rate of publication has certainly not slowed down during the eight years since then; it is clear in fact that feminist criticism continues to be one of the most lively, productive and influential of the current approaches to Shakespeare.

Shakespeare and the Nature of Women has just been reissued (London: Macmillan, 1996) with a substantial new Preface by Dusinberre entitled 'Beyond the Battle?'. The interrogative mode seems appropriate both in relation to the state of feminist scholarship itself – *is* the battle lost or won? – and to the extent to which the whole enterprise has been about asking questions: asking *different* questions about the Shakespearean texts themselves and using those texts to interrogate 'women's place in culture, history, religion, society, the family'. It seems to me that these questions are now inescapably on the agenda of academic enquiry, and that they have moved from the margin to the centre. The growth and variety of feminist approaches in Shakespeare studies has been complemented and supported by work in feminist theory, women's history, the study of women's relationship to language,

and the study of women's writing. A summary of the achievements of feminist criticism of Shakespeare in its first 21 years
would for me include the following:

1 Since *Shakespeare and the Nature of Women* looked at Shakespeare's
   works in the context of the history of contemporary ideas about
   women, drawing on non-literary texts to do so, feminist studies
   have contributed to the now widely accepted view that works of
   art can and should be treated within a social frame of reference.

2 While sharing some features of their work with new historicist
   critics, feminist critics have also provided a critique of new
   historicism, notably by objecting to its neglect of gender issues
   and its concentration on male power relationships, and by
   resisting the conservative idea that subversion is a calculated
   form of license, always in the end contained.

3 Feminist critics have changed what scholars and students read:
   there are many more texts by women of the Renaissance period
   available now, and more studies of women as writers, readers,
   performers, patrons and audiences. Publishers are responding
   to the demands of feminist critics and their students for more
   and different texts from those traditionally taught.

4 Feminist critics have changed how we read: women readers no
   longer have to pretend to be men. Reading is seen as a complex
   interaction between the writer, the text and the reader in which
   the gender of the reader is not necessarily irrelevant.

5 The performance tradition has been affected, with feminist
   approaches making new stage and screen interpretations possible. Supportive relationships exist between feminist scholars,
   directors and performers, and a female-centred study of Shakespeare in performance is burgeoning.

6 Our perceptions of dramatic texts have been changed by work
   on women's access to language and women's use of language.
   We are opening up the discussion of the gendering of rhetoric,
   public and private voices, the stereotypes of the 'bad' vocal
   shrew and the 'good' silent woman.

I believe of course that the five books in this series will help to
consolidate these achievements and further the aims of feminist
criticism of Shakespeare in a number of ways. The books are
generically based studies by authors who would define themselves as feminist critics but who would not see this as an
exclusive or narrow label, preventing them from being, at the

same time, traditional scholars, psychoanalytic critics, textual critics, new historicist critics, materialist critics and so forth.

When I first proposed the series in 1990 I wanted to commission books which would on the one hand outline the current positions and debates within the field and on the other hand advance original feminist readings of the texts in questions. I wanted the books to demonstrate the full range of possibilities offered by feminist criticism and to challenge the standard over-simplifications voiced by hostile critics, namely that feminist criticism is limited to the study of female characters and that it is driven by a desire to co-opt Shakespeare on behalf of the feminist movement.

Certainly the authors of the books in this series are not un-interested in female characters, but they are also interested in male characters. The first two books to appear are on the history plays and the Roman tragedies – not on the whole noted for their wealth of substantial female roles. The authors are not asking 'Is this woman a good or bad role-model for women today?', as nineteenth-century writers did, or 'Is Shakespeare capable of creating strong females?' as some early feminist critics did, but 'How does Shakes-peare construct femininity and masculinity?' and 'How has thea-trical and critical tradition represented and re-read these texts in relation to the issue of gender difference?' They accept that systems of gender differentiation are historically specific, and they seek to relate the practices of Shakespeare's theatre to their contemporary context as well as to the range of literary and historical materials from which the narratives are derived. They feel no obligation to claim that Shakespeare was a feminist, or to berate him for not being one, but they are interested in exploring ways in which his work can at times seem feminist – or can be appropriated for feminist purposes – while still being totally consistent with Renais-sance conceptions of patriarchy.

The study of Shakespeare in the late 1990s is a vigorous and exciting field to which feminism is making a major contribution. In just 21 years it has become quite difficult for anyone to perform, read, teach or study Shakespeare without an awareness of gender issues, and I am confident that this will prove to be a permanent and positive change in our attitude to the plays and their extra-ordinarily rich afterlife in international culture.

Ann Thompson

ACKNOWLEDGEMENTS

Many people have helped with the making of this book. Our biggest debt is recorded in our dedication. Our second is to our students who constantly remind us what a privilege it is to be teachers and who have helped in countless ways to generate and refine the ideas found in this book.

We were also lucky in our readers, Ann Thompson and Alan Sinfield, both of whom helped to guide the argument into its final form. Ann is also responsible for the existence of this series dedicated to feminist inquiries into all of the major dramatic genres in which Shakespeare wrote. She has been a patient but persistent general editor. Along the way, a number of friends and colleagues provided excellent suggestions for making the book better and in other ways sustained our intellectual work. We cannot list them all here, but special thanks go to Nina Auerbach, David Lorenzo Boyd, Catherine Belsey, Lynda Boose, Greg Bredbeck, Rebecca Bushnell, Caroline Bynum, Dympna Callaghan, Bill Carroll, Marlene Clark, Elaine Combs-Shilling, Fran Dolan, Ann Douglas, Heather Dubrow, Lucienne Frappier-Mazur, Margie Ferguson, Margreta de Grazia, Kim Hall, Margo Hendricks, Martha Howell, Susan Jeffords, Ann Rosalind Jones, Constance Jordan, David Kastan, Gwynne Kennedy, Kate McLuskie, Barbara Mowat, Genevieve Muinzer, Stephen Mullaney, Felicity Nussbaum, Lena Orlin, Gail Paster, Jean Peterson, Mary Beth Rose, Carroll Smith-Rosenberg, Cheryl Shipman, Peter Stallybrass, Barbara Traister, Valerie Traub, Virginia Vaughan, Wendy Wall, Linda Wiedmann, and Marilyn Williamson. Talia Rodgers has provided excellent and remarkably good-tempered editorial support and counsel.

For help in securing the illustrations used in this book, we are

xvii

especially grateful to Daniel Traister, Lynne Farnington, and John Pollack, The Furness Library, The University of Pennsylvania; Georgianna Ziegler and Theresa Helein, the Folger Shakespeare Library; Wayne Furman, Ted Teodoro, and Radames Suarez, the New York Public Library; Dr Tony Trowles, The Muniment Room and Library, Westminster Abbey; Christine Reynolds, Westminster Abbey Library and Michael Mayne, Dean of Westminster Abbey; Paul Cox and James Kilvington, the Picture Library, the National Portrait Gallery. We also wish to thank Mark Frezzo for photographing the statue of Queen Margaret in the Luxembourg Gardens, Paris.

Earlier versions of portions of this book have been published as follows.

Chapter 2: part by Phyllis Rackin previously published as "Engendering the Tragic Audience," in *Studies in the Literary Imagination* 26 (1993), pp. 47–65, and as "History into Tragedy: The Case of *Richard III*," in *Shakespearean Tragedy and Gender*, ed. Shirley Nelson Garner and Madelon Sprengnether (Indiana UP 1996), pp. 31–53.

Chapters 2 and 3: parts by Phyllis Rackin previously published in *Stages of History: Shakespeare's English Chronicles* (Cornell UP and Routledge 1990).

Chapter 3: part by Jean Howard previously published as "Forming the Commonwealth: Including, Excluding, and Criminalizing Women in Heywood's *Edward IV* and Shakespeare's *Henry V*," in *Privileging Gender in Early Modern England*, ed. Jean R. Brink, vol. XXIII of *Sixteenth Century Essays and Studies* (1993), pp. 109–21. Other parts by Phyllis Rackin previously published in *Privileging Gender* (see above), pp. 37–63, and in *Enclosure Acts: Sexuality, Property, and Culture in Early Modern England*, ed. Richard Burt and John Michael Archer (Cornell UP 1994), pp. 68–95.

J.E.H. and P.R.

Part I

MAKING GENDER VISIBLE

A re-viewing of Shakespeare's history plays

1

THOROUGHLY MODERN HENRY

Twice in the twentieth century, *Henry V*, one of Shakespeare's plays about fifteenth-century English history, has provided the basis for a highly successful commercial film. Laurence Olivier's 1944 production helped to solidify his reputation as the pre-eminent Shakespearean actor of his time. Now, more than fifty years after the event, the ideological implications of Olivier's project are clear. Produced in a time of national emergency and dedicated "To the Commandos and Airborne Troops of Great Britain" (quoted in Holderness 1985: 184), Olivier's film was explicitly designed as World War II propaganda. It celebrated an embattled English nation in what Winston Churchill had called its "finest hour" (Churchill 1940), confronting the terrifying forces of Nazi Germany. In this context, Henry V's miraculous victory over the French at Agincourt in 1415 was taken to reveal those strengths of national character that would once again allow Great Britain to prevail over its enemies. In 1989 Kenneth Branagh, a young Irishman who had been raised in England and had made a name for himself as an up-and-coming Shakespearean actor, challenged Olivier's achievement with his own version of Shakespeare's *Henry V*, updated to address the anxieties and to satisfy the desires of his own generation. Like Olivier's, Branagh's film was a major commercial success.

What has made this play, first staged in 1599, the subject of two such successful movies in the twentieth century? A feminist critique can suggest answers to that question. It can also begin to indicate why all of Shakespeare's plays about English history are important subjects for feminist analysis. Let us begin with a brief look at the plot of *Henry V*. Having inherited the English throne at his father's death – along with a legacy of civil war and the

3

opposition of powerful nobles – Henry attempts the conquest of France in order to solidify his authority at home and to unify his country. Much of the play (and of both movies) depicts the difficult but ultimately successful French campaign, which ends not only with the conquest of French territory but also with Henry's marriage to the French king's daughter. When the play was first put on in London in 1599, Queen Elizabeth I, near the end of her long and successful reign, was plagued by a lingering war in Ireland as well as by anxiety about who would succeed her on the throne (Neale 1934: 351–90). *Henry V* may have been popular in 1599 in part because it depicts the rule of a male monarch, a king who is also a martial hero and who serves as a point of identification for those audience members weary of the rule of a woman (Eggert 1994: 526). Henry's chief accomplishment in the play is to lead his small army to glorious victory over the much larger army of France. The play is premised on the consolidation of national identity through violence against foreign enemies. In war, Henry's men – whether Irish or English, Scottish or Welsh, yeoman or earl – temporarily become a band of brothers, the many differences among them rhetorically and emotionally elided by the moving eloquence of the young king and the common experience they share.

But where are the woman in this male fantasy of cross-class brotherhood? English women hardly exist in Shakespeare's playscript. One, Mistress Quickly, a tavern keeper, has a small part in the early scenes. She nurses Falstaff, a debauched knight, as he lies dying. Once a good friend of the young prince, Falstaff has been cast aside as too lawless and disorderly to associate with Henry after his ascent to the throne. Mistress Quickly, Falstaff, and the other inhabitants of the tavern define the limits of what can acceptably be included within the new king's charmed band of brothers – Quickly is excluded because of her gender, the others for their undisciplined behavior. Among the French, unlike the English, female characters do appear in the royal court, but with one important exception (the French princess, Katherine) these women are not visible or prominent in the play. The French princess, of course, has to be foregrounded because she is the chief prize of war. By wedding her after he has defeated her father's forces in battle, Henry can consolidate his control over the territory of France.

But there is at least one other crucial moment in this text when

French women become rhetorically important, even though visibly absent, and that is when Henry stands before the gates of the French city of Harfleur and threatens its destruction if the governor does not surrender. He thunders:

> The gates of mercy shall be all shut up,
> And the flesh'd soldier, rough and hard of heart,
> In liberty of bloody hand, shall range,
> With conscience wide as hell, mowing like grass
> Your fresh fair virgins and your flow'ring infants.
> What is it then to me, if impious War,
> Arrayed in flames like to the prince of fiends,
> Do with his smirch'd complexion all fell feats
> Enlink'd to waste and desolation?
> What is't to me, when you yourselves are cause,
> If your pure maidens fall into the hand
> Of hot and forcing violation?[1]

(III.iii.10–21)

Later in the same speech Henry again evokes the specter of daughters defiled, fathers with heads dashed against the wall, infants spitted, and mothers run mad with grief.

The speech acknowledges what the rest of the play seems to deny, that women are indeed present everywhere in the territories of England and France and that war is a nasty, brutal business which powerfully affects women even if it is waged by men. The speech also constructs these women in a certain way: in terms of their sexuality and their family status. The women most emphasized are "fair virgins" and "pure maidens," women not yet married whose virginity is the guarantee of their worth. The potential rape of these women is meant to be horrifying, though the speech is directed not to the women whose bodies would be violated but to the governor of the town. Henry is a man speaking to another man, and what he emphasizes is that the French are about to lose control over "their" women and children. In the struggle for power between men of two nations, the sexualized bodies of women become a crucial terrain where this battle is played out.

In early modern England, fathers held authority over the households in which they lived. Servants, children, wives – all were theoretically subordinate to the father, even in those situations where the bond between husband and wife was promoted as one of affection and near equality (Stone 1977: chapters 4 and 5; Haller 1941–2: 235–72). Henry's speech depicts the prospect of a father's family wrested from him by other men. His daughters will be raped, making them unfit for marriage; his infants killed, leaving him without lineage; his wife run mad, no more a fit companion and helpmeet. In short, Henry's speech directly threatens Frenchmen's patriarchal authority within their domestic domains, and it reduces women to sexual counters in a struggle between the English and French forces. What matters to Henry about the women he abstractly describes in this speech is not their education, their eloquence, their capacity for military action, or even their productive labor. What matters is their status as the signifiers of patriarchal power and possession, and their capacity to be victimized and sexually violated. Here, as in the rest of *Henry V*, women are sexualized figures, regardless of their nationality or place in the social hierarchy. The position of the French princess, for instance, may appear to be quite different from that of Mistress Quickly, the keeper of a London tavern, which, it is insinuated, may also be a place of prostitution. But, like the imagined women of Harfleur, both Katherine and Quickly are defined in terms of their sexuality and marriageability. Quickly's hand in marriage is the object of contention between Pistol and Nym; Katherine's is the final prize in Henry's French war, sealing his power over the French king as surely as his soldiers' rape of the women of Harfleur would have sealed his power over those women's fathers and husbands. Henry's masculinity is defined by his dually compelling performances as warrior and wooer.

In 1989 when Branagh's film was released, England was once again engaged in protracted and seemingly futile military action in Northern Ireland and once again subjected to female rule at home – doubled in the persons of Queen Elizabeth II and the Tory Prime Minister, Margaret Thatcher, both of whom elicited anxious hostility as well as loving admiration from their countrymen. England had never regained the military and economic prominence on the world stage that the country had enjoyed in the years leading up to World War II. In the unheroic 1980s, *Henry V* provided Branagh with a story of English heroism of a decidedly masculine sort. Branagh's depiction of war, of course, differs greatly from Olivier's, and the two films are worth comparing on this point. Produced during World War II, when leadership at home rested securely in the hands of men, but also when the country was confronted by the terrifying prospect of conquest by a foreign enemy, Olivier's film makes Henry V's campaign against the French a prophecy of England's longed-for victory over the Nazis on French soil. Beginning with an aerial shot of a picturesque reconstruction of Elizabethan London and of the Globe Theatre, where *Henry V* is by tradition believed to have first been performed,[2] Olivier enlisted the cultural authority of Shakespeare in the Allied cause. His was a celebratory and sanitized version of the play. The horrors of battle were muted, for example, and all mention of the treachery to King Henry by the English nobles, Cambridge, Scroop, and Grey, was deleted. Except for the comically cowardly Pistol and his confederates, the English forces were depicted in idealized terms. Also deleted was the graphic speech in which Henry threatens Harfleur with rape and plunder (Hodgdon 1991: 195–6). Olivier's Henry is the perfect king of courtesy, and the English victory, bloodless and miraculous, is presented as a sure sign of God's grace to the Elect Nation.

Branagh's is a grittier depiction of war. After television had graphically revealed the horrors of war in Vietnam and in the back streets of Belfast and Beirut, Olivier's prettified representation of battle would no longer do. Consequently, in Branagh's film Henry's army wallows in mud and blood during much of the action (Donaldson 1991: 64). Branagh's focus is the depiction of male bonds and male heroism under conditions of extreme hardship. The camera lingers on shots of brothers at war together: marching together, talking together, and, above all, fighting together. In the crucial battle of Agincourt, which the English so miraculously win, Branagh suddenly employs slow motion to depict the hand-to-hand combat in the mud. Male bodies leap up, lunge forward, crash into one another – all in a beautifully choreographed synchronicity. It is like ballet, with the emphasis on the grace and the power of the male body in moments of strenuous exertion.

So just how do women figure in this film? To understand this point, let us return to the siege of Harfleur. In Olivier's version, the siege takes place in the daylight, and the city's capitulation is accomplished with relative ease. But in Branagh's film, the struggle over Harfleur is a dreadful one. The final scene of this struggle is shot at dusk. Henry's men are weary; the city of Harfleur is in flames, but still resisting; Henry, on horseback, keeps rallying his soldiers so that they will attack the breach in the wall. Finally, with concentrated ferocity, he delivers his terrifying speech about the slaughter and rape that will ensue should the city not yield. When it finally does, he slumps forward in relief. Branagh's Henry does not *want* to rape and murder innocent people: he only threatens to do so from necessity. What immediately follows this scene is a direct cut from the flames and darkness of the battlefield to the French princess's starkly virginal bedroom. Since no women were visible in the actual assault on Harfleur, the clean white bedroom seems, in the logic of the film, to stand for the private place of women and for the domestic life that Henry has just threatened to violate. Katherine, in effect, becomes the potential rape victim we never actually saw at Harfleur. In this scene the French princess is oddly vulnerable. Accompanied only by a wizened and desexualized older female companion, she is attempting to learn English by naming the parts of her body. In the process, she mispronounces words in ways that produce obscene results. No matter how high-spirited the actress playing Katherine, the context frames her as a woman preparing to be the bride of a conquering enemy, struggling to learn the language of that conqueror and to know her own body in the self-alienating terms provided by another's tongue (Newman 1991: 97–108). Like the French territory she symbolizes, Katherine is preparing to be occupied, although her occupation will be called marriage.

When the film was first released, the grim undertones of this scene were mitigated by the fact that many viewers knew that the French princess was played by Emma Thompson, who married Branagh that same year. Thompson's appearance as Katherine encouraged the notion that Henry's love for her was to be "real," rather than instrumental, that theirs was to be a marriage of love, not of political necessity. For those viewing the film now, who know the marital history of Thompson and Branagh, the fact of their subsequent separation can add a poignant irony to all the scenes involving Katherine and her courtship by the young English king. In real life, love can be as brief as was the historical Henry's reign. Whenever it is viewed, however, the scene in Katherine's bedchamber, following directly upon the rhetorical and actual violence of the siege of Harfleur, can have the disconcerting, if unintentional, effect of undermining the mythologies of modern marriage. The context of violence with which the scene is framed associates the English soldiers' potential violence against enemy women with the potential violence of husband against wife within the "protected" space of the household. For women, the fact that this space can be claustrophobic and suffocating is strongly indicated in Branagh's film at the end of the language lesson when Katherine, laughing with her companion, opens the door and with a start sees the French king and his train grimly passing by in the corridor. Harried by Henry's successes on the battlefield, the king glares at his daughter, reproving her laughter, driving her back into her bedroom. That bedroom is, in effect, her prison. Katherine has no place and no agency within the public arena, even though it is her body that will be bartered away in the final negotiations between Henry and the King of France.

Olivier's film, which cast Renee Asherson as Katherine, made the women's world less claustrophobic than in Branagh's version and less shadowed by violence. With Henry's speech threatening the sack of Harfleur cut, the ensuing scene between Katherine and her attendant, in which Katherine learns to give English names to her body parts, is not framed by displays of male aggression. In Olivier's version, the two women are outside cutting roses during the "language lesson." At both the beginning and the end of the scene they glance over the edge of the castle's inner wall and see the French king and his nobles riding out or messengers riding into the fortress. But the king waves gaily to his daughter; there is no anger directed toward her; and the war seems a distant, not an imminent, threat. Olivier's film, unlike Branagh's, does not reproduce Shakespeare's representation of the violence framing Katherine's marriage. Both films, however, follow their source in unmistakably separating the central actions of the public realm, dominated by men, from the private world of women.

The twentieth-century popularity of these two film versions of *Henry V* suggests a public longing for narratives of strong male heroes who embody national prowess through their military achievements and their mastery of the women of other nations. Shakespeare's play enables a fantasy of an England reborn to former greatness through a reconstruction of heroic masculinity and the reconstruction of women as sexual and domestic beings. The fact that this fantasy is based on a play written by Shakespeare gives it added weight and authority because Shakespeare in many ways has come to stand for England's past greatness. As the English author known throughout the world, he still represents the cultural authority that once accompanied England's imperial power (Hawkes 1986: 51–72). Shakespeare's representations of England's medieval past, moreover, have done more to shape popular conceptions of English history than the work of any professional historian. In short, Shakespeare not only represents the greatness of his nation's heritage; he also serves in the popular imagination as the leading historian of England's past. As a result, when this play is used in modern productions to figure gender in a specific way, one can be sure that those figurations will have immense cultural authority. It is our contention in this book that Shakespeare's cultural authority is deeply implicated in the production of the very ideology that Branagh's film expresses. The history plays Shakespeare wrote in the 1590s helped produce what are now regarded as "traditional" gender relations and the divisions between what we now call the public and private domains. The interconnections between Englishness, aggressive masculinity, and closeted womanhood that emerge so clearly in Branagh's film are present in Shakespeare's text, marking it with a modernity that bears investigation.

2

THE HISTORY PLAY IN
SHAKESPEARE'S TIME

There were no buildings dedicated solely to the public, commercial performance of plays in England until 1576, when James
Burbage built The Theatre on the south bank of the Thames and
opened the doors to paying customers (Gurr 1992: 31). Before that,
religious theater had been performed, usually by town guild
members, on wagons in the street; or traveling players had
performed in the great houses of the nobility or had rented
temporary playing spaces in inns and innyards. Shakespeare came
to London sometime in the late 1580s from his home in Stratford
and quickly – as writer and actor – became involved in what was
thus a relatively new and rapidly expanding commercial theater
industry. By the 1590s various kinds of plays were being written
for that theater, including a number that dramatized events from
the reigns of England's former kings. Collectively, these have
become known as English "history plays." What distinguishes
them from other types of drama is above all their subject matter.
They deal with *English* history, and they typically focus on the
reign of a particular monarch. The sources for many of these plays
lie in the great prose chronicles written during the sixteenth
century – works such as Raphael Holinshed's *Chronicles of England, Scotland and Ireland* (2nd edn. 1587) and Edward Hall's
*The Union of the Two Noble and Illustre Famelies of Lancastre &
Yorke* (1548).

The interest of the sixteenth-century English in the history of
their own country can be seen as one aspect of the complex process
by which England was slowly emerging as a modern nation state.
In the medieval period, states were typically decentralized entities. Their boundaries were fluid, readily changed when dynastic
marriages united them or when conquest led to the absorption of

11

one state by another (Anderson 1974: 31–2). Medieval subjects owed allegiance to a feudal overlord and to the monarch, but not to the fixed entity we usually designate as "a nation." England was one of the first European powers to develop some of the practices and institutions of a modern nation state (Smith 1984; Greenfeld 1992). The Tudors came to the throne in 1485, and for the next one hundred years they worked to wrest political power from the feudal barons and centralize it in the person of the monarch, and to wrest religious authority from the Church of Rome and vest it, as well, with the king. When Henry VIII through the Act of Supremacy in 1534 became head of the Church of England, he united – at least symbolically – temporal and spiritual authority in one person. Equally important, the Tudors developed a centralized administrative infrastructure for the country, making local justices of the peace, for example, accountable to London authorities, and extending bureaucratic control of taxation and judicial review. Ironically, however, the Tudors' relative success at building a more unified and centralized state created conditions in which the centrality of the monarch as the focus of allegiance could diminish. England's geography, commercial vitality, laws, and language could all become points of pride that focused attention less on the monarch than on what were perceived as the natural and essential aspects of the country itself as an entity with an organic and essential integrity (Helgerson 1992).

Of course, no nation is a "natural" entity. Nations are artificial creations, and the unity of a nation is a carefully constructed fiction. In Benedict Anderson's telling phrase, nations are "imagined communities," that is, they are communities that are imagined into being by certain cultural practices and ideas, rather than pre-existing entities that have only to be recognized and named (Anderson 1983: 14–16). In sixteenth-century England, trade between London and the rest of England increased markedly (Thirsk 1995). As products moved from Bristol to London, for example, people, money, and ideas moved with them. This material practice – increasing internal trade – helped to bind England's different regions together. Discursive innovations such as mapmaking, linguistic standardization, and the development of a self-consciously national literature also contributed to the nation-building process. In short, conceptions of national unity both enabled and were enabled by a set of evolving material practices.

It is important to recognize, however, that an imagined community can never be as unified as it is represented as being. In sixteenth-century England, for example, many Catholics still lived in what had supposedly become a Protestant country. If, to many, Englishness became synonymous with Protestantism, then Catholics could easily be seen as non-English. This was certainly the case with John Foxe whose immensely popular *Book of Martyrs* represented Catholics, in particular, as conduits through whom dangerous foreign ideas and practices entered the body of the nation (Helgerson 1992: 254–68), even though many of these "foreign" Catholics had been born in England. As critics of nationalism have repeatedly shown, the fictive unity of a nation is often created by insisting on the utter difference between those who are designated as belonging to the nation and those, whether inside or outside the nation's boundaries, who are seen as alien on the basis of religion, complexion, or customs.

Modern forms of racial distinctions, supposedly based on somatic differences, were also beginning to emerge in this period. The word "race," which earlier referred simply to lineage, designating those persons descended from a common ancestor, was beginning to take on its modern meaning of a tribe, nation, or people distinguished by common physical characteristics such as color or physiognomy (Hall 1996). By the late sixteenth century, England was beginning to solidify its national identity and its commercial strength through a vast expansion of overseas trading activities; the opening decades of the seventeenth century saw English ships sailing the shores of Africa and India, Java and North America, while English overland traders were established in Moscow and in Fez (Brenner 1993: 51–91). As England consolidated as a nation state, English traders were increasingly involved in a global economic system in which their ability to extract maximum profits from their endeavors was facilitated by the gradual racialization of those with whom they came in contact (Newman 1991: 73–93; Hendricks and Parker 1994). By the midseventeenth century, among the goods regularly carried in English ships were African slaves. In short, as scholars such as Etienne Balibar and Samir Amin have made clear, European nationalism was from its inception intertwined with the emergence of modern forms of racialization (Balibar and Wallerstein 1991: 37–67; Amin 1989).

But one did not have to look so far afield in the late sixteenth

13

century to see how much English nationalism depended on the racializing of other groups, especially when colonization was the objective. England's war against the Irish in the 1590s was often described as a war against a racialized other (Jones and Stallybrass 1992: 157–71; Neill 1994: 1–32). English texts depicted the Irish as different from the English in language, religion and dress, and even in the way they wore their hair. At the same time, the leaders of the invading forces feared that English soldiers sent to fight these Irish kerns might intermarry with them, adopt their customs and language, and cease to be English. This anxiety tellingly reveals the fragility of fictions of racial and national difference. Englishness could not be an essence if it could so easily evaporate through contact with the Irish. With Scotland and with Wales the story was equally complicated. Wales had been officially incorporated into England in 1535 and the use of the Welsh language forbidden in many contexts. Neither the Welsh tongue nor Welsh national feeling was eradicated, however, and in many texts of the period Wales is still imagined as a foreign and threatening place, rather than as a region of England like any other region. In the first decade of the seventeenth century James I tried to effect a formal union between the kingdoms of England and Scotland. He failed, and the union did not occur until 1707. In the early modern period, therefore, there was always potential ambiguity about the very territory which the word "England" was to designate. In this book we speak of "English" nationalism and the "English" nation, but with the recognition that these are problematical terms. Great Britain did not exist in the 1590s, but to use "England" to refer to any entity containing part or all of Wales, Ireland, or Scotland can be a form of verbal imperialism that elides the historical struggles, and the perceived differences, among these regions. We will indicate when, in plays such as *Henry IV* and *Henry V*, such struggles are part of the historical material being negotiated.

Viewed in the context of this process of national consolidation and national self-definition, the vogue for national history and the national history play in late sixteenth-century England appears as an important component of the cultural project of imagining an English nation. Like their historiographic sources, the plays performed the necessary function of creating and disseminating myths of origin to authorize a new national entity and to deal with the anxieties and contradictions that threatened to undermine the nation-building project. These stories had an obvious selective function as well; that is, they highlighted some players in the nation's history and sidelined or erased others.

The history play was probably one of the first types of drama in which Shakespeare worked. Of the plays we have, most scholars agree that among the earliest written are three plays we now know as *Henry VI, Part I, Part II,* and *Part III* (usually dated 1589–92) and *Richard III* (*c.* 1593).[1] These four plays together comprise what has become known as "the first tetralogy," a term used by modern scholars to indicate both that the plays dramatize historically connected events and that they were written before the other history plays with which Shakespeare's name is associated. Many scholars have argued, however, that the Henry VI plays were not entirely Shakespeare's work. Collaborative authorship was common in the period, and as a young playwright Shakespeare may have joined with others in composing these early works (Taylor 1995). However, by 1592 at least one of those plays was clearly associated with his name. Robert Greene, in *Greene's Groatsworth of Wit*, made fun of his rival playwright by saying he fancied himself "the onely Shake-scene in a countrie" and describing him as "an upstart Crow, beautified with our feathers, that with his *Tygers heart wrapt in a Players hide*, supposes he is as well able to bombast out a blanke verse as the best of you" (Greene 1592, in Chambers 1923: 4: 241–2). This is an echo of a famous line in *Henry VI, Part III* in which the Duke of York reproaches Margaret, Henry's queen, for tormenting him after his capture by her forces at the Battle of Wakefield. In rage and grief, York lashes out at the ruthless queen, accusing her of having a "tiger's heart wrapp'd in a woman's hide" (I.iv.137). This scene apparently lingered in the memory of spectators, and Greene uses this particular line to deride the rival who was obviously making a name for himself as a writer of bravura dialogue.

Perhaps encouraged by the success of these early plays, Shakespeare continued writing English histories. *King John* was probably composed some time between 1594 and 1596; and in the period 1595 to 1599 Shakespeare wrote the plays that are now known as "the second tetralogy": *Richard II, Henry IV, Part I* and *Part II,* and *Henry V.* It is these nine plays with which we will be chiefly concerned in the following pages.[2] Two of these plays, *Henry VI, Part I* and *King John*, were never published in Shakespeare's lifetime. Along with about half of Shakespeare's entire canon, they were first printed in the 1623 folio in which John

Heminges and Henry Condell, senior members of The King's Men (the theatrical company with which Shakespeare had been associated for most of his career), published the first collected edition of his plays. The other seven history plays, like many of his other dramatic works, appeared in individual quarto or octavo versions before the folio was issued. The titles of Shakespeare's plays in these early printed versions were sometimes different from those in the folio, and sometimes there were major textual differences among various versions of one play. The play we have come to know as *Henry VI, Part II*, for example, appeared in the 1623 folio as *The Second Part of Henry the Sixth*, but it also appeared in a quarto version of 1594 with the title *The First part of the Contention betwixt the two famous Houses of York and Lancaster*. Quarto versions bearing approximately the same title appeared again in 1600 and 1619. While the folio title focuses attention on the reigning king, Henry VI, whose weak rule invited usurpers to lay claim to his throne, the quarto title draws attention to the warring dynastic factions who, capitalizing on Henry's weakness, embroiled England in civil war.

How the quarto and folio versions of this play are related to one another is a puzzle that has long occupied editors. The quarto is one third shorter than the folio text, and it has very full stage directions, suggesting that it may record some version of a performance of the play. Since the 1920s these features have led most editors to conclude that *The First part of the Contention* is a memorial reconstruction of the folio text; that is, that it represents a transcript of what actors who had performed in the folio version could remember (Wells and Taylor 1987: 175). If this theory is correct, the many differences between the quarto and the folio, and the quarto's shorter length, could be explained by the imperfect memories of the actors who were reconstructing the text. On the other hand, some scholars such as Stephen Urkowitz feel that the quarto text may represent Shakespeare's own early draft of the play, that the folio represents a later draft, and that each text has its own integrity and should be studied as an independent entity (Urkowitz 1988b). The real question is whether the folio text represents the only authoritative version of the play, while the quarto is a "bad" redaction of it; or if the quarto is of interest in and of itself, either because it is Shakespeare's early draft or because, whatever its origins, it represents a version of the play in circulation, on stage and on the page, in the 1590s.

Differences among various versions of these plays can have important interpretive consequences. The 1600 quarto version of *Henry V*, for example, includes neither the Choruses which open each act of the folio text nor the concluding epilogue. These may have been excised because one of the Choruses contains a controversial comparison of Henry V to the Earl of Essex, one of Elizabeth's nobles who in the late 1590s led a campaign to subdue the Irish. When the play was initially written, hopes were high that the campaign would be successful. It failed, however, and Essex returned home in disgrace. Soon thereafter he led an unsuccessful attempt to seize the throne from Elizabeth, an action for which he lost his life. With the excision of the Choruses, the 1600 quarto omits all reference to Essex. It also deletes a number of other passages, such as the discussion in the first scene between two prominent churchmen in which they consider offering to support the king's war in France in order to prevent him from supporting a bill seizing ecclesiastical property. (For a fuller account of the differences between the two versions see Patterson 1989: 71–92.) Read on its own, the quarto *Henry V* is more unabashedly patriotic and less politically ambiguous than the folio version.

These examples suggest that for at least some of the multiple-text history plays, the differences among the existing versions deserve careful critical attention. We do not believe that it is always possible to determine how much responsibility Shakespeare himself had for the various texts that have survived, but in our view that is less important than acknowledging that there are striking differences between many quarto and folio versions of the same play. It is at least as important to discuss the theatrical and critical consequences of those differences as to speculate about their origins. Many modern editions of the plays, however, do not foreground these textual matters. *The Riverside Shakespeare* does not, and it is the text we cite in this book when referring to any of Shakespeare's plays. We chose to use this edition because for some time it has been one of the most widely used single-volume texts of Shakespeare's plays available. At some points in our analysis we supplement *The Riverside* by discussing important points of difference between folio and quarto versions of the history plays, but an examination of the facsimile reproductions of the First Folio and the early quarto and octavo texts will provide many other examples.

The number of dramatic histories which Shakespeare wrote or helped to write indicates the popularity of this genre in the 1590s. Clearly, theatergoers had a taste for these plays; and the number of early printed versions that were produced suggests that readers did, also. Collectively, in their multiple versions, these plays incited patriotic interest in England's past and participated in the process by which the English forged a sense of themselves as a nation. When apologists for the theater wished to defend it against attacks from critics who saw it as a place of idleness and moral danger, they often held up the history play as an example of theater's value. And they did so in terms that stressed the role of history plays in preserving the memory of English heroes and of encouraging patriotic feelings in the spectators. Thomas Nashe, for example, praised the genre because in it "our forefathers valiant acts (that have line long buried in rustie brasse and worm-eaten bookes) are revived, and they themselves raised from the Grave of Oblivion, and brought to pleade their aged Honours in open presence.... How would it have joyed brave *Talbot* (the terror of the French) to thinke that after he had lyne two hundred yeares in his Tombe, hee should triumphe againe on the Stage, and have his bones newe embalmed with the teares of ten thousand spectators at least (at severall times), who, in the Tragedian that represents his person, imagine they behold him fresh bleeding?" (Nashe 1592, in Chambers 1923: 4: 238–9). The reference to Talbot suggests that Nashe had in mind Shakespeare's *Henry VI, Part I*, in which Talbot and his son are slaughtered in a battle against the French in which they face overwhelming odds but from which they refuse to flee. For Nashe, what matters is that the history play lets English heroes from the past live forever in the memories of ordinary Englishmen, many of whom would not have been able to read the sixteenth-century prose chronicles by Holinshed, Hall, and others from which much of the subject matter of these plays was drawn. The stage makes the dead arise, forging a continuity between those who have embodied English-ness in the past and those who are the heirs of that legacy.

Thomas Heywood's *An Apology for Actors* also described the inspiring effects of "our domesticke hystories." "What English blood," he wrote, "seeing the person of any bold English man presented and doth not hugge his fame, and hunnye at his valor, pursuing him in his enterprise with his best wishes, and as being wrapt in contemplation, offers to him in his hart all prosperous performance, as if the Personator were the man Personated, so bewitching a thing is lively and well spirited action, that it hath power to new mold the harts of the spectators and fashion them to the shape of any noble and notable attempt" (Heywood 1612: I: sig. B4ʳ).[3] The theater makes the dead arise, but it also has the power to refashion the malleable spectator into a person fit for heroic action. It helps, in short, to create subjects defined by a common "English blood," who identify with the notable deeds of their "forefathers."

3

FEMINISM, WOMEN, AND THE SHAKESPEAREAN HISTORY PLAY

One notable feature of both of these accounts is their androcentrism. Both Nashe and Heywood seem to assume that history plays are about male heroes such as Talbot and produce their ravishing effects primarily upon male spectators. In this Nashe and Heywood both were and were not right. On the one hand, none of Shakespeare's history plays has a female protagonist. Chronicle history, upon which these plays were largely based, took the reign of the individual monarch as its point of departure, and monarchs were, except in unusual circumstances, male. Moreover, the arenas most often visited in these chronicles – the battlefield and the court – were typically regarded as the sites of masculine power and authority. When Holinshed's 1577 *Chronicles* incorporates the story of how Arden of Faversham was killed in his own house by his wife and her lover, the narrative voice apologizes for doing so, saying that Arden's murder may seem to be "but a private matter, and therefore as it were impertinent to this history" (quoted in Orlin 1994: 16). History, in short, does not deal with private and domestic matters, but with public matters and affairs of state.

On the other hand, of course, the chronicles write some women into history, especially those who are queens, the wives of nobles, or warriors such as Joan of Arc. Shakespeare's history plays also contain women characters, and it will be important to examine how the roles assigned to women change from the early histories to the late. What is most important about these plays from a feminist standpoint, however, is not primarily the images of women they construct (which are relatively few and often sketchy), but rather the impact the plays have had on the ways we imagine gender and sexual difference, the institution of marriage, and the gulf between "public" and "private" life. These are part of the legacy affecting the lives of all women who inhabit the cultures these plays helped to shape.

Despite the many achievements of twentieth-century feminist Shakespeare criticism, feminists have devoted much less attention to the history plays than to Shakespeare's comedies, in which women have prominent roles, or to the tragedies. The history plays that feminists have chosen to discuss, however, provide a revealing illustration of the impact of gendered interests on the process of canon formation. For mainstream Shakespeare scholarship, as for the general public, the canon of Shakespeare's English histories consists of *Richard III* and the second tetralogy. *Richard III* has been popular with feminist critics as well (although for different reasons and with very different emphases), but otherwise the emerging "feminist canon" looks very different from the mainstream canon. Evidence as to which histories have seemed to Shakespeare scholars most worthy of critical treatment is perhaps best provided by the annual *MLA Bibliographies of Books and Articles on the Modern Languages and Literatures*. The *Bibliographies* tabulate the number of times each play has been discussed in the scholarly literature – each of the times, that is, that critics and scholars have found a play worth writing about and academic editors have found it a worthwhile subject for published discussion. Not surprisingly, the plays with the largest numbers of references in the *MLA Bibliographies* are the ones generally considered, in this century, to be Shakespeare's "best." During the twelve years from 1975 to 1988, for instance, the *Bibliographies* listed 153 items pertaining to *Richard II*, far and away the greatest number for any of Shakespeare's history plays. *Henry VI, Part I*, by contrast, has only 17 entries for those same twelve years: *Henry VI, Part II* and *Part III* have only 23 apiece. The "ratings" to be derived from the entries for the other plays are equally predictable. *Richard III* and the plays of the second tetralogy do significantly better than *King John, Henry VIII*, and the Henry VI plays; and of the plays in the second tetralogy, the only one to receive fewer than 100 entries is *Henry IV, Part II*.

In striking contrast to these numbers, recent feminist critics have devoted considerable attention to the *Henry VI* plays. We restricted our search of the *MLA Bibliographies* to the years 1975–88 because those are the years covered in Philip Kolin's bibliography of feminist Shakespeare criticism, and we wanted to compare the two lists.[1] *Richard II* is the runaway winner in the *MLA Bibliography*, with 153 entries. Interestingly, Kolin lists only 3 feminist studies of that play. No other history play has fewer references in his index, and only one has so few.

At the opposite end of the scale, the history play that received the lowest number of listings (17) in the *MLA Bibliographies*, *Henry VI, Part I*, was the subject of 12 items in Kolin's list, and the other two parts of *Henry VI* also came out near the top in Kolin's bibliography. Here, as in the case of every play except *Richard III*, there is a striking difference between the amount of attention a history play has received from scholarship in general and the number of feminist studies it has attracted.

Although the current scholarly consensus about the relative merits of the different plays is generally regarded as "traditional," it has very little to do with the judgment of Shakespeare's contemporaries. In the case of *Henry VI, Part I*, for instance, Thomas Nashe wrote in 1592 that "ten thousand spectators (at least)" had wept at the spectacle of Talbot's death (Nashe 1592, in Chambers 1923: 4: 239) and recent scholars report that Nashe actually underestimated the play's popularity by at least one-half, for Henslowe's records of the receipts for its initial run suggest a figure closer to twenty thousand: only one other play Henslowe produced earned more.[2] Its popularity did not survive the advent of modernity, however. There is only one recorded revival of *Henry VI, Part I* during the Restoration and eighteenth century – at the request, according to a contemporary report, of "several Ladies of Quality" (Hattaway 1990: 43). By the eighteenth century, Maurice Morgann was dismissing the play as "that Drum-and-trumpet Thing . . . written doubtless, or rather exhibited, long before *Shakespeare* was born, tho' afterwards repaired, I think, and furbished up by him with here and there a little sentiment and diction" (Quoted in Ryan 1989: xxiii). *Part II* and *Part III* did no better. According to the nineteenth-century critic William Hazlitt, for instance, all "three parts of Henry VI . . . are inferior to the other historical plays. They have brilliant passages; but the general groundwork is comparatively poor and meagre, the style 'flat and unraised'" (Halliday 1958: 133).

The *Henry VI* plays still do well on stage – at least when they are given the opportunity. Consider Barry Kyle's 1995 production of them at the Theatre for a New Audience in New York. The New York newspaper critics were generally agreed that Kyle's production was a stunning success. The *Post* called it a "thrilling theatrical experience" (Barnes 1995); the *Daily News* declared that "no fan of the Bard should miss" it (Disch 1995). Even the reviewer for the *New York Times* was impressed, despite his anxious awareness of the plays' low status among scholars. "Thanks to good performances in the main roles," he wrote, "the productions are effective and surprisingly engaging. . . . [This] is no small feat. There are problems with the plays" (Hampton 1995).

The *New York Times* reviewer cited three "problems," two of which were really reservations about the plays' lack of canonical status. He warned prospective playgoers that aside from "Let's kill all the lawyers," "there are few recognizable lines" in the Henry VI plays, and he also raised the issue of authenticity: "some scholars believe," he cautioned, "that the plays were a collaborative effort." Finally, he seems to have been afraid the plays would mislead their audience about the facts of medieval history: "Relying on Shakespeare for a true account of the Wars of the Roses," he wrote, "is like learning about the Kennedy assassination from Oliver Stone's film 'JFK'" (Hampton 1995). (Of course, if this is really a problem, then most of Shakespeare's other history plays are equally defective. Richard III was actually a fairly good king, and there is no reliable historical evidence that there was anything wrong with his body. Falstaff and the entire crew at the Eastcheap Tavern are unhistorical, and so is the Bastard in *King John*.)

Although numerous, and conflicting, reasons have been given to explain the popularity – or superiority – of the later plays, one seldom-discussed factor may be worth noting: the presence and prominence of female characters in the represented action. Or perhaps we should say, "the lack thereof," for there is a striking correlation – or rather a striking inverse correlation – between the amount of space any of these playscripts allows to female characters and its status in the Shakespeare canon. *Henry IV, Part I*, for instance, was the subject of 132 entries in the *MLA Bibliography* as well as the winner of that ultimate mark of canonicity, inclusion in the *Norton Anthology of English Literature*. It is also the play which most marginalizes the roles of women. There are only three female characters in *Henry IV, Part I*, and the total number of lines they speak constitutes less than 4 percent of the script: female characters have less to say in *Henry IV, Part I* than in any of Shakespeare's other English history plays.[3] Moreover, even when women do speak in this play, the language they use signals their exclusion from its dominant discourse. Mistress Quickly uses malapropisms that serve as constant reminders of her inability to master the King's English, and Mortimer's wife speaks no English at all. Instead of lines in the playscript, her language is represented by stage directions ("the lady speaks in Welsh"), and its meaning comes to the audience only through the medium of her father's translation. Hotspur's wife is the only woman in the play who manages to speak good English, but she speaks only 1.7 percent of the words in the script, and even then her husband criticizes her choice of language: "Swear me, Kate," he orders " like a lady as thou art,/ A good mouth-filling oath, and leave 'in sooth,'/ And such protest of pepper-gingerbread,/ To velvet-guards and Sunday-citizens" (III.i. 253–6).

In the less canonical plays, by contrast, female characters have no difficulty in making their voices heard. Joan's, in fact, is the most vivid and memorable voice in *Henry VI, Part I* – at least in the folio text, for modern professional productions typically diminish her role and de-emphasize the importance of her character (Ryan 1989: 248). In the first tetralogy, *King John*, and *Henry VIII*, the playscripts assign over four times as many lines to female characters as they as they do in the canonical plays, although here again the women's parts are often cut in modern productions.

Female characters do much more than talk in the less canonical plays, however; they also have important roles in the historical action. All three parts of *Henry VI* feature women in what are now considered "untraditional" roles – as generals leading victorious armies on the battlefield and as political actors who exercise significant power in the conduct of state affairs. In *Henry VI, Part I* Joan leads the French armies to repeated victories. In the subsequent Henry VI plays, Margaret turns out to be a better general than her husband, and she has no difficulty in overriding Henry's efforts to make peace with his Yorkist antagonists.[4] In the nineteenth century, the role of Constance in *King John* was an important star vehicle, but the play is relatively unpopular today (Dusinberre 1990: 37–8). In the canonical plays of the second tetralogy, by contrast, not only are women's roles reduced both in size and in number, but the field of women's action is also constricted: the few female characters who appear on stage are typically confined to domestic settings and domestic roles – as wife, prospective wife, mother, widow, lady-in-waiting. The only

English queen who appears in the canonical histories is the wife of Richard II. Nameless, she has very little time on stage and no function in the plot of Richard's fall. She weeps at her husband's infidelities, and she weeps again at the news of his downfall, but she has no existence except as his wife.

Given these characteristics, it is not surprising that there were only 3 feminist studies of *Richard II* during the twelve years when the *MLA Bibliography* records the impressive total of 153. The statistics, however, tell only part of the story. Although there is a general inverse correlation between the mainstream canonicity of a history play on the one hand and both its popularity with feminist critics and the prominence of female characters within it on the other, *Richard III* is a revealing exception. Unquestionably canonical, it ranks fourth in the number of references in the *MLA Bibliography*, but it also ranks first among the feminist studies listed in Kolin's bibliography. Moreover, *Richard III* has an un-usually large cast of female characters: women are assigned over 22 percent of the lines in this play, by far the greatest number in any of Shakespeare's English histories.

What, then, accounts for the interest of this play to a critical establishment that generally prefers male-centered historical drama? For one thing, of course, it *is* male-centered drama: the entire action focuses on the story of a powerful male protagonist, Richard III, who has captured the imagination of scholars and playgoers alike. In this respect, it prefigures the canonical plays of the second tetralogy and differs strikingly from the *Henry VI* plays and *King John*, which are notable for their diffusion of royal and patriarchal authority, and often criticized for their lack of dramatic focus.[5] Second, although the women's roles in *Richard III* are relatively extensive for a Shakespearean history, they are fre-quently disregarded in mainstream criticism and cut in theatrical performance. Margaret, the most powerful of the female char-acters in the play, often disappears entirely. As long ago as 1700, Colley Cibber eliminated Margaret from his revised text, a practice which continues to this day, most notably, perhaps in Laurence Olivier's influential and widely acclaimed film (Dash 1981: 197), but certainly not confined to it. Although we no longer live in the days of actor-managers, the politics and economics of theatrical production still require a male star, and he in turn is likely to resent any threat to his onstage dominance. In the nineteenth century, actor-managers such as Henry Irving reshaped the plays as

25

vehicles for themselves. Today *Richard III* is still seen as a vehicle for the actor who plays Richard's part, and the fame of that actor is still a major factor in calculations of the likely commercial success of a production, as witnessed by the emphasis placed upon Ian McKellen as the star of the 1995 film version of the play, a version which also eliminated Margaret's part. Finally, although female characters have relatively prominent roles in *Richard III* – a fact which probably helps to explain the popularity of the play among feminist critics – the nature of those roles prefigures the more domesticated women in the second tetralogy rather than reiterating the dangerous, demonic otherness of female characters in the early plays.

It might seem strange that feminist critics have valued plays that represent women in demonic terms, but although the early plays tend to demonize female characters, they also record women's power as orators, as warriors, as custodians of dynastic legitimacy. Institutions often depend on the very elements they feel compelled to dismiss or derogate, such as women's labor. So long as the authority of monarchs rests on genealogy, as in the first tetralogy, its guarantors – and its potential subverters – are women; for no man could know that he was truly the son of his mother's husband or the father of his wife's son. Because the transmission of patrilineal authority could take place only through the bodies of women, it was vulnerable at every stage to subversion by female sexual transgression. In the first tetralogy and *King John*, characters like Joan and Margaret and Lady Faulconbridge register masculine anxiety about female sexual independence.

Comparing the *MLA Bibliographies* with Kolin's bibliography of feminist criticism reveals something about how feminist critical concerns can alter what is taken to be of interest in the Shakespeare canon. In this book, of course, we are not interested only in those plays in which female characters have the largest speaking parts, even though we do share with other feminist critics a real sense of the value and interest of the Henry VI plays and *King John*. Our intention, however, is to look at even the canonical plays in new ways, particularly at how, in helping to fashion a nation, they also helped to fashion the regimes of gender and sexuality that we still inhabit today.

A great deal of work on the family and social history of the sixteenth and early seventeenth centuries suggests that the process of national consolidation was accompanied by changes in family form. As Lawrence Stone has argued, part of the consolidation of monarchial authority in the period depended on weakening the extended kinship networks of the great noble families while putting more emphasis on the immediate conjugal unit, its children and servants (Stone 1977: 123–50). As countless Protestant marriage manuals of the time proclaim, the household was to be a little seminary with the father at its head, but the wife installed as his companion and near equal (Haller 1941–2: 235–72). In the medieval period aristocratic marriages were unabashedly made to strengthen political alliances and economic well-being. "Love" was a suspect emotion, connected with irrationality and likely to lead one to make imprudent marriage choices. By the late sixteenth century, however, love and conjugal affection were in some quarters being praised as things good in and of themselves, and marriage was valued as a source of affection and companionship (Belsey 1985a: 166–90).

These changes at first probably affected the "middling sort" of people and the gentry most strongly. It was centuries before the nobility ceased to marry primarily to cement alliances and family fortunes. Yet it is unnecessary to construct arranged marriages and love matches as mutually exclusive phenomena. Increasingly in the period, fathers were urged to consider the wishes of their children when deciding on their marital futures. Forced unions were seen as dangerous, likely to lead to unhappiness and disobedience. A number of plays of the period, such as *The Witch of Edmonton* and *The Miseries of Enforced Marriage*, depict the disastrous consequences of loveless matches.

In a parallel process, what we now call private life was slowly being defined as a sphere separate from public life. As with other cultural distinctions we assume to be timeless and natural, the division between the public and private has not always existed, at least in its contemporary form (Orlin 1994: 15–78). In the medieval period, modern ideas of privacy were tenuous at best. Much of daily life, at every social level, was lived before the eyes of neighbors, retainers and servants. "The great hall" of the late medieval country house expressed the public nature of the aristocratic household and the activities that went on there. It was the heart of the estate, the place where the household ate, often in the company of neighbors and retainers, the place where it conducted business and entertained itself (Girouard 1978: 34). Only gradually did family life separate itself from this public space and architecture begin to reflect the desire for more private spaces: private dining chambers, studies, and bedrooms. By the late sixteenth century, for example, most aristocratic families no longer dined in the great hall. Nonetheless, they did not yet have the private bedchambers that most of us take for granted, for the corridors that allow sleeping chambers to be closed off from one another and entered individually were a later architectural innovation. In the Tudor period, bedrooms generally opened into one another, with tenuous "privacy" provided only by the curtains around the bed (Orlin 1994: 185).

In the late sixteenth century, home and the workplace had also not yet become separate spheres. Domestic spaces were still frequently used as places of productive labor. Moreover, in yeoman and artisan households, women took part in economic production: in spinning wool, in raising and selling crops for local markets, and in supervising apprentices (Clark 1919; Howell 1986: 9–46; Weisner 1993: 82–114). As public and private spheres were gradually demarcated and separated from one another, and as productive work ceased to occur mainly in the household, gender roles and ideologies were further transformed. Valued work – work that produced money or brought public recognition – was increasingly gendered masculine, and the public world of government, business, and citizenship came to belong to men. By the eighteenth century, bourgeois women in particular were defined by their roles as wives and mothers in the private sphere of the home. If marriage had in theory become a valued affective and companionate institution, it nonetheless restricted the horizons of the middle-class woman's life in ways unthinkable for men.

The changes in family form and gender ideologies we are sketching here took several centuries to develop. We are not suggesting that they were accomplished primarily in the decade of the 1590s when Shakespeare wrote most of his history plays, or even in his lifetime. Moreover, Shakespeare's history plays neither caused nor simply reflected these changes. Rather, they themselves were part of the cultural and material struggles that resulted over time in a changed gender system and an altered understanding of the relationship of private life to the public world of the nation state. Keeping in mind the overarching social context in which these plays were written, our focus will be on their particularity. Genres develop specific conventions for representing the worlds in which they are produced. They are mediations – reworkings – of reality, not the thing itself. What concerns us is how this genre, in telling stories about England's past and in using those stories to create an imagined community in the present, inevitably also told stories about gender: that is, about how masculinity and femininity differ and about the ways those differences are to be linked to specific social arrangements involving work, marriage, citizenship, and cultural power.

Of course, the nine plays that are the focus of our inquiry do not reveal a simple or neatly developmental narrative. They are as interesting for their contradictions, symptoms of conflict and unresolved struggle as for their coherence. Both older and emerging models of marriage and gender relations were available to Shakespeare and his original audiences, and they appear in different configurations in plays written throughout his professional career. Nonetheless, in the analysis that follows, we will be suggesting several broad lines of development. First, we will be tracing the greater "modernity" of the second tetralogy in comparison to the first. In terms of subject matter, while the second tetralogy was composed after the first, it deals with historical material that occurred earlier. Paradoxically, however, although the later plays dramatize earlier history, they bear the imprint of modernity in ways the earlier plays do not

The first tetralogy and *King John* imagine the past as a world where marriages are dynastic and the state is organized around, and is conceived as inseparable from, the body of the monarch. Because genealogy authorizes social position and title, claims to the throne are repeatedly asserted by recitation of male lineage, beginning typically with Edward III, moving to an enumeration of his seven sons, and then to an elaboration of the claims to the throne of the offspring of one of those sons. These set pieces are crucial to an imagined world in which legitimacy descends through a blood line. In these early plays, women, often tainted by insinuations of sexual promiscuity, figure most frequently as threats to the purity of those blood lines. Their power to undermine patriarchal authority (here meaning the authority of the father) is indirectly registered in the degree of demonization attending their representation. Joan is accused of being a witch; Eleanor Cobham of consorting with conjurors; and Margaret of being a cursing shrew.

By the end of the second tetralogy all this has changed. In *Richard II*, England is conceived as a hierarchically ordered medieval kingdom, authorized by divine right and threatened by the degrading forces of modernity, but the England of Henry V looks very much like one of Benedict Anderson's imagined communities, a nation conceived in strikingly modern terms. Even in the Henry IV plays, England is represented as a bounded geographical space with borders, landmarks, cities, and local histories. No longer centered in the symbolically resonant locales of "court" and "battlefield," the action occupies a variety of specific geographical locations as it moves from Gadshill near Rochester to Gloucestershire to a tavern in the Eastcheap district of London. Each locale has its distinctive customs, qualities and inhabitants, and often its distinctive idiom as well. Less defined by reference to the monarch and the upper nobility than before, the nation becomes a geographical and cultural entity composed of distinct, particularized regions. Simultaneously, in these plays kingship is secured less by genealogy than by performance, and women cease to be represented primarily as warriors, witches, or monstrous adulteresses. Rather, women in the later histories are strategically peripheralized. They often reside, literally, in the subplots of the narrative and in the borderlands of the plays' geographic economy. Sometimes they function to define what is not English, what is foreign and dangerous. Mortimer's Welsh wife is the prototype of such a figure, never speaking English and luring her husband away from his public duties. Other women in the second tetralogy, Mistress Quickly and Doll Tearsheet, inhabit not a geographical borderland, but an Eastcheap tavern, a sort of anti-nation or kingdom of rogues tucked inside the larger entity called England. And finally there is the figure of Katherine, Princess of France, whose marriage to Henry V we have already briefly discussed in regard to Branagh and Olivier's film versions of *Henry V*, and who inhabits a space largely set apart from the world of public action. One purpose of this book is to explore why the roles of women and the representation of gender relations should shift so markedly between the two tetralogies and to investigate the relationship of this change to other factors that differentiate the two sets of plays from one another.

30

4

THE THEATER AS
INSTITUTION

In addressing these questions, it is important to consider the fact that the plays were designed for performance in a public, commercial theater. Peter Womack has argued that as an urban and commercial institution, London theater helped to make the playgoers themselves members of a new kind of imagined community (Womack 1992: 91–145). In traditional guild theater, which was performed in, by, and for specific local communities, actors and audience were known to one another. On religious holidays a series of plays based on stories from the Old and New Testaments was performed sequentially at various stations or places within a medieval town. Rather than formal theaters, the place of performance was often a pageant wagon. Numerous members of the community were involved in these productions, each of which was sponsored by one of the town guilds. Those who were not actors in the performance helped with preparation or participated as audience members watching the enactment of the timeless truths of biblical history. The London commercial theater, however, operated on different principles. The actors were professionals; the scripts were usually secular in content and were produced as commercial entertainments; novelty was as important as familiarity in making these scripts commercially successful; members of the audience were not necessarily known to one another or to the actors. In such conditions, the practice of playgoing helped to establish community in conditions of anonymity. This imagined community was not so much based on personal acquaintance and familiarity, shared history, and prior relationships, as on the shared conditions of theatrical spectatorship in a commercializing culture and the shared temporality of theatrical enactment.

The status of women within this theatrical culture was complicated. Although women did perform in guild drama and in various other forms of dramatic entertainment such as court masques and itinerant shows (Stokes 1993), scholars are generally agreed that none of the London professional companies of players included women and that female parts were performed by boys (or perhaps sometimes by men). There is evidence that women conducted some of the pawnbroking activities by which costumes for these professional companies were often acquired (Korda 1995), but women's primary place in the commercial theater was as consumers of theatrical entertainment, not as laborers who produced it. Even the women's participation as spectators, however, was condemned by those who found the commercial theater a dangerous addition to London life. The litany of charges against the theater included the following: theaters encouraged idleness by taking apprentices from their work; they promoted illicit sexuality by inflaming the passions of the spectators; they violated God's injunctions against wearing the clothes of the opposite sex; they were places where disease, especially the plague, could be spread (Barish 1981: 80–190; Howard 1994: 47–72). Women, being the weaker sex, were deemed more vulnerable than men to all the allurements and dangers associated with theater. Moreover, because playgoers did not sit in darkness as they usually do in modern theaters, members of the audiences were visible to one another and to the actors. The amphitheaters, for instance, were open-air structures where performances were staged in daylight. Because women were highly visible in the playhouses, even though they were not actors, moralists repeatedly warned of the risks they incurred by exposing themselves to the dangers of such places. Yet women kept coming to the theaters, exercising the prerogatives of paying customers not only to judge the play before them, but also to participate in the exchange of gazes, words, and touches that was part of the playgoing experience (Howard 1994: 73–92).

Many texts from the period record, some matter-of-factly, some with anxiety and disapproval, the presence of women in the commercial theaters. Stephen Gosson, in a concluding epistle to his *School of Abuse*, warns city wives to keep away from the theater and to stay in their houses, for, as he says: "Thought is free: you can forbidd no man, that vieweth you, to noute you and that noateth you, to judge you, for entring to places of suspition"

(Gosson 1579: sig. F2^r). For Gosson, this implies that in the theater all women could be read as whores. Michael Drayton's late sixteenth-century collection of verse epistles about women who suffer for love or are abandoned by their lovers has the fifteenth-century city wife, Jane Shore, anachronistically describe how husbands keep their wives from the public theater so that the wives will not

> heare the Poet in a Comick straine,
> Able t'infect with his lascivious Scene;
> And the young wanton Wits, when they applaud
> The slie perswasion of some subtill Bawd;
> Or passionate Tragedian, in his rage
> Acting a Love-sick Passion on the Stage.
> (Drayton 1961: 2: 257)

Jane, rehearsing her husband's fears, connects theater with sexual temptations; yet she goes on to complain that women who are denied liberty and remain cloistered at home have no pleasures worth enjoying and are reduced to playing with the dog or walking in the fields. A gendered struggle is implied here. While even Jane acknowledges that the theater (and by extension the wider public world) is a place of temptation, she is clear that it is hypocritical for men to enjoy pleasures they deny women and boring for women to be kept from the sophisticated pastimes of urban life.

The fact of women's attendance at the theater reveals some of the contradictions surrounding women's place in early modern urban culture and in the public, commercial theater. Increasingly, women of the middling sort in particular were being inculcated with an ideology of domesticity. Marriage defined their social status; the home constituted their main arena of activity. Yet city women were obviously not simply staying at home. They were going to the theaters, and they were shopping, working in shops, visiting Bedlam to view the antics of the mad inmates, and taking part in other public pleasures (Newman 1991: 111–43; see also Plate 1). In part, the strident injunctions for women to stay at home, such as those registered by Gosson, are a good indication that they were not doing so. The theater was just one of the many institutions in urban London that took women out of the home, even as the home was being more insistently constructed as woman's proper place.

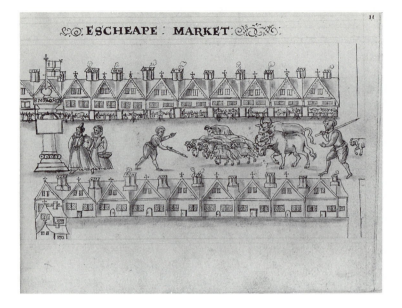

ESCHEAPE : MARKET

Plate 1 Pen and wash picture of the Eastcheap market, from *Hugh Alley's Caveat* (1598). Here, as in other street scenes illustrated in the book, women move freely in the public places of London. In this case, two women walk together, but in others, women appear alone, sometimes carrying market baskets, sometimes selling in the public markets, sometimes simply strolling in the streets.

Source: Reproduced by permission of the Folger Shakespeare Library

This is not to suggest that the theater was an inherently liberatory site for the women in the audience. As we have noted, women were not allowed to act in these theaters. And in some discussions of the theater, such as Nashe's description of the effect of history plays on English men, even women's place in the audience seems to be elided. Yet, increasingly, playwrights acknowledged the woman spectator's presence. In 1607 Beaumont in *The Knight of the Burning Pestle* wrote a play in which a London grocer, his wife and apprentice go to a theater to see the play *The London Merchant*. They are unhappy, however, with what they feel is the work's negative picture of the merchant class. They want something more heroic. In fact, they want a grocer to go on a quest, fight monsters and rescue maidens. The wife, who plays the major role in interrupting the play and lodging these objections and suggestions, finally pushes their apprentice, Rafe, onto the stage to play the hero's part. *The Knight of the Burning Pestle* satirically but unmistakably registers the role of citizen taste, especially the tastes of city wives, in determining the repertory of the theater companies (Osborne 1991: 491–517).

Plays for this theater could, of course, respond to the presence of women in the audience by presenting them with fictions designed to inculcate their subordinate place in patriarchal structures. As many recent critics have demonstrated, there are innumerable instances of misogynist dramas in the period (McLuskie 1985: 88–108). But it simplifies both the nature of theatrical scripts and the nature of the viewing experience to assume that the theater was simply a site where patriarchal norms were reinforced. Foreign visitors to England were impressed by the fact that English women attended the playhouses so freely (Harbage 1941: 76–8). As we have seen, their status as paying customers meant that women's tastes and interests as well as men's had to be taken into account by the players. Moreover, as part of a larger and changing social environment, playscripts embodied the contradictions of that larger arena. Sometimes the gender ideologies deployed in a single play were inconsistent, showing that there was not one true version of masculinity and femininity, but competing versions serving different social interests. Sometimes the theatergoing experience itself may have contradicted the conservative gender ideologies of particular scripts. How would women spectators, for example, have understood their own relationship to representations that equated "good" women with those who stayed within the household and did not gad about – exactly what these theatergoing women were themselves, in fact, doing?

One must also ask whether men and women, or different members of each of those groups, might not have had divergent responses to the dramatic fictions they watched. In *A Midsummer Night's Dream*, Theseus and Hippolyta, the Duke of Athens and his Amazonian bride, react quite differently when told the story of four young lovers who ran from Athens in pursuit of love and spent the night in the woods. The lovers claimed to have undergone mysterious transformations, to have lost themselves as in a dream. To Theseus the lovers' tales are "antic fables" and "fairy toys" (V.i.3); Hippolyta interprets them less dismissively. As she says to Theseus:

But all the story of the night told over,
And all their minds transfigur'd so together,
More witnesseth than fancy's images,
And grows to something of great constancy;
But howsoever, strange and admirable.

(V.i.23–7)

Hippolyta can hear in the lovers' mingled and fantastic-sounding tales the ring of truth, but to Theseus they are mere fables. His response is in character for the rational, masculine ruler of Athens, who has no time for what he sees as nonsense: stories of magic and irrational transformations. Hippolyta, by contrast, is a conquered Amazonian queen being forced into a marriage with her captor. In accepting the lovers' consensus as a kind of authority for their story, she is willing to entertain the possibility of a realm of experience that Theseus neither dominates nor acknowledges. One can read Hippolyta's responses as covert or perhaps unconscious resistance to Theseus' way of making sense of the world.

We would argue, then, that the often-stated anxiety about women's attendance at the commercial theaters had some legitimacy in the sense that it could not be clear in advance how women would interpret the expanded range of narratives and images to which the theater exposed them. Even the history plays, Shakespeare's most seemingly androcentric productions, might, we have to assume, produce a different response among English women than the patriotic excitement Nashe assumed they evoked from English men. Even as women were slowly excluded from productive occupations and even as the household was increasingly defined as their proper sphere, the theater, in part through its commercial drive for profits, continued to draw women out of the house, put them into public circulation, and make them judges and interpreters of public entertainments.

Before turning to the explicit analysis of Shakespeare's plays in the ensuing chapters, we ought to note, of course, that in his own day Shakespeare was not the only dramatist to write histories. Peele's *Edward I* (1591), Marlowe's *Edward II* (1592), Heywood's *Edward IV* (1599), Ford's *Perkin Warbeck* (c.1632) – these are but a handful of the English history plays written by other dramatists. Paul Dean estimates that Shakespeare's ten history plays represent about one eighth of those produced between 1580 and 1620, approximately half of which survive (Dean 1990: 415) There are

36

considerable differences among these plays. Recently, Richard Helgerson has argued that some of the history plays written for playhouses connected with the theater manager Philip Henslowe embody a vision of the commonwealth different from Shakespeare's (Helgerson 1992: 195–245). He suggests that after Shakespeare's early play, *Henry VI, Part II* (*The First part of the Contention betwixt the two famous Houses of Yorke and Lancaster*), Shakespeare lost sympathy for forms of popular radicalism as embodied in that play by the figure of Jack Cade. Helgerson sees Shakespeare as increasingly concerned with "the consolidation and maintenance of royal power," while those history plays written for some of the other theater companies "give their attention to the victims of such power" (Helgerson 1992: 234). We are going to argue a somewhat different case in this book, finding in Shakespeare's later histories an expansion of dramatic focus well beyond the court and the monarch, as well as an anatomy of changing forms of royal power. It can be argued in fact that by insisting upon the performative nature of "modern" kingship, Shakespeare's histories finally reveal the radical contingency of monarchial authority.

Not all of the Henslowe histories, moreover, embrace popular radicalism. In Thomas Heywood's *Edward IV*, for instance, first published in 1599, the opening scenes show the apprentices of London, under the leadership of the Lord Mayor, defeating in battle an army of disaffected common men marching on the city. Ostensibly these rebels are backing the Bastard Falconbridge's attempt to reseat Henry VI on the English thone; in actuality, they are interested in plundering the shops inside the city walls. They are poor men, the sort of disorderly and envious commoners feared by the good property holders of London. These rebels are roundly defeated and driven off; Falconbridge is executed. The play evinces little sympathy for the plight of these, the most disenfranchised members of the commonwealth. Rather, it celebrates the valor and virtue of the propertied citizens within the city walls. The tradition of popular radicalism which held that wealth should be redistributed is discredited in this play: characters who espouse such views are idle, envious, and violent – as ready to rape the citizens' wives as to steal the citizens' household goods and the contents of their shops.

The London citizens who emerge as the heroes of Heywood's play have little time for the practices and discourses of popular radicalism. They are too busy defending their property. Nor are

37

these citizens interested in subverting the monarch or in protesting monarchial abuses. Even when Edward seduces Matthew
Shore's wife, Jane, Matthew refuses to oppose or confront him.
The other citizens are depicted much less as victims of royal
authority than as heroic embodiments of civic virtue, and loyalty
to the monarch is celebrated as an unquestioned citizen value.
However irresponsible Edward's actions, all the play's good
characters insist on obedience to him. Although *Edward IV* reduces
the role of the king in the dramatic action, it is hardly an expression
of a popular tradition of radical thought. The only figures who
speak of making property common are the discredited lower-class
rebels; there is no direct critique of the monarch, even though he
is irresponsible, uxorious, and lustful; and it is the city's property-
loving artisans and merchants whose values and way of life are
most firmly applauded (Howard forthcoming).

Where Shakespeare's histories really do differ from a play such
as *Edward IV* is that they never take London's artisans and
merchants as their overt focus of attention. Monarch and nobles
are foregrounded in most of Shakespeare's histories, but over the
course of these plays the representation of monarchy changes, as
does the source of monarchial authority and power, as does the
England the monarch rules (or attempts to rule). The Shakespearean history play thus helped to invent new ideas of both
monarch and nation. David Kastan has argued that simply by
representing kings upon the public stage, history plays undermined the cultural authority of the monarch by showing that
kingship was a role even a common player could personate
(Kastan 1986). They revealed that successful kingship was at least
in part a matter of successful performance. Shakespeare's history
plays, in our view, seem to express an increasing recognition of
this fact, along with an increasing emphasis on the performative
basis of all authority. Concurrently, the histories point to other
changes in the larger social context in which monarchy exists. In
short, if Shakespeare's histories do not oppose or subvert monarchy, they nonetheless alter its nature, anatomizing and transforming both royal power and also the England in which such
power is exerted.

The transition to modernity, which we feel these dramas helped
to effect, cannot fail to be of concern to feminists, for in this
transition the world we have inherited was emerging. The history
play may seem to be simply about England's medieval past, and

in the most obvious sense it is. But in putting England's fifteenth-century kings upon the sixteenth-century stage, the theater was creating a sense of national identity by producing a collective history for its audiences. Moreover, these plays sometimes directly acknowledge the conditions in which they were produced by anachronistically mingling scenes from contemporary London life, such as those set in Quickly's Eastcheap tavern, with events supposedly occurring nearly two hundred years before. At other times the plays explicitly point to the contemporary relevance of past events. In one of the best-known of these instances, the Chorus in the folio text of *Henry V* compares Henry's victorious return from conquered France to the longed-for return of one of Elizabeth I's generals, the Earl of Essex, from a campaign against the Irish:

> Were now the general of our gracious Empress,
> As in good time he may, from Ireland coming,
> Bringing rebellion broached on his sword,
> How many would the peaceful city quit,
> To welcome him!
>
> (V. Cho. 30–4)

The past is here used to express a wish about the present, that Essex would achieve the victory in Ireland that Henry had achieved at Agincourt. But more important than explicit contemporary references such as this one is the pervasive evidence that in his history plays Shakespeare was negotiating the social disruptions that attended the beginnings of modernity. As we have suggested above and will elaborate below, the transformation of England into a nation state and a major mercantile power entailed changes in the nature of monarchy, in the bases for personal status, in family life, in the gendered division of labor, in gender ideology, and in the relationship of private and public spheres. These changes, moreover, have had continuing social and cultural implications still felt in the late twentieth century.

For some time, historical and materialist feminists have argued that it is not possible to talk about women monolithically, as if all women shared a common essence, or to speak of gender in isolation from other aspects of a social formation (Hennessey 1993; Wayne 1991: 1–26). This book treats gender as a variable historical construction and recognizes the interconnections between the economic, political, and cultural levels of a social formation.

Gender is constructed in and through the entire fabric of a society. Economic systems affect, for example, how work gets gendered – that is, what work men and women do, where they do it, and how it is labelled and valued. Political systems affect who is or is not empowered as a citizen or subject and policies on matters as diverse as how reproduction is regulated and how access to law courts and education is determined. Cultural productions, such as plays, circulate and naturalize contesting ideologies of gender. None of these levels is discrete from the others: together they help to create the gendered matrix in which subjects live, move, and have their beings.

Shakespeare's history plays seem to deal primarily with the political realm and with the men who dominate the political landscape of an imagined England of the past. But as we hope to demonstrate, it is a mistake to conclude that the plays therefore have little to do with the gendering of social life in either the 1590s or in the present.

Part II

WEAK KINGS, WARRIOR WOMEN, AND THE ASSAULT ON DYNASTIC AUTHORITY

The first tetralogy and *King John*

5

HENRY VI, PART I

The first wave of twentieth-century feminist Shakespeare criticism focused on the comedies, especially the ones with cross-dressed heroines, to theorize a theater in which female spectators could find liberating images of powerful, attractive women who violated gender restrictions and were rewarded for those violations with admiration, love, and marriage – a utopian fantasy in which gender identity was as changeable as the theatrical costumes that transformed boy actors into female characters. The romantic comedies were doubly satisfying to these feminist critics because they answered desires for personal liberation without disturbing the dominant gender ideology of our own time. The stories they told resolved early modern social conflicts in marriage; and in so doing, they also helped to produce the modern ideological construction of heterosexual passion as the basis for the ideal nuclear family, held together by the love between husband and wife, the avenue for personal self-fulfillment and the foundation for the good order of society. In recent years, feminists have considerably revised this early account of the comedies, recognizing the sobering persistence within them of patriarchal power, the temporary nature of the heroines' holiday freedoms, and the price which heterosexual marriage usually exacts from women at the plays' ends. Nonetheless, Shakespearean comedy is still generally viewed as the genre with the fullest roles for women and the most optimistic view of their autonomy and power.

Shakespeare's history plays, however, tell a different, much less optimistic story. In a recent survey of feminist Shakespeare criticism, Ann Thompson remarks that feminist critics have tended to neglect the English history plays (Thompson 1988: 85). Given the roles of women in those plays, this omission is not surprising.

The hierarchy of dramatic genres was also a hierarchy of social status: the subjects of history were kings and the great noblemen who opposed them; women and commoners occupied only marginal places in historical narratives. Antagonists and consorts, queens and queans, witches and saints: women play almost every conceivable role in Shakespeare's history plays. But there is one role that is always reserved for a man – that of the protagonist. Female characters can threaten or validate the men's historical projects, but they can never take the center of history's stage or become the subjects of the narratives of patriarchal succession where it was recorded.

To move from comedy to history is to move up the social and generic hierarchy to an aristocratic world where patriarchal domination is assumed and female characters marginalized. The comedies look forward with some effort to the emergent bourgeois ideal of the loving, nuclear family, but the histories for the most part look backward to an older conception of marriage as a political and economic union between feudal families – a model that did in fact last longer at the higher levels of the social hierarchy. In the first tetralogy, heterosexual passion is always represented as a dangerous, destructive force, even when it leads to marriage. Shakespeare's Henry VI and Edward IV both reject prudent dynastic marriages in order to marry on the basis of personal passion; both marriages are represented as disastrous mistakes that weaken the men's authority as kings and destabilize the political order of their realms. By contrast, the desirable marriage between Richmond and Elizabeth, the foundation of the Tudor dynasty, is totally uncontaminated by any hint of romantic love – or even by any appearance on stage of the bride-to-be.

The difficult transmission of patrilineal authority from one generation to the next is the subject of the history plays, but they marginalize the roles of the wives and mothers, centering instead on the heroic legacies of the fathers, the failures and triumphs of the sons. The privileged scene of heroic history, the battlefield, is a problematic place for women. In the early history plays Joan and Margaret and Elinor do usurp masculine prerogatives and turn soldier, but always at the risk of stigmatization. The most powerful of these female warriors, Joan, is also the most demonic. Her inexplicable military power, first explained as deriving from the Blessed Virgin, is finally defined as witchcraft and punished with burning. Initially portrayed in positive terms – as "Deborah"

(I.ii.105) and "Astraea's daughter" (I.vi.4) – that associate her with Queen Elizabeth, Joan is finally degraded to resolve the ideological paradox of female power (Jackson 1988). By the end of *Henry VI, Part I*, her shocking military success is explained as the the illicit supernatural power of a disorderly woman who has refused to abide by the limits of her natural role.

Joan's witchcraft is closely related to her appropriation of masculine dress and masculine behavior. Edward Hall, a major historiographic source for *Henry VI, Part I*, links Joan's masculinity with her demonic power when he describes her as "this wytch or manly woman" (Jackson 1988: 64; Hall 1548: 157). Using the two terms as if they were synonymous and interchangeable, Hall suggests an unexamined connection between them in Renaissance ideology. Sexual difference constituted the necessary ground of patriarchal order. For a woman to perform manly deeds and so to transgress gender categories could render her and her deeds demonic (witchlike) or literally unspeakable.[1] When the Welsh women intrude on the battlefield in *Henry IV, Part I* to mutilate the corpses of the fallen warriors, they commit an act that "may not be/ Without much shame retold or spoken of" (I.i.45–6). The single combat between Joan and Talbot (an encounter that Shakespeare invented) is characterized in similar terms – as emasculating, shameful, and indescribable. Deprived of his "strength," "valor," and "force" (*Henry VI, Part I*: I.v.1), Talbot cannot understand the female power that makes him impotent: "My thoughts are whirled like a potter's wheel,/ I know not where I am, nor what I do" (I.v.19–20). All he can do is lament the "shame" (I.v.39) of his defeat at Joan's hands and, ascribing it to supernatural forces, conclude that Joan is a witch.

The emblem of social and spiritual transgression, Joan's transvestite costume associates her with accounts of Queen Elizabeth's appearance at Tilbury dressed in armor, but it also prepares for Joan's final association with the demonic.[2] As Leah Marcus points out, "The figure of Joan airs a wide range of anxious fantasies which had eddied about the English queen in the years leading up to the Armada victory and in the Armada year itself, fantasies which could be allowed to surface only after the worst of the Catholic threat had receded."[3] A complicated, troubling presence in the patriarchal world that Elizabeth ruled, female authority is always absent in Shakespeare's histories, but it hovers at the edges of the stage, a repressed knowledge that escapes the historio-

45

graphic narrative. Essential to the exercise and transmission of patriarchal authority, the women in Shakespeare's histories can never exercise authority in their own right. Some of the women have power, but authority – the right to exercise power – is always defined in patriarchal terms, so whatever power the women exercise is defined in terms of menace to the patriarchy that contains them.

Gabrielle Bernhard Jackson suggests that Joan may have been the first female character to appear on stage in armor and that she was one of the first to appear there in masculine attire of any kind (Jackson 1988: 54). In Shakespeare's later romantic comedies, when the vogue for transvestite heroines was well established and real women in Shakespeare's London had also taken to wearing masculine dress, fashion collaborated with generic convention to allow positive, as well as negative and ambivalent, responses to cross-dressed heroines. In the masculine world of the histories, however, it serves as the mark of transgression. Joan's masculine attire, like the beards of the witches in *Macbeth*, is the sign of the uncanny. It associates sexual ambiguity with the dangers that lurk at the boundaries of the known, rationalized world of sexual difference and sexual exclusion constructed by patriarchal discourse. It is no surprise, then, when in Act V Joan is accompanied on stage by literal demons.

Tudor fascination with history – and the popularity of Shakespeare's history plays – were both fueled by the need to rationalize a changing world. For subjects and sovereigns alike, the residual structures of genealogy provided a traditional rationale for newly acquired power and privilege. Invoking the legendary names of Brute and Arthur, Tudor historians produced fables of ancient descent and providential purpose to validate a new dynasty's claim to the English throne. Living in a time of unprecedented social mobility, Shakespeare and his contemporaries provided a thriving business for the heralds who constructed the genealogies by which they attempted to secure their places in an unstable social hierarchy (Stone 1966: 15–55). The Tudor chronicles were organized by the same principle of genealogical patriarchal succession, and for a similar purpose. Divided into chronological segments that represented the reigns of successive kings, they imposed the structures of patriarchal genealogy upon a heterogeneous assemblage of material, the products of disparate authorial voices and divergent social interests.

Even in Shakespeare's time, the history play was identified, as we saw in Chapter 1, as a specifically masculine genre, and its masculinity was identified with its function as an ideological apparatus for the construction of an emergent national consciousness. That ideology was not monolithic, however, and neither were the conceptions of national identity and masculine authority it produced. On the one hand, it looked nostalgically back to an older, feudal paradigm based on dynastic succession. On the other, it attempted to rationalize an emergent conception of a nation as defined by its geographical boundaries and an emergent conception of masculine authority based on personal achievement.

Shakespeare's historical sources colonized the past, assembling disparate local records preserved in manuscripts into gigantic printed volumes that constructed a national history for England. The book known as "Holinshed's" *Chronicles* is a good case in point; for it was actually the product of many writers – predecessors whose work was incorporated, successors who augmented the narrative after Raphael Holinshed's death, and collaborators at the time of its first production (Rackin 1990: 23–4; Patterson 1994: 3–70). The first edition included William Harrison's chorographic descriptions of Britain, England, and Scotland and Richard Stanyhurst's description and history of Ireland; its sources ranged from Caesar's account of his invasion of Britain to sixteenth-century chronicles of London life. The edition Shakespeare used, published after Holinshed's death, was greatly augmented, perhaps most notably by Abraham Fleming's moralistic commentary on historical events and repeated reminders that they were the work of Divine Providence.

Disparate sources and authorial voices produced a text in which the same event could be represented by divergent accounts and contradictory interpretations, one the expression of pragmatic skepticism, the other of providential moralizing. Material from city chronicles that expressed the interests of London merchants rubbed shoulders with heroic legends that expressed the nostalgic ideals of a feudal aristocracy (Rackin 1990: 7–8, 23–5; Patterson 1993: 185–208). Harrison's chorography, with its "rehersall of the nature and qualities of the people of England and such commodities as are to be found in the same" (Holinshed 1587: I: 1) adumbrated an emergent conception of England as a nation defined by its geography, inhabitants, and economic resources.

47

But just as the coats of arms purchased by upstart commoners like William Shakespeare used genealogical fictions of hereditary entitlement to rationalize the status purchased by new money (Schoenbaum 1978: 227–32), the genealogical organization of the bulk of "Holinshed's" text, divided by the reigns of kings and subdivided by regnal year, imposed the structures of royal succession upon a collection of material as disparate as the sources it incorporated. (See Plate 2, which reproduces two pages from Hall's *Union*, the other principal source for Shakespeare's histories, which was also divided by royal reigns and subdivided by regnal years.)

Despite their coexistence in Holinshed's *Chronicles*, the emergent conception of England implicit in the new genre of chorography was to come into increasing conflict with the residual

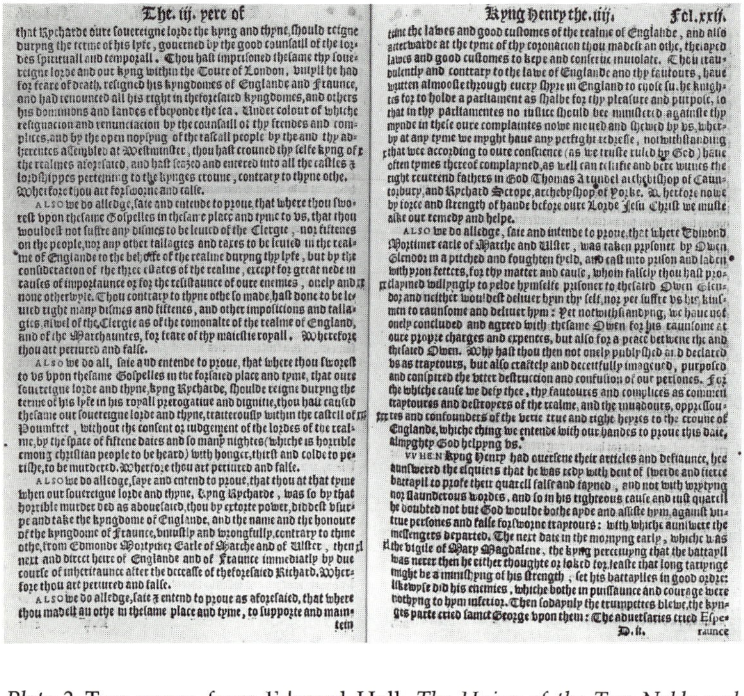
The .iii. yere of

Kyng Henry the .iiii. Fol.xxii.

Plate 2 Two pages from Edward Hall, *The Union of the Two Noble and Illustre Famelies of Lancastre & Yorke* (1550), recounting events from the third year of the reign of King Henry IV (sigs. D1ᵛ–D2ʳ).

Source: Reproduced by permission of the Furness Collection, Department of Special Collections, Van Pelt-Dietrich Library, University of Pennsylvania

conception of England as a dynastically defined royal kingdom which was implicit in the chronicle structure. (Helgerson 1992: 107–47; Levy 1990: 869–70). Organized by temporal sequence, chronicles told the histories of royal dynasties, which acquired and protected their domains by inheritance and warfare. Chorography assembled a picture of national identity from the maps and geographical descriptions that moved in spatial order from one part of the land to another. Substituting land, people, and commodities for king as the embodiments of national identity, and space for time as its medium, it constructed the nation as a material place rather than a royal domain. In so doing, the chorographers mapped not only the country but new conceptions of national and personal identity.

Put in its simplest terms, the chief differences are these: chronicle history constructs its readers as hereditary subjects of the English kings whose narrative of dynastic succession it recounts. To be English is to be a subject of the English king. Chorography, by contrast, constructs its readers as inhabitants of the geographical place called England. To be English is to be native to a particular place. This is not to say, however, that the adoption of the new required the abandonment of the old. In Shakespeare's time, the two models of national identity coexisted. Often, in fact, they were combined (as in the inclusion of Harrison's chorography in Holinshed's *Chronicles*). Even in the twentieth century the vestiges of an international feudalism can be seen as the last remnants of European royalty marry across national boundaries but not across the barriers of social rank that divide aristocrat from commoner. Nonetheless, the emergence of the nation state increasingly privileged geographical difference as the defining mark of national identity.

Shakespeare's history plays, like their historical sources, combined residual and emergent versions of national and personal identity. In the first tetralogy, the older model is clearly privileged. In *Henry VI, Part I*, for instance, hereditary entitlement authorizes English claims to France, while the newer discourse of the nation is associated with French resistance and a form of subversion that is gendered feminine. Joan appeals to Burgundy's loyalty to the French land to persuade him to join her forces, while the English nobility condemn his defection as disloyalty to his nephew, the English king.[4] Joan pleads with Burgundy in heavily gendered language to

Look on thy country, look on fertile France,
And see the cities and the towns defac'd
By wasting ruin of the cruel foe.
As looks the mother on her lowly babe
When death doth close his tender-dying eyes,
See, see the pining malady of France!
Behold the wounds, the most unnatural wounds,
Which thou thyself hast given her woeful breast.
. . . .
One drop of blood drawn from thy country's bosom
Should grieve thee more than streams of foreign gore.
Return thee therefore with a flood of tears,
And wash away thy country's stained spots.

(III.iii.44–57)

Despite the eloquence of Joan's pleading, the playscript is clearly designed to condemn Burgundy's action. Abandoning his alliance with the "lordly nation" of "English Henry" (III.iii.62, 66) and adopting the role of a weeping mother to a dying babe, Burgundy assumes a feminized French identity, a degen(d)eration that leads to dishonor. The news of Burgundy's defection is brought to the English court by a figure who in this play is presented as a paragon of knightly dishonor, Sir John Falstaff (IV.i.9–12); and the English nobles predictably condemn Burgundy's alliance with France as shameful disloyalty to his true sovereign, Henry VI.

The incident of Burgundy's defection identifies the emergent conception of national identity as French (i.e. as not-English) and as feminine; it associates both with the instability of an identity defined (and always subject to redefinition) in performance. Joan's cynical comment on the success of her eloquence – "Done like a Frenchman – turn and turn again!" (III.iii.85) – identifies the new, geographical concept of nationality that makes Burgundy French with the destabilizing effects of the transition from a genealogical to a performative model of masculine identity .

As we saw in Chapter 1, Thomas Nashe based his defense of theatrical performance on the masculinity of the English chronicle play. He also invoked the masculine purity of English acting companies. "Our Players," he boasted, "are not as the players beyond Sea, a sort of squirting baudie Comedians, that have whores and common Curtizens to playe womens partes" (Nashe 1592, in Chambers 1923: 4: 239). Nashe invoked the authority of

English history to defend theatergoing as an elevating, manly activity; but in the eyes of its opponents, the theater was associated with the destabilizing and effeminating forces of social change. English antitheatrical invective focused obsessively on the sexually corrupting allurements of bawdy comedies, the immorality of boys in female costume, and the contaminating presence of women in the theater audiences, especially the prostitutes who were said to haunt the playhouses in search of customers. Nonetheless, Nashe's contrast between the masculine purity of English acting companies and the "baudie Comedians" from "beyond Sea" reflects a literal fact about the theaters of Shakespeare's time; for although English women never appeared on stage, French and Italian companies, which included women, did occasionally perform in England.[5] Nashe's comparison also carried a powerful symbolic charge, for it invoked the same emergent conception of England as a nation and a geographical entity, which associated the foreign with the female, that helped to determine the marginal locations of female characters in Shakespeare's English histories.

Aliens in the masculine domain of English historiography, the women in Shakespeare's English history plays are often quite literally alien. Female characters are often inhabitants of foreign worlds, and foreign worlds are typically characterized as feminine. These associations are overdetermined: representatives of the unarticulated residue that eluded the men's historiographic texts and threatened their historical myths, women were inevitably cast as aliens in the masculine domain of English historiography; but, in addition to reproducing the marginal status of women in the discourse of English history, the separation of female characters from the central scenes of English historical representation expressed the gendered distinction between the authoritative masculine discourse of history and the disreputable feminized world of the playhouse, although the theater was an arena Nashe clearly thought could be recruited to the service of patriotic and male-centered drama.

In *Henry VI, Part I*, these oppositions between masculine English history and feminine theatrical subversion can be seen in their simplest terms, and history is clearly privileged. Here, as in Nashe's defense of playgoing, theatricality is associated with the effeminating forces of a degenerate modernity, history with the redeeming virtues of a heroic masculine English past. The protagonists of Shakespeare's narrative are aristocratic English men.

Conceived both as subjects and as writers of history, they repeatedly allude to history, past and future. They define their military struggle to retain Henry V's French conquests as an effort to preserve his historical legacy and add their own names to the historical record. And they present themselves as the sons of noble fathers. The leader of the opposing forces, by contrast, is not only French and female but also low-born, sexually promiscuous, and insistently theatrical. Just as Nashe's contemptuous reference to the "players beyond Sea," displaces the contaminating effects of theatrical performance onto foreign "common Curtizens," *Henry VI, Part I* associates them with a common French woman who, in a vain attempt to save her life, claims to have engaged in illicit sexual liaisons with virtually every member of the French court.

An important function of history, in the Renaissance as in antiquity, was to repair the ravages of mortality. Nashe wishes to enlist the power of the theater in that task. "How would it have joyed brave *Talbot*," he writes, "to thinke that after he had lyne two hundred yeares in his Tombe, hee should triumphe againe on the Stage, and have his bones newe embalmed with the teares of ten thousand spectators at least (at several times)" (Nashe 1592, in Chambers 1923: 4: 238–9). Like the Greek epic, heroic history, on the page or the stage, is motivated by a sense of loss. As Foucault explains in the case of the epic hero, "if he was willing to die young, it was so that his life, consecrated and magnified by death, might pass into immortality" (Foucault 1979: 142). The process by which human mortality (to which all men and women are subject) is translated into textual immortality (which was typically associated with heroic men) was a frequent theme for Renaissance theorists of historiography as well as for Shakespearean sonnets (where the aristocratic young man but not the dark lady is promised eternity in verse).

In *Henry VI, Part I*, as in Nashe's reference to "these degenerate, effeminate dayes of ours," the past is idealized in heroic terms as the repository of English honor, and its loss is defined as a process of effeminization. The play begins in a dangerously degenerate and unstable world mourning the death of an idealized hero. The opening scene depicts the funeral of Henry V, the legendary warrior-king who was, we are told, "too famous to live long" (I.i.6). Other deaths of England's great warriors punctuate the action. Salisbury is cut down at Orleans, Bedford at Rouen, Talbot and his son on the plains before Bordeaux. The entire play can be seen as a series of attempts on the part of the English to preserve Henry's fame, along with the fame of English martial heroes, and with them the manhood of the English nation. These are associated from the first scene when Bedford proclaims,

> Posterity, await for wretched years,
> When at their mothers' moist'ned eyes babes shall suck,
> Our isle be made a nourish of salt tears,
> And none but women left to wail the dead.
> Henry the Fifth, thy ghost I invocate:
> Prosper this realm, keep it from civil broils,
> Combat with adverse planets in the heavens!
> A far more glorious star thy soul will make
> Than Julius Caesar or bright–
>
> (I.i.48–56)

Bedford's speech defines the English predicament in this play by constructing a gendered antithesis: if Henry's heroic legacy is lost, England will become an island of weeping women. What interrupts Bedford's funeral oration, and with it his attempt to establish the dead king's place in history, is a messenger who rushes in to announce that eight French cities have been lost. The Arden editor speculates that the folio dash at the end of Bedford's speech "probably indicates illegibility of the copy or MS" (Cairncross 1962: 7, note to line 56), but the dash works very well as an indication that Bedford's speech is in fact interrupted – cut short in mid-sentence by the news of French victories that threaten England's control over the territories Henry V conquered, and threaten thereby to erase Henry's name from the historical record. In this play, and even more so in *Henry VI, Part II*, the loss of Henry's French territories is blamed in part on dissension among the English nobility. Winchester, the churchman, and Gloucester, the Lord Protector, fight. In the Temple Garden, the descendents of the two branches of England's ruling dynasty – Yorkists and Lancastrians – pluck white and red roses to symbolize their opposing allegiances. In France, quarrels among the English nobles prevent reinforcements from being sent to Talbot at Bordeaux. But in this play an even greater threat to Henry's legacy in France are the French themselves, especially when they are led by the charismatic and wily Joan of Arc.

Joan explicitly identifies the French effort to drive the English from their country with the erasure of Henry's and England's place in history when she claims,

> Glory is like a circle in the water,
> Which never ceaseth to enlarge itself,
> Till by broad spreading it disperse to nought.
> With Henry's death the English circle ends,
> Dispersed are the glories it included.
>
> (I.ii.133–7)

Implicit in Joan's entire performance, however, is a threat to English historical renown even more dangerous than her military victories: the vivid theatrical presence that makes her the most memorable character in the play.

Joan's only rival for theatrical pre-eminence is Talbot. Henry VI, the boy king who gives the play its name, does not even appear on stage until Act III (Watson 1990: 35); and the gendered opposition between Joan and Talbot defines the meaning of the conflict between France and England. A chivalric hero who fights according to the knightly code, "English Talbot" represents the chivalric ideal that constituted an object of nostalgic longing for Shakespeare's Elizabethan audience (Riggs 1971: 22–3, 100–13). A youthful peasant whose forces resort to craft, subterfuge, and modern weapons, Joan embodies a demonized and feminine modernity threatening to the traditional patriarchal order. Shakespeare invented the single combat in which Joan fights Talbot to a draw (I.v), and he also shaped their characterizations around a series of binary oppositions. He repeatedly calls attention to the fact that the French champion is a woman, defining the conflict between England and France as a conflict between masculine and feminine force, as well as between chivalric virtue and pragmatic craft; historical fame and physical reality/theatrical presence; patriarchal age and subversive youth; high social rank and low. It is significant that the great Salisbury is shot by a French boy sniper and that Joan recaptures Rouen by sneaking in, disguised as the peasant she really is, to admit the French army. Joan's disguise is the visible emblem of her theatricality as well as her low social rank and anti-heroic status.

Most obvious in this moment of explicit role-playing, Joan's theatricality is actually her salient quality. Her role as leader of the French army involves her in the same transgressions against God and the social hierarchy that were repeatedly charged against the players in Shakespeare's England: wearing a costume and playing a part that belie her true social rank and natural sex. Moreover, her female gender, her sexual promiscuity, and her deceptiveness all imply the vices that were associated with theatrical performance. Paradoxically, the only time when Joan's "true" identity appears on stage is in that tiny scene at the gates of Orleans. As an actor, Joan is most truly herself only when she is explicitly playing a part. Dressed as a peasant woman, she also declares her true station in life when she responds to the watchman's challenge, *"Qui là?"* by announcing, *"Paysans, la pauvre gens de France"* (III.ii.13–14). But in the very next line she returns to English, and to deception, when she continues, "Poor market folks that come to sell their corn." The fleeting moment of truth, and of social and national identity, is immediately subsumed within the frame of deceptive play-acting.

Although Joan is repeatedly identified as French, this is the only time in the play when she speaks the French language, and there is very little sense of "France" as either a nation or a kingdom in this play. The Countess of Auvergne charges that Talbot has "Wasted our country, slain our citizens,/ And sent our sons and husbands captivate" (II.iii.41–2); and Joan's dialogue with Burgundy provides a momentarily poignant image of a French nation; but in the authoritative words of the English men who define the terms of the conflict, France is simply a rebellious English territory. Talbot explains to the countess that the French have "rebellious necks" which he has "yoke[d]" (II.iii.64). The messenger who comes to the English court with the bad news that the Dolphin has been crowned king in Rheims defines the meaning of the coronation by announcing that "France is revolted from the English quite" (I.i.90). And even when Joan comes to the Dolphin with the claim that "God's Mother" appeared to her in a vision and willed her to "leave my base vocation/ And free my country from calamity" (I.ii.78, 80–1), the liberation of France is associated with the insubordinate act of abandoning a "base vocation."

The glimpses of a sense of French national identity that can be dimly seen in the words and actions of the French women and in the language that Joan attributes to the Virgin Mary are superseded by the insistent and explicit sense of hereditary entitlement that authorizes the English right to France, along with Englishmen's understanding of their own identities. The messenger who interrupts the funeral of Henry V to announce that seven French cities have been "lost" uses heraldic terms to describe the loss as a destruction of the English nobles' dynastic identity: "Cropp'd are the flower-de-luces in your arms,/ Of England's coat one half is cut away"(I.i.80–1). At Orleans, Talbot charges his troops to "either renew the fight,/ Or tear the lions out of England's coat" (I.v.27–8). Similarly, Richard Plantagenet spends much of the play attempting to recapture the lands and title he feels he should rightly have inherited from his father, the Earl of Cambridge, both of which had been lost when Cambridge was put to death for treason. Richard's family honor, and his identity, are only restored to him when King Henry reinstates him in "the whole inheritance" "that doth belong unto the house of York,/ From whence you spring by lineal descent" (III.i.163–5). "Rise, Richard," he says, "like a true Plantagenet,/ And rise created princely Duke of York" (III.i.171–2). The principles of inheritance that warrant the English claim to territories in France also determine personal identity.

The same indifference to geographical origin as a mark of nationality or basis of entitlement informs Talbot's denunciation of Sir John Falstaff for cowardice unbecoming a knight of the Garter: he cries, "Shame to the Duke of Burgundy and thee!" (IV.i.13), making no distinction between Burgundy's decision to join the French forces and the English knight's defection in battle. It also seems to inform Shakespeare's decision to have Talbot bury Salisbury, one of the last English heroes of the former age, in France. The real Salisbury was buried in England, but Shakespeare's Talbot announces that he will erect Salisbury's tomb in the "chiefest temple" (II.ii.12) of the French "Upon the which, that every one may read,/ Shall be engrav'd the sack of Orleance,/ The treacherous manner of his mournful death,/ And what a terror he had been to France" (II.ii.14–17). His purpose, he says, is so "that hereafter ages may behold/ What ruin happened in revenge of him" (II.ii.10–11). Talbot's desire here, as in his military campaign to secure Henry's French conquests, is to preserve and augment the historical record of English martial achievement. France is simply the place where English history is written.

The motivation of the French is defined in strikingly different terms. More than a record of heroic names and glorious deeds or an aggregate of individual biographies, dynastic history tells a connected story, authorizing present power in genealogical myths of patriarchal succession. The Dolphin and his courtiers make no claims to textual or dynastic authority. They do promise Joan immortal fame, but they cite as precedents an eclectic assortment of famous women from world history and legend – including, among others, Deborah, St Helen, and the Greek courtesan Rhodope (I.ii.105, 142; I.vi.22). The Countess of Auvergne adds to this list when she declares that if her plot to capture Talbot succeeds, "I shall as famous be by this exploit/ As Scythian Tomyris by Cyrus' death" (II.iii.5–6). If the women succeed, they will be rewarded by personal fame – or infamy – but the heterogeneous collection of famous names, united only by their sex, carries the implicit message that although extraordinary women can enter the historical record, female achievement is always isolated and exceptional, and it can never provide the basis for the construction of a national history. Talbot, by contrast, is identified with a collective, English project. He declares that the English army is his "substance, sinews, arms, and strength" (II.iii.63); and he dedicates himself to the preservation of the English legacy. The French struggle to destroy that legacy, but there is no sense that they have a historical legacy of their own to preserve.

The only reference to a French historical text is Alanson's statement, after the initial English victory at Orleans,

> Froissard, a countryman of ours, records
> England all Olivers and Rolands bred
> During the time Edward the Third did reign.
> More truly now may this be verified.
>
> (I.ii.29–32)

In Alanson's statement, as in the case of Froissart's actual chronicle, what the French historian writes is English history. Temporally situated by reference to the reign of an English king, both the French historian's record and the legendary symbols of ancient French chivalry are subsumed into a chronicle of English heroic achievement.

As Alanson's statement implies, what is most at stake in the battles between France and England is the verification of English history. The issue of verification frames the conflict between Joan and Talbot as an opposition between the historical record that Talbot wishes to preserve and the physical reality that Joan invokes to discredit it. Joan's challenge takes two forms. What she does threatens to deprive the English of their martial honor by defeat at the hands of a woman; and what she says attacks both the English version of history and the values it expresses, with an earthy iconoclasm that threatens to discredit the traditional notions of chivalric glory invoked by the English heroes. We see this opposition in its purest form after Talbot's death when Sir William Lucy calls for him in heroic language:

> But where's the great Alcides of the field,
> Valiant Lord Talbot, Earl of Shrewsbury,
> Created, for his rare success in arms,
> Great Earl of Washford, Waterford, and Valence,
> Lord Talbot of Goodrig and Urchinfield,
> Lord Strange of Blackmere, Lord Verdun of Alton,
> Lord Cromwell of Wingfield, Lord Furnival of Sheffield,
> The thrice-victorious Lord of Falconbridge,
> Knight of the noble Order of Saint George,
> Worthy Saint Michael, and the Golden Fleece,
> Great marshal to Henry the Sixth
> Of all his wars within the realm of France?
>
> (IV.vii.60–71)

Rejecting the grandiose pretentions in the string of titles Lucy uses to mark Talbot's absence, Joan invokes the here and now of physical presence to debunk the titles and deride Lucy's language:

> Here's a silly stately style indeed!
> The Turk, that two and fifty kingdoms hath,
> Writes not so tedious a style as this.
> Him that thou magnifi'st with all these titles
> Stinking and fly-blown lies here at our feet.
>
> (IV.vii.72–6)

Lucy describes Talbot as history was to describe him, decked in the titles that designate his patriarchal lineage and heroic military achievements. Joan relies on what she can see, rejecting the masculine historical ideals and significance that Lucy's glorious names invoke, and Joan's subversive speech has an obvious appeal for an audience. Her vigorous, colloquial language, tied to the material facts of earth, threatens to topple the imposing formal edifice Lucy has constructed with his tower of names. Despite her lack of ideological authority, Joan's vivid voice and energetic theatrical presence provide the basis for a serious challenge to the logocentric, masculine historical record.

In Shakespeare's later history plays, but especially in *King John*, those subversive voices will become more insistent, threatening to invalidate the nostalgic myths of an heroic past, implying that before the voice of official history can be accepted as valid, it must come to terms with the unauthorized voices empowered by the disorderly milieu of theatrical performance. However, once Shakespeare attempts to come to terms with his theatrical medium and incorporate those oppositional elements, historiography itself is revealed as problematic. Instead of speaking with the clear, univocal voice of unquestioned tradition, it is re-presented as a dubious construct, always provisional, subject to erasure and reconstruction, and never adequate to recover the past in full presence.

In the later plays, many of those disorderly voices will belong to men: the most memorable of all, in fact, will be those of Falstaff in the Henry IV plays and the Bastard in *King John*. In *Henry VI, Part I*, however, the gendered distinctions between masculine historical and genealogical legitimacy and feminine theatrical subversion are relatively uncomplicated. All of the women are French, and none of the English are women. The manhood of the French men, moreover, is always compromised by their dependence upon Joan's military leadership. After the French victory at Orleans, Alanson gloats, "All France will be replete with mirth and joy,/ When they shall hear how we have play'd the men" (I.vi.15–16). The very terms in which Alanson exults undermine any claim to French manhood by identifying it as playacting. Moreover, the Dolphin immediately rebukes him: "'Tis Joan, not we, by whom the day is won" (I.iv.17).

The female characters in *Henry VI, Part I* – Joan, the Countess of Auvergne and Margaret of Anjou – are united not only by gender and nationality but also by the threats they pose to the English protagonists and to the heroic values associated with history as the preserver of masculine fame and glory (Bevington 1966; Burckhardt 1968: 47–77; Kastan 1982: 116). Like Joan, the countess attacks Talbot; like Joan, she resorts to craft and stratagem; and like Joan she threatens to subvert the English historical project by calling attention to the difference between Talbot's unimpressive physical presence in the person of the actor who played his part and the verbal record of the historical Talbot's heroic honor. The countess says she wants to verify the reports of Talbot's glory by seeing his person: "Fain would mine eyes be witness with mine ears/ To give their censure of these rare reports" (II.iii.9–10). What she sees – "a child, a silly dwarf . . . this weak and writhled shrimp" (II.iii.22–3), in short, the actor's body – convinces her that "report is fabulous and false" (II.iii.18).

The countess's preference for physical evidence over historical report associates her with the French and female forces in the play as a theatrically empowered threat to the authority of English history, but Shakespeare resolves that threat in an antitheatrical joke which insures that the countess, and the audience along with her, will be clearly instructed in the superiority of historical report over theatrical presence.[6] Just before Talbot summons the hidden soldiers who will free him from her trap, he announces, "I am but shadow of myself./ You are deceiv'd, my substance is not here" (II.iii.50–1); and a minute later the countess acknowledges that the verbal reports she doubted were really true. For the audience, Talbot's lines were doubly significant: a "shadow" was a common term for an actor, and in that sense the man who spoke those lines was quite literally "but a shadow" of the elusive Talbot, the emblem of a lost historical presence, celebrated by historiographer and playwright, but never present in substance even to the countess who thinks she has him captured in her castle.

The issue of physical presence vs. historical record, dramatized in *Henry VI, Part I* as a conflict between English men and French women, is central, not only to this particular play, but to the history play genre itself. Nashe's description of Talbot raised from the tomb of historical writing to "triumph again on the stage" reminds us that the audience went to the history play hoping to see those historical records brought to life and to make direct contact with the living reality that was celebrated but also entombed by the "worme-eaten" books of history. For Shakespeare's audience, as for the characters in the play, Talbot's "glory [still] fill[ed] the world with loud report" (II.ii.43). His mere name, like the name of God, is sufficient to rout the French soldiers (II.i.79–81); and although Talbot is finally killed, his glory survives his physical death. Like the countess, Shakespeare's audience wanted to *see* the renowned Talbot, and like her, they were likely to be disappointed. Talbot's antitheatrical joke exploits the inadequacies of theatrical representation to validate the historical record, instructing the potentially irreverent audience in the playhouse, along with the countess, that the sight they see on stage is only a "shadow" of Talbot – that history and renown portrayed him more truly than physical presence ever could do. The masculine authority of history is thus sustained against the feminine challenge of physical presence as the play is revealed as a representation. Presence remains ineluctably absent – the elusive Other, that, like the feminine principle itself, must be suppressed in order to sustain the masculine historiographic narrative. The theatrical challenge posed by the women's appeals to physical fact is discredited by reminders that the drama contains no physical facts, and the verbal construction of Talbot's glory survives.

In this context the scene of Talbot's death is instructive. A long contention between Talbot and his son – a son repeatedly addressed by his father as "Talbot," the father's own name – in which each urges the other to save his life by fleeing from battle and in which neither, of course, will flee, ends with the death of both. Despite Talbot's paternal solicitude, the boy refuses to leave because "flight" would "abuse" his father's "renowned name" (IV.v.41): "Is my name Talbot? and am I your son?/And shall I fly?" (IV.v.12–13). Shakespeare lowers the historical character's age and makes him Talbot's only son to insure that the boy's filial devotion, along with both Talbots' devotion to honor, will prevent the possibility that any survivor will carry their name into the future. The boy's willingness to die means that only the name will survive – stripped of any living human referent but glorious in historical memory.

The argument that finally convinces Talbot to allow his son to stay with him and die in battle is the boy's claim that if he runs away, he will lose his patriarchal English title and become "like . . . the peasant boys of France" (IV.vi.48): "if I fly, I am not Talbot's son. . . . If son to Talbot, die at Talbot's foot" (IV.vi.51–3). Talbot and his son both make the traditional heroic choice to sacrifice their lives in order to preserve their honor and their heroic titles. The son must sacrifice his life to secure his legitimate place in the patriarchal line: "O, if you love my mother,/ Dishonor not her honorable name/ To make a bastard and a slave of me!/ The world will say, he is not Talbot's blood,/ That basely fled when noble Talbot stood" (IV.v.13–17).

In direct contrast, Shakespeare contrives Joan's final interview with her father to show her placing life above historical glory. We see her rejecting her father, revealed as a bastard, and claiming to be pregnant with yet another bastard, all in a futile effort to save her life (V.iv). The historical prototype for Talbot's son was already in his late twenties when he died, and already had children (Saccio 1977: 109). Moreover, he was not the only son of Talbot's to die at this battle. Hall's *Union*, a major source for this play, reported that Talbot's bastard son Henry was also killed there (1548: 229). Shakespeare rewrites the historical record to produce a final schematic contrast between the strong bond that unites the male Talbots and Joan's denial of her peasant father, thus completing his representation of Talbot and Joan as opposites and connecting the various terms in which their opposition has been defined – historian vs. anti-historian, noble man vs. peasant woman, dynastic pride vs. the shame of bastardy.

Joan's sexual promiscuity and her association with bastardy are hinted even in her first appearance, when she is introduced to the Dolphin (and to Shakespeare's audience) by the Bastard of Orleans and quickly becomes the object of the courtiers' lascivious jokes (I. ii). The suggestion of illicit sexuality that always surrounds Joan associates her with the third French woman in the play, Margaret of Anjou, soon to become the adulterous queen of Henry VI. Immediately linked to Joan in the audience's eyes, Margaret is introduced as a captive led onto the stage at the same time that Joan is led off it as a prisoner of the English.[7] Moreover, as we quickly learn in *Henry VI, Part II*, the marriage between Margaret and Henry threatens to erase history itself:

> Fatal this marriage, cancelling your fame,
> Blotting your names from books of memory,
> Rasing the characters of your renown,
> Defacing monuments of conquer'd France,
> Undoing all, as all had never been!
> (I.i.99–103)

Besides Joan, Margaret is the only woman who plays a major part in the *Henry VI* plays and the only character of either sex who appears in all four plays of the first tetralogy. Margaret's disruptive role becomes increasingly prominent as the story progresses and the world of the plays sinks into chaos. Shakespeare follows Hall in making her "a manly woman, usyng to rule not to be ruled," and he also exploits the old Yorkist slander that she was an adulteress (Hall 1548: 249). Like Joan's sexual promiscuity, Margaret's adultery has no real impact on the action of the *Henry VI* plays. In both cases, the women's sexual transgressions seem almost gratuitous – dramatically unnecessary attributes, at best added to underscore their characterization as threats to masculine honor, at worst unwarranted slanders, like the slander by which Renaissance women who transgressed in any way, even by excessive gossip and railing, were often characterized as whores. Shakespeare does not elaborate the relationship between sexual transgression and historical subversion until he comes to *King John*, but the relationship is always there, even though in the Henry VI plays it remains implicit. Winchester, the most villainous of the contentious nobles who undermine the stability of the English state, is identified as "lewd," "lascivious, wanton" (III.i.15,19), and as a bastard (III.i.42). In a social order based on patrilineal inheritance, adulterous wives (like Margaret) and their male paramours (like Suffolk), are the primary agents of subversion, but any illicit sexual liaison is threatening, even when neither of the parties is married. Bastard children represent a threat to established order because without legitimate fathers they are unrestrained by any authorized place in the social hierarchy. Although Winchester is an aristocratic English man and Joan a French peasant woman, both aspire to power and authority to which they are not entitled by birth; and in both cases their aspirations threaten to destroy legitimate order.

Winchester's characterization is inscribed in the same register of debasement and subversion as that of the women. When Gloucester charges that Winchester gives "whores indulgences to sin" (I.iii.35), he reiterates the Bishop's association with sexual license, but he also associates him with the disorderly milieu of theatrical performance; for the insult would have reminded Shakespeare's audience that the Bishop of Winchester did, in fact, receive revenues from the houses of prostitution in Southwark, the same disreputable neighborhood where the playhouses were also located. Women and sexuality belong to the degraded milieu of the playhouse, and to the lower, and most explicitly theatrical, genre of comedy. When Burgundy hears that the Countess of Auvergne has invited Talbot to visit her castle, he protests, "Nay, then I see our wars/ Will turn unto a peaceful comic sport,/When ladies crave to be encount'red with" (II.ii.44–6). Dalliance with ladies has no place in the heroic world of patriarchal history.

The dynastic imperatives which shape that history give a negative valence even to the idealized discourse of courtly love. Suffolk's description of Margaret's dazzling beauty –

As plays the sun upon the glassy streams,
Twinkling another counterfeited beam,
So seems this gorgeous beauty to mine eyes.
(V.iii. 62–4)

employs the same term, "counterfeit," that was used in contemporary writing to describe the deceptive powers of actors. The
only times the discourse of courtly love appears in *Henry VI, Part
I* are to express the Dolphin's infatuation with Joan and Suffolk's
infatuation with Margaret, and in both cases it is associated with
the loss of manhood and royal authority. Shamefully overcome by
Joan in single combat, the Dolphin is immediately overcome by
sexual passion as well. Imploring the peasant to "look gracious on
thy prostrate thrall" (I.ii.117), he declares, "My heart and hands
thou hast at once subdu'd . . . Let me thy servant and not sovereign
be" (I.ii.109–11). Emphasizing the impropriety of his abjection, he
immediately adds, "'Tis the French Dolphin sueth to thee thus"
(I.ii.112). In *Henry VI, Part II* and *Part III* Margaret's sexual allure
will produce a similar abdication of English royal authority.
Suffolk ends this play, in fact, by declaring, "Margaret shall now
be Queen, and rule the King;/ But I will rule both her, the King,
and realm"(V.v.107–8).

In considering the power of illicit sex and the bastards it could
produce to undermine the historical project, it is important to
remember the ideological functions of dynastic history. Designed
to authenticate the relationships between fathers and sons, it
constructed a verbal substitute for the visible, physical connection
between a mother and her children. That essential act of displacement became a focus of anxiety because the invisible, putative connection between fathers and sons that formed the basis for
patriarchal authority was always dubious, always vulnerable to
subversion by an adulterous wife. In the case of a king, moreover,
cuckoldry constituted a threat to royal succession and therefore a
serious crime against the state. Political authority based on
hereditary right required the repression of women for the same
reason that it could never do without them. The necessary
medium for the transmission of patrilineal authority, women were
also the only custodians of the dangerous knowledge that always
threatened to dishonor the fathers and disinherit the sons and in
so doing, subvert the entire project of patriarchal history (Kahn
1981: 13, 17; Rackin 1990: chapter 4).

6

HENRY VI, PART II

Although Joan is burned at the stake at the end of *Henry VI, Part I*, the subversive forces she embodies survive in *Part II* in the persons of unruly women and rebellious commoners. Unlike *Part I*, where much of the action takes place on French soil, *Part II* is set entirely in England, an England descending rapidly into the chaos of civil war; and the domestic dissension already represented in *Part I* becomes the focus of the action. These two early plays are united, however, in their representation of women as a principal cause of England's problems. Foretold at the very end of *Part I* and announced in the opening scene of *Part II*, Margaret's marriage to Henry VI brings the subversive forces embodied by the French women in *Part I* to the heart of the English court. The French women who threaten to subvert the English historical project in *Part I* are unmarried; in *Part II*, the dangers they embody quite literally come home to England in the form of ambitious wives, married to the men who govern the land. These women threaten both the authority of their husbands and the stability of the kingdom. Margaret openly defies her husband, engages in an adulterous love affair with an ambitious courtier, and takes a leading role in dangerous court intrigues. Eleanor Cobham, wife of Gloucester, the upright Lord Protector, defies his wishes, scheming to put him on the throne so she herself can become queen. Fundamental to the play's brutal representation of political disorder, then, is its emphasis on the gender disorder at the heart of the English state and the English family.

Scholars are still debating which of these two plays was written first, but whatever their order of composition, the narrative links between them suggest an effort to tell a connected story. Thus, the play that we have come to know as *Henry VI, Part II* could have been written either as a sequel or a prequel to *Henry VI, Part I*. If Shakespeare began by writing about the earliest part of Henry VI's reign, then *Henry VI, Part I* came first, for it begins with the funeral of Henry V and concentrates on the struggles of Henry VI's forces, especially those of Lord Talbot, to retain the French territories Henry V had conquered. *Henry VI, Part II* and *Part III*, by contrast, focus on the ensuing civil war in England, the so-called Wars of the Roses. *Henry VI, Part II* represents the early stages of that struggle. There is no certainty, however, that Shakespeare did write the plays in the same order as the events they depict. It is odd, for example, that *Henry VI, Part II* makes no mention of Joan of Arc or of Talbot, key figures in *Part I*, and no mention of the Temple Garden scene from that play in which the followers of York and Lancaster pluck the white and red roses that will become their emblems. In fact, *Part II* makes very little use of the color symbolism so prominent in *Part I*. Moreover, the title *The First part of the Contention* might imply that when first published this play did not advertise itself as the continuation of an earlier play, but rather as the beginning of a projected two-part play on the Wars of the Roses.[1]

What is clear, however, is that the world of *Henry VI, Part II* is defined by extraordinary social chaos. The greatness of Henry V is only a memory in the England ruled by his ineffectual son, and the territories in France won by the warrior father are quickly lost or bartered away by this young and "bookish" king and his contentious peers. Internal divisions wrack the commonwealth. The Cardinal, Winchester, feuds with the Lord Protector, Gloucester; Suffolk and Margaret join with York, Winchester and others to kill Gloucester, but this alliance, like most in the play, is unstable. Where the king is weak and ambition unchecked, each ally is also a potential rival for power. Moreover, not only the nobility is fractious. In Shakespeare's most extensive representation of a plebeian insurrection, English commoners, led by Jack Cade, rise up against the learned, rich, and powerful men whom they see as their oppressors.

One unforgettable manifestation of the breakdown of order in the play is the startling amount of brute violence it depicts, especially in the form of decapitation. Suffolk is beheaded at sea, but his head is sent back to the English court. Cade also loses his head, and it is brought to the king to earn his killer, Alexander Iden, the reward promised for cutting down a traitor. Cade, in his turn, had already had Lord Say beheaded, along with Say's son-in-law, James Cromer; and he had ordered their heads to be placed on poles and made "to kiss" at every corner. The severed heads symbolize the dismemberment of the troubled kingdom, where the head of state is unable to rule. Other bodies suffer different kinds of violence in the play. For her part in witchcraft and conjuration, Gloucester's wife, Eleanor Cobham, is made to walk barefoot in a sheet through the streets of London. William Stafford, killed by Cade's men, has his body dragged to London behind Cade's horse. Gloucester, Protector of the realm, is strangled in his bed, and his corpse is gruesomely described with bulging eyes, a face blackened with blood, hands outstretched and grasping for life.[2] All this physical violence visited upon individual bodies makes tangible the more invisible violence inflicted by civil strife on the body of the kingdom, but it also transforms this carnage into theatrical entertainment. The play is perfectly orthodox in its depiction of the horrors of civil war and the dangers of a weak king, but it transforms those horrors into scenes of spectacular and sadistic stage violence, destabilizing by theatrical re-presentation the cultural orthodoxies the story it tells is designed to express.

Henry VI, Part II makes the young King Henry responsible for much of the disorder in his kingdom, and it insistently connects his failures as monarch to his failures of masculinity. The play opens with Henry receiving his new French bride from Suffolk. The young king's excessive passion for Margaret marks him instantly as an effeminate or womanish man. In early modern sexual discourses, an effeminate man was typically one who, like the inferior being, woman, let passion control his reason. To love a woman too much marked a man as effeminate, at the mercy of his emotions and his desire (Sinfield 1992: 127–42). When he first sees Margaret and hears her speak, Henry exclaims:

> Her sight did ravish, but her grace in speech,
> Her words yclad with wisdom's majesty,
> Makes me from wond'ring fall to weeping joys,
> Such is the fullness of my heart's content.
>
> (I.i.32–5)

Ravished by the sight of Margaret, Henry is further undone when she speaks, unable to keep himself from weeping. Such overflowing emotion signals a loss of self-control, and his subsequent actions confirm his loss of judgment. As the articles of marriage are read, it becomes plain that Margaret is a bride without a dowry and that King Henry must cede to her father both the Duchy of Anjou and the County of Maine, territories which the forces of Henry V had with great sacrifice conquered. The consternation caused by King Henry's immediate acceptance of these terms, a consternation shared even by Gloucester, suggests how far the young king has ventured into the domain of the irrational and how little, his authority thus undermined, he will subsequently be able to use his monarchial position to quell the mounting dissension among his nobles.

Henry's lack of manly self-control is matched by what is represented as Margaret's unwomanly self-assertiveness. She does not reciprocate her husband's affection, but openly prefers the courtly Suffolk. In *Henry VI, Part I*, Shakespeare shows Suffolk arranging the marriage between Margaret and Henry to satisfy both his own adulterous desire for her and his political ambitions (V.iii.81–195; V.v). In this play, Margaret frankly declares disappointment with Henry:

> I tell thee, Pole, when in the city Tours
> Thou ran'st a-tilt in honor of my love
> And stol'st away the ladies' hearts of France,
> I thought King Henry had resembled thee
> In courage, courtship, and proportion;
> But all his mind is bent to holiness,
> To number Ave-Maries on his beads;
> His champions are the prophets and apostles,
> His weapons holy saws of sacred writ,
> His study is his tilt-yard, and his loves
> Are brazen images of canonized saints.
> I would the college of the Cardinals
> Would choose him Pope and carry him to Rome,
> And set the triple crown upon his head –
> That were a state fit for his holiness.
>
> (I.iii.50–64)

In Margaret's contemptuous description, Henry appears more fit for a cloister than a throne (or a marriage bed), while Suffolk is endowed with all the glamour of a figure from Castiglione's *The Book of the Courtier*. This popular sixteenth-century conduct book instructed gentlemen in graceful deportment not only in chivalric arts such as horsemanship, but also in conversation and in the other social pastimes appropriate to a courtier. Suffolk has all the courtly skills; Henry none. Pious and ineffectual, the king dotes on Margaret but is unable to please her. The courtly glamour she prefers, however, is itself suspect, as the sign of a degenerate modernity.

Henry VI, Part II has no idealized figure such as Talbot through whom to articulate nostalgia for a vanished era of masculine heroism. The wise governor, the Duke of Gloucester, however, comes closest to setting the play's standard for proper English manhood, and his behavior quickly reveals Suffolk's deficiencies. Suffolk, for example, shows no respect for England's martial heritage when, in exchange for making Margaret Henry's bride, he barters away the French territories won by Henry V. By contrast, Gloucester is allied from the first scene with those who despise Suffolk's easy surrender of these territories. Suffolk's adulterous passion for Margaret, moreover, is a sign of his own lack of self-control, and one which reveals his fundamental disloyalty as a subject of the king. Gloucester, by contrast, despite his devotion to his wife, reproves her ambition and acquiesces in her punishment for crimes against the state. Suffolk fails in other ways to demonstrate the regard for the English commonwealth exemplified by the good Duke Humphrey. This contrast between the two is shown early in the play (I.iii) when the common people mistake Suffolk for Gloucester, thus allowing the predatory courtier to intercept the petitions they have prepared asking Gloucester to redress their grievances. One of those grievances is "Against the Duke of Suffolk, for enclosing the commons of Melford" (I.iii.20–2). In the sixteenth century, enclosures were a common cause of plebeian riots and protests, when land once devoted to the common use of many villagers was fenced or enclosed to allow the grazing of sheep or other forms of "efficient" agriculture that would profit only the landowner. In brushing aside this petition and another protesting the unjust actions of one of Cardinal Winchester's followers, Suffolk shows his disregard for the common good and contempt for the rights of the common people. If Gloucester is magnanimous in opening his own purse to supply the English armies in France and merciful to common offenders (III.i.115–18 and 124–7), Suffolk is self-serving in making a profit for himself when he brings Margaret from France (I.i.132–4) and rapacious in his enclosure of common land. Old-fashioned in the weapon he uses – a "two-hand sword" (II.i.45) – Gloucester also exemplifies the traditional aristocratic function of benevolent concern for those beneath him. Suffolk, by contrast, has nothing but contempt for the common people: even when he is captured by pirates, he execrates the "obscure and lousy swain" (IV.i.50) who has taken him prisoner. Suffolk may have courtly graces, but he is unlikely to have been a sympathetic figure to the socially heterogeneous audience in Shakespeare's commercial theater. Paramour of the king's French wife, contemptuous of the English commons, and one of the chief conspirators in Gloucester's murder, he appropriately loses his life to men he regards as "paltry, servile, abject drudges" (IV.i.105) in the watery no man's land between England and France.

Shakespeare's idealized portrait of Gloucester also makes strikingly apparent the degree to which Henry has degenerated from the greatness of his forefathers. Made Protector by order of Henry V, Gloucester is linked to this revered figure from the past and set apart from the corrupt peers who otherwise surround the young king. Henry's dependence on Gloucester throughout the first half of the play underscores the fact that the king has not yet, and perhaps may never, attain perfect manhood. For example, when confronted at St Albans with a supposed miracle, the young king is credulity itself. Simpcox, allegedly blind from birth, claims to have regained his sight; Henry believes his every word. It is the Lord Protector who discerns that Simpcox is a theatrical imposter, pretending to be what he is not, and contrives a means of exposing his fraud. Of even greater importance are Gloucester's attempts to keep the young king from falling prey to the lies and machinations of the corrupt peers. In singling out Gloucester as a rival to be eliminated, Margaret both acknowledges Gloucester's power and recognizes that Henry cannot pretend to control the realm while Gloucester holds the staff that symbolizes his authority as Lord Protector. Although Margaret and her fellow conspirators at court eventually do undermine Gloucester, forcing King Henry to take his staff of office (II.iii.23–4), Henry never commands the authority signified by this phallic emblem. He does not even use his authority to save Gloucester's life when Gloucester is accused by his enemies of crimes against the state. Henry tearfully professes his faith in Gloucester's innocence, but does nothing to help him. Withdrawing from the Parliament, he tells Margaret: "my heart is drown'd with grief,/ Whose flood begins to flow within mine eyes" (III.i.198–9). Praising Gloucester as the "map of honor, truth, and loyalty" (III.i.203), he describes both his uncle and himself in an extended simile that portrays them both as victims, and himself as a feminized victim.

> And as the butcher takes away the calf,
> And binds the wretch, and beats it when it strays,
> Bearing it to the bloody slaughter-house,
> Even so remorseless have they borne him hence;
> And as the dam runs lowing up and down,
> Looking the way her harmless young one went,
> And can do nought but wail her darling's loss,
> Even so myself bewails good Gloucester's case
> With sad unhelpful tears, and with dimm'd eyes
> Look after him, and cannot do him good,
> So mighty are his vowed enemies.
>
> (III.i.210–20)

Compared to a mother cow bewailing the loss of a calf carried off to slaughter, the King of England is refigured as a lowly domestic animal and regendered as a bereaved – and helpless – mother. Himself the author of the comparison, the king is also the author of his own disempowerment.

Henry's failings as a king are thus presented in part as failings of masculinity. He can neither fight with a sword; tilt with a lance; nor effectively wield the staff of office once held by Gloucester. His excessive love for Margaret makes him act unwisely in regard to her dowry and the territories demanded by her father; and his response to the turmoil in his land is to pray and weep. Only once does Henry act decisively, and even then he does so at the behest of Salisbury, Warwick, and the enraged commons. After Gloucester's death, the commons in anger demand Suffolk's death or banishment. For a moment, Henry acts like a king, ignoring Margaret's pleas and giving Suffolk just three days to leave the realm. It is an action that rids him both of one of the peers who plotted Gloucester's death and also of his chief rival for Margaret's affections. It is also an action whose decisiveness he does not repeat. For most of the rest of the play Henry is on the run, forced to flee London before the force of Jack Cade's attack and forced to flee back to London before the fact of York's victory at St Albans. The leadership of his troops falls largely to his wife, the warlike Margaret, and to Clifford and Somerset.

It was a commonplace of early modern thought that mannish women – that is, those who assume the prerogatives of men – emerge when men are womanish and fail to assert control over their wives and daughters.[3] One of the many signs of gender disorder in this play is the spectacular rise of Margaret to fill the vacuum created by Henry's ineffective performance as king. This Margaret is neither the beautiful bride courted by Suffolk at the end of *Henry VI, Part I*, nor the cruel virago who dominates the action of *Part III*. Rather, she is a woman whose sexuality and ambition place her quite beyond her husband's control and who increasingly assumes the public roles he has abdicated. Anxious to be rid of Gloucester's interference in state matters, she plays a leading part in engineering his death; and by Act V she is herself on the battlefield, actively participating in the military decisions in the campaign against York and telling Henry when he must flee and what he must do.

Shakespeare's representation of Margaret makes her appear morally worse than she does in his sources. The Margaret of the chronicles does not scheme against Eleanor Cobham, Gloucester's wife, nor does she participate in the plot against Gloucester himself (Pugliatti 1992: 460). Shakespeare has her do both, and, as with Joan of Arc, he associates her outspoken strength with heightened sexuality. In Shakespeare's play, Margaret's adulterous association with Suffolk is not just a rumor or a surmise, as it was when mentioned in his historical sources; rather, the two lovers appear frequently on stage together, and when Suffolk is banished, their farewell is an impassioned aria punctuated with kisses and tears. This scene is remarkably sensual, and it once again reveals the dangers, to men, of excessive passion for a woman. Suffolk is undone by the prospect of parting. Margaret reproves him as a "coward woman and soft-hearted wretch" (III.ii.307) for his inability to overcome his grief and rail and curse at his enemies. When they are finally at the point of parting, Suffolk expresses his abject dependence on Margaret as he contemplates staying in order to die in her presence:

> If I depart from thee, I cannot live,
> And in thy sight to die, what were it else
> But like a pleasant slumber in thy lap?
> Here could I breathe my soul into the air,
> As mild and gentle as the cradle-babe

Dying with mother's dug between its lips;
Where, from thy sight, I should be raging mad,
And cry out for thee to close up mine eyes,
To have thee with thy lips to stop my mouth;
So shouldst thou either turn my flying soul,
Or I should breathe it so into thy body,
And then it liv'd in sweet Elysium.
To die by thee were but to die in jest,
From thee to die were torture more than death.
O, let me stay, befall what may befall.

(III.ii.388–402)

Suffolk's neediness is embarrassingly apparent. He cannot imagine living outside of Margaret's presence. Throughout the speech, his language of death and dying puns on the Renaissance meaning of death as sexual orgasm. To die in Margaret's presence would be like slumbering in her lap (often a word implying female genitalia), or like dying while nursing at her breast. Away from her, by contrast, death would be terrifying. The sensuous immediacy of Suffolk's language testifies to the erotic power Margaret exercises over him, a man who possesses some of the political and courtly skills Henry lacks, but who is equally vulnerable to Margaret's sexual attractiveness. His desire infantilizes him and renders him passive. He imagines slumbering in Margaret's lap or nursing at her breast or, his soul having gone from his body, waiting for her kiss to draw that soul back to his – or to her – body.

While Joan in *Henry VI, Part I* is accused of various kinds of sexual impropriety and often talked about in sexualized terms, Margaret in this scene commands the stage as a sexually mature and erotically powerful figure in a way Joan never does. This sexuality is in part what makes her a powerful stage presence in the play, but it is clearly represented as dangerous to men and to the good order of the kingdom. It impairs Henry's judgment, and here it renders Suffolk passive and immobile. While there is no overt mention of the fact that Margaret's adulterous relationship with Suffolk could call in question the legitimacy of Henry's heirs, the ship's officer who indicts Suffolk for various crimes before having him killed specifically mentions kissing the queen's lips as one of the crimes for which he must suffer (IV.i.75), along with wasting the treasury of the realm, marrying the king to a woman without a dowry, and contributing to the loss of the French territories.

Perhaps the most egregious sign of the inordinate passion that Margaret herself feels for Suffolk occurs when the severed head of her lover is sent back to Henry's court. Margaret insists on carrying it about, mourning, weeping, and vowing revenge even in the presence of the king. The public nature of her grief and her fetishizing of this severed body part characterize Margaret as a figure of willful passion, dangerously oblivious to the decorum that should govern the behavior of the king's wife. By way of reproach, however, all the timid Henry does is to lament that should he die, his queen would mourn less for him than she does for Suffolk.

To depict Margaret as a figure of open and unrestrained sexual passion is one way of demonizing her and representing the dangers of a femininity not firmly under the control of a father or husband. But the figure of the strong-willed wife is doubled in this text, compounding and underscoring the threat. Even the good Duke Humphrey has a wife, Eleanor Cobham, whom he cannot control. Depicted as enemies and rivals, Margaret and Eleanor are, nonetheless, united by their assertive, ambitious natures. Against Gloucester's express wishes, Eleanor aspires to put him on his nephew's throne in order to make herself the Queen of England. The competing dreams Gloucester and Eleanor recount in I.ii underscore the differences that separate husband and wife and the danger she poses to his public position. Troubled, he tells her that he dreamed his staff of office (that often-mentioned and crucial stage prop) had been broken by the Cardinal and the heads of Somerset and Suffolk set on the two pieces. The broken staff foreshadows the end of Gloucester's political power as well as the later deaths of Somerset and Suffolk, but Eleanor reads the dream only as a sign that those who oppose Gloucester will lose their heads. Rushing to recount her own dream, Eleanor inadvertently reveals the role she will play in Gloucester's impending downfall.

> Methought I sate in seat of majesty
> In the cathedral church of Westminster,
> And in that chair where kings and queens were crown'd,
> Where Henry and Dame Margaret kneel'd to me,
> And on my head did set the diadem.
>
> (I.ii.36–40)

The ambition Margaret expresses here leads her immediately after this encounter to turn to a witch and a conjurer for information about the fate of those she perceives as blocking her way to the throne – an action that leads to her downfall and eventually to Gloucester's. As it turns out, his dream of the broken staff signals not only the end of his public power but the end of his patriarchal authority in the family as well. His wife's willful decision to ignore his command that she "banish the canker of ambitious thoughts" (I.ii.18) undoes the entire edifice of his authority both at home and in the state. Again, an ungovernable wife is represented as a danger, here to the authority of the kingdom's wisest governor.

Eleanor's dream reveals much about the exact form of her transgression. Significantly, the person crowned in the dream is Eleanor alone, although it is Gloucester who as brother to Henry V has a blood claim to the throne if Henry VI dies without issue. Perhaps even more significant is the association of her treasonous ambition with images of theatricality. Dreaming of sitting on the coronation throne, a diadem on her head, with the former king and queen kneeling at her feet, Eleanor's fantasy of usurpation focuses on her theatrical assumption of the clothes and symbols of royalty. Her taste for theatrical self-display is also represented as a distinctively feminine form of ambition. Angry that her husband will not move to seize the throne, she declares,

> Follow I must, I cannot go before
> While Gloucester bears this base and humble mind.
> Were I a man, a duke, and next of blood,
> I would remove these tedious stumbling-blocks,
> And smooth my way upon their headless necks;
> And being a woman, I will not be slack
> To play my part in Fortune's pageant
>
> (I.ii.61–67)

Eleanor's frequently noted sartorial extravagance is another signal of her ambition, as well as making plain the fact that the Lord Protector's wife is much more wealthy than the poverty-stricken queen. So convincingly does Eleanor act and dress the part of royalty in the daily life of the court that, by Margaret's own testimony "Strangers in court do take her for the Queen" (I.iii.79). Eleanor's is an essentially theatrical challenge to Margaret. Not born a queen, she plays the part of one by her sartorial displays and troops of followers (Willis 1995: 187). As throughout the first tetralogy, this form of theatricality is suspect (Howard 1994: 130–9), disruptive of the "natural" order of society. Whether it is Cade pretending to be a descendent of Edmund Mortimer or Simpcox pretending to be the special beneficiary of a miraculous healing, acting a part above one's station or concealing one's true identity constitututes a subversive challenge to legitimate authority.

Eleanor's subsequent traffic with priests, witches, and conjurors further discredits her, just as Margaret was discredited by her sexualization. It also connects Eleanor to Joan of Arc in *Part I*, another woman shown summoning spirits to her aid. In the early 1590s there was considerable interest in England in the question of witchcraft. Writers such as Reginald Scot and George Gifford had recently (1584 and 1587) published treatises about the phenomenon, and in 1591 word reached England concerning James VI's prosecution of witches in Scotland (Jackson 1988: 61). As Peter Stallybrass has argued (1982: 190–1), anxieties about female challenges to patriarchal authority frequently lay at the root of early modern witchcraft hysteria. Considerable powers were attributed to women believed to be witches, including the ability to harm or kill their victims and to bring bad luck upon anyone they cursed. When the ambitious and powerful Eleanor is shown in the company of Margery Jordan, a witch, and two of her companions, a conjuror and two priests, the effect is damning. In Protestant England, Catholic priests were themselves widely regarded as dangerous and deceptive figures, in part because fear of persecution forced them to use both caution and secrecy in propagating their faith. Throughout Elizabeth's reign Protestants worried that Catholic supporters of the King of Spain or of Mary Queen of Scots were attempting to overthrow her. Eleanor is thus represented as subversively "unEnglish" when she consorts with Catholic priests in what could be construed as a plot to bring down an anointed King of England. What Eleanor asks of the conjuror and the witch is knowledge of the fates of King Henry and of Suffolk and Somerset, two of his most powerful peers. The spirits they summon deliver three cryptic prophecies. The first, regarding Henry, is typical in its ambiguity: "The duke yet lives that Henry shall depose;/ But him out-live, and die a violent death" (I.iv.30–1). This sentence may mean that a duke will depose Henry or that Henry will depose a duke; one of them will die a violent death after outliving the other, but it is impossible to tell which is which. Such riddling prophecies were especially feared by the authorities, for their ambiguities could be exploited to promote rebellion or sedition among the common people. Political prophecies had specifically been banned by Henry VIII, Edward VI, and Elizabeth herself (Hobday 1979: 72). Caught soliciting such prophecies, Eleanor is subjected to a shaming ritual and banished to the Isle of Man. Her confederates, unprotected by her high rank, are hanged and burned. That Eleanor ended up on the Isle of Man is historically accurate; but it is also symbolically appropriate. A female over-reacher, she is condemned to live out her life in the space of "man."

The shaming of Eleanor makes this ambitious woman a public spectacle in a way that ironically literalizes her earlier anxiety about the "tedious stumbling-blocks" (I.ii.64) that stood in the way of her ambition and punishes her transgressive fantasy of playing the part of the queen "in Fortune's pageant" (I.ii.67). Her rich attire is exchanged for a white robe of penitence, and her troops of followers are replaced by jeering crowds who mock her as she stumbles, barefoot, over the flinty stones of London's streets. Shakespeare puts this theatrical spectacle of a proud woman tamed near the visual center of the play (II.iv), and it is an enactment of a special kind of gendered violence. While her rank saves Eleanor from burning, the progress through London's streets strips her of her social identity. She is no longer the second-greatest woman in England, the Lord Protector's wife, but a criminal displayed to public view.

Not only the punishment for her own illicit ambition, Eleanor's humiliation is also the prelude to Gloucester's fall. With his death, chaos descends on England. As the king has been rendered effeminate by his strong-willed queen, so Gloucester has been fatally undermined by the actions of his ambitious wife. In both cases, the men's failure to control their wives has more than personal consequences; it also undermines the stability of the kingdom. In *Henry VI, Part I*, where the emphasis is on a foreign threat to English greatness, Joan endangers Talbot's attempt to retain control of the French territories that represent Henry V's legacy. In *Part II*, where the focus is on the internal dissension that threatens England's unity, Margaret and Eleanor are convenient figures of domestic disorder – unruly women whose transgressive ambitions are inextricably implicated in the political disorder that overtakes the realm.

In *Part II*, Margaret continues to wield power to the end, which is one reason the play concludes so open-endedly. Female ambition has not been entirely quelled. But while Margaret escapes

Eleanor's fate, she loses Suffolk, who is banished, and after Gloucester's death she is faced with her most formidable opponent in the person of Richard, Duke of York. York embodies a martial, self-enclosed masculinity untainted by womanly affections and unweakened by sexual desire. His success seems in part to be attributable to his isolation from the female ambition and female sexuality that undermine Gloucester, Henry, and Suffolk. Significantly, York is never represented as having either a mistress or a wife, but he does have sons, who support and underwrite his growing authority.

York's autonomy and his power are both revealed in III.i when word comes to Henry's court that the Irish are in rebellion. Given an army to quell this rebellion, York seizes the occasion to facilitate his usurpation of the English throne. In a long, breathtakingly energetic soliloquy, he reveals his plans to the audience:

> My brain, more busy than the laboring spider,
> Weaves tedious snares to trap mine enemies.
> Well, nobles, well; 'tis politicly done,
> To send me packing with an host of men:
> I fear me you but warm the starved snake,
> Who, cherish'd in your breasts, will sting your hearts.
> 'Twas men I lack'd, and you will give them me;
> I take it kindly. Yet be well assur'd
> You put sharp weapons in a madman's hands.
> While I in Ireland nourish a mighty band,
> I will stir up in England some black storm
> Shall blow ten thousand souls to heaven or hell;
> And this fell tempest shall not cease to rage
> Until the golden circuit on my head,
> Like to the glorious sun's transparent beams,
> Do calm the fury of this mad-bred flaw.
>
> (III.i.339–54)

Soliloquies are a device for creating intimacy between an audience and a character. York here gets the play's big soliloquy, and in it he seductively confesses to an overweening ambition, using this intimacy with the audience to rivet their attention and make them complicit with his agenda. It is a device Shakespeare will use again, in *Henry VI, Part III* and in *Richard III*, in constructing the theatrical charisma of Richard of York's villainous son, Richard of Gloucester. In this speech, York declares that his desire for the crown will make him busy as a spider, venomous as a snake, and wild as a madman. These images dehumanize York, but they also reveal his singleness of purpose. Policy, not love, governs his actions. Having some claim to the throne as a descendent of the third son of Edward III, York scruples at nothing to make good on that claim. The seductiveness of this chilling speech owes much to the fact that few of the male figures in the play possess a similar singleness of focus or seem so immune to the dangers represented by women.

Importantly, the immense danger that York represents to Henry's authority and England's well-being, as well as the ruthless violence he is prepared to set loose, are displaced in the second half of the play onto a lower-class figure, the infamous Jack Cade. In *Henry VI, Part I*, the threats to the English patriarchy are concentrated in the figure of Joan, who embodies the transgressive power of feminine theatricality and and also speaks with the subversive voice of lower-class self-assertion. In *Part II* these subversive forces are separated. Ambitious, demonized, but nobly-born wives, Margaret and Eleanor threaten patriarchal order, while the rampaging commoner, Jack Cade, exhibits some of Joan's earthy effrontery before established authority. Cade respects neither the privileges nor the laws of his social betters. At York's behest (III.i.355-9), he claims to be a descendent of Edmund Mortimer, Richard II's designated successor to the English throne. Like Eleanor Cobham and like Joan, Cade is thus a theatrical role-player, one whose impersonations subvert Henry's authority. As Mortimer's supposed descendent, Cade plays on the grievances of the common people, inciting them to march against London to unseat the king. Although both the women and Cade are demonized in this play, neither Eleanor nor Margaret evinces any sympathy for the commons. Margaret, in fact, is with Suffolk when he is beset by common petitioners in I.iii., and in the folio text it is she who tears up their petitions, commanding, "Away, base cullions!" (I.iii.40). And as we shall see, Cade's supposed concern for the poor does not preclude brutality toward lower-class women. In that regard, Cade reinforces, rather than contests, the patriarchal power of his social superiors. In this play, then, the forces of female and of lower-class subversion are not only kept separate, but to some extent pitted against one another.

York's initial description of Cade emphasizes his warlike masculinity and his duplicitous cunning. York remembers Cade fighting with the Irish kerns until his thighs were impaled with so many arrows that he looked like a porcupine. But rather than being weakened by these darts, Cade capered about like a Morris dancer, shaking the arrows like a dancer's bells (III.i.360–6). Penetration by arrows does not effeminate Cade; rather, it energizes him. Impervious to pain, he can turn his astonishing energies to the defense of England against foreign rebels, but he can also turn those energies against England itself. Cade's treacherous side is hinted at when he is described as not only fighting the Irish, but also mimicking them. Disguised as a shaggy-haired Irish kern, Cade penetrates the Irish encampments, bearing their secrets back to his English masters.[4] Nonetheless, Cade's ability to play the kern discredits him as a stalwart defender of the English state, revealing the theatrical skill which later allows him to adopt the persona of Mortimer's descendent and connecting him to the dangerous and subversive theatricality often associated with women.

Much recent criticism of the play has focused on the degree to which it presents a sympathetic portrait of Cade and of the rebellion he leads (Greenblatt 1983; Patterson 1989: 32–51; Rackin 1990: 207–21; Helgerson 1992: 195–245; Pugliatti 1992; Wilson 1993: 23–44; Cartelli 1994). His status as York's henchman clearly undercuts Cade's credibility as a spokesperson for popular grievances, and his connection with Ireland and the Irish kerns associates his actions with a dangerously foreign territory. It is as if Cade brings Irish wildness into England with his march on London. Yet Cade and his followers articulate a critique of social and economic inequality that had a history in peasant revolts stretching back well into the fourteenth century but alive in the London of the 1590s. Historically, Cade's rebellion took place in 1450, but in representing it Shakespeare borrows details from accounts of other protests. For example, it was in the Peasants' Rebellion of 1381 that rebels such as Wat Tyler marched on London, burned London Bridge, and attacked the Savoy – John of Gaunt's house – and the Inns of Court. Shakespeare attributes these actions to Cade. Other rebellions occurred throughout the fifteenth and sixteenth centuries, and the decade of the 1590s saw a number of riots in the city of London. Some of these were directed against foreign workers; some were protests against the high cost of food or the granting of monopolies that put the control of a valuable commodity in the hands of a tiny group (Manning 1988: 187–219).

Cade and his followers repeat many of the complaints voiced in these rebellions and riots. They attack the idleness and the privileges of the rich, including the privilege of literacy, and Cade speaks to the poverty and hunger of his followers when he promises that when he rules, bread will be cheap, beer of the highest quality, and all goods held in common. The rebels insist that working men, and only working men, should be magistrates and rulers. As one of the rebels opines: "it is said, labor in thy vocation; which is as much to say as, let the magistrates be laboring men; and therefore should we be magistrates" (IV.ii.16–18).

While Cade thus gives voice to popular grievances, his position is nonetheless undermined and his character blackened in countless ways. He is a counterfeiter, playing the role of nobleman when he is only a commoner, and he is a tool of York. He is also brutal, having men killed because they can read and write or because they address him by the wrong title. What is less often noted is that Cade is also guilty of promoting sexual assaults on women. In the 1594 quarto version of the play, *The First part of the Contention betwixt the two famous Houses of Yorke and Lancaster*, one of Cade's men rapes a sergeant's wife, and Cade refuses to punish the offender. In fact, he has the sergeant's tongue cut out for complaining of the crime, and then has him put to death. This passage is missing in the folio version of the play, although in the folio Cade says, "There shall not be a maid be married, but she shall pay to me her maidenhead ere they [the women's husbands] have it" (IV.vii.121–3). Women are thus among the things Cade would make common, at least in regard to his own "right" to all their maidenheads. Ironically, Cade here is copying a supposed medieval custom, the *droit de seigneur*, by which members of the nobility assumed the right to the maidenheads of women who married men on their estates. But in Shakespeare's play, it is the lower-class rebels, and not the nobility, who engage in predatory sex or express their imagined right to the maidenheads of other men's wives. By this act of displacement, the sexual exploitation practiced by the dominant members of society is attributed to those most usually victimized by it.

Along with Eleanor and Margaret, Cade serves as a convenient scapegoat for the disorder that is the central fact of the world of *Henry VI, Part II*. Cade himself ends the play dead, killed while stealing food from a country gentleman's garden. He has, however, served the purpose York intended: that is, he has driven King Henry from the city of London and given York an excuse to bring in his army in supposed defense of the monarch. Yet York himself is shielded from committing the atrocities attributed to Cade. At St Albans, York defeats Clifford, Henry's champion, in a chivalric hand-to-hand encounter. In *Henry VI, Part II*, the lower class rebel and the play's women, along with the effeminate king, thus bear the brunt of the blame for the disorder and violence that overtakes England. Henry's weakness as a ruler and his failings of masculinity have alienated many of his peers and made it possible for rebels to rear their heads. By the end of the play the king retains little of the authority that was his father's legacy to him.

The subversive power of Margaret, however, has not been quelled. While Eleanor has been banished and Cade is dead, the queen lives. On the battle field of St Albans, she is still chiding Henry for his failures of masculinity – "What are you made of? You'll nor fight nor fly" (V.ii.74). She takes command of their battered army, ordering the retreat to London. By the end of this play, which clearly looks ahead to its sequel, Margaret has grown into the first tetralogy's most sustained example of the danger which ambitious and sexual women pose to English manhood and to English monarchy. At the same time, she embodies perhaps the only power that can match the unalloyed ferocity of Richard, Duke of York. As the play has made theatrical pleasure from the horrors of civil war, so it has, in demonizing Margaret, also invested her with astonishing sensuality and power. In *Henry VI, Part III*, Margaret will dominate the play as does no other woman in any of Shakespeare's historical dramas.

7

HENRY VI, PART III

E. M. W. Tillyard said of *Henry VI, Part III* that when Shakespeare wrote it he was "tired or bored: or perhaps both" (Tillyard 1944: 190). Editors are no longer sure that Shakespeare was the sole author of this play, but contemporary critics, especially feminist ones, have found it considerably more interesting than Tillyard did. Civil war dominates *Henry VI, Part III*. The cast of characters is narrowed almost exclusively to members of the nobility, and battle scenes regularly punctuate the action. With the sitting king, Henry VI, impossibly weak, the English crown becomes a trophy various factions attempt to seize, rather than a lineal and sacred inheritance. But while *chaos* is the word probably used most often in conjunction with this particular play, that chaos allows interesting and anomalous figures to emerge and social boundaries and roles to be tested and contested, including those of gender. The most prominent of these transgressive figures is Margaret. Assuming male prerogatives, she initiates much of the action. She takes charge of Prince Edward when his father in effect disinherits him; she leads the Lancastrian forces repeatedly into battle against their Yorkist foes; when defeated in battle, she goes to France for aid; finally captured, she continues to inveigh against her enemies. Quick, decisive and clever, Margaret gives the lie to those who feel they have nothing to fear because "a woman's general" (I.ii.68). In fact, this woman is one of the play's most impressive and most successful martial figures.

When the play was first published in a quarto version in 1595, it bore a title, *The True Tragedy of Richard, Duke of York*, that might have misled readers as to which figure would dominate the action. Because the Duke of York had played such a commanding role in *Henry VI, Part II*, where he suborned Jack Cade to foment popular rebellion, killed Clifford, and routed the king's forces, audiences would have been primed to expect his pre-eminence in the ensuing play. But in *Part III* Richard is dead by the end of the first act, and it is Queen Margaret's army that has defeated him, Margaret herself who delivers one of the stab wounds that cause his death. Subsequently Margaret goes on to defeat many other antagonists before herself suffering her one inconsolable loss: the murder of her young son.

Margaret's prominence in the action immediately suggests a weakness in the patriarchal structures that should have rendered her less visible and less powerful. In fact, *Henry VI, Part III* represents an extraordinary breakdown in the male bonds of filiation and loyalty, some biological and some not, that underwrote the feudal social order represented in this play (Kahn 1981: 59). The symbolic center of the social system, the king, is so little invested in the continuation of his genealogical line upon the English throne, that in the first scene of the play he agrees to the self-defeating bargain with the Duke of York allowing York to "Enjoy the kingdom after my decease" (I.i.175) as long as Henry can hold the throne in peace during his own lifetime. This unnatural act is fatal both to Henry's position as father in his own family and as ruler in his own kingdom; and it becomes the paradigm for the repeated betrayals that pepper the play's action. Its most immediate consequence is to alienate Henry from some of his most important nobles, particularly Northumberland, young Clifford, and Westmerland, and from his wife and son, as well.

In addition, Henry's act frees Margaret to become the family's patriarch in the sense that she not only assumes authority in the family and in the state, but also takes upon herself the burden of guaranteeing Prince Edward's succession to the English throne. She begins by an act of divorce. To Henry she says:

> . . .thou prefer'st thy life before thine honor;
> And seeing thou dost, I here divorce myself
> Both from thy table, Henry, and thy bed,
> Until that act of parliament be repeal'd
> Whereby my son is disinherited.
> The northern lords that have forsworn thy colors
> Will follow mine, if once they see them spread;
> And spread they shall be, to thy foul disgrace,

And utter ruin of the house of York.
Thus do I leave thee. Come, son, let's away.
Our army is ready; come, we'll after them.
(I.i.246–56)

Crucially, Edward has become *Margaret's* son here, and he not only stays in her company for most of the rest of the play, but echoes her warlike words and manner. In early modern culture, children were assumed to belong to their fathers, who determined their disposition and place of residence. Women were simply the vessels that delivered the father's progeny to the world and transmitted the father's lineage to his sons. It is remarkable, therefore, when Margaret claims Edward as *her* son and bears him away from his father (see Plate 3). Paradoxically, however, it is Margaret's strength and support that empower the young prince to claim the patriarchal legacy his father has betrayed. At the end of the play, captured by King Edward and Richard of Gloucester and facing what he knows must be his own death, the young prince defies his enemies and claims his own right to the throne: "Speak like a subject, proud ambitious York!/ Suppose that I am now my father's mouth:/ Resign thy chair, and where I stand kneel thou" (V.v.17–19), To this speech of defiance, which sounds very much like one of Margaret's own defiant proclamations, she responds approvingly, "Ah, that thy father had been so resolv'd!" (V.v.22).

In separating herself from Henry's bed and table and taking on the job of championing her son's rights to the throne, Margaret is in a contradictory position within the patriarchal structures of family and state, but she is also a vehicle for exposing the ideological nature of many of patriarchy's claims. In *Henry VI, Part I* and *Part II*, Margaret was consistently represented as a danger to Henry and a threat to his kingship. Foreign-born, lacking a dowry, adulterously consorting with the Duke of Suffolk, Margaret was easily demonized as the cause of the Lancastrian misfortunes. Henry is admittedly weak, pious, and ineffectual in the earlier plays, but it is only in *Part III* that the hollowness at the center of the patriarchal edifice is fully exposed. The scandal of *Henry VI, Part III* is not that a woman is a general, but that a man, and an anointed king to boot, can perform none of the actions expected of a father and king. He is less fit to rule than his French-born wife. Ironically, she, accused by all of undermining the

Plate 3 Heroic statue of Queen Margaret with her young son, presumably Prince Edward, in the Luxembourg Gardens in Paris. Margaret is identified on the pedestal as "Marguerite d'Anjou Reine d'Angleterre 1429–1482."

Source: Reproduced by permission of the photographer, Mark Frezzo

Lancastrian dynasty, becomes its staunchest upholder, vowing to place her son on the throne he lineally inherited. Yet the play also demystifies the idea that patriarchal blood lines, even ones unadulterated by bastardy, guarantee the valor or worth of the father's descendents. Henry V was a revered king and martial hero; but his son is a failure at both. That Prince Edward is valiant seems to owe much more to his mother's example, and perhaps her blood, than to that of his pusillanimous father. Edward claims the throne in his father's name, but he does so in his mother's spirit. It is really no surprise that after a play such as *Henry VI, Part III*, Shakespeare would turn in the later histories to the examination of monarchs whose claims to the throne, while still often expressed as lineal claims, are in actuality anchored in their own performative skills.

Henry's initial transgressive act of confounding his own son's claim to the throne is, moreover, only the first of many actions that unravel the male networks by which the patriarchal culture of the play is supposed to be sustained (Berman 1962). The civil war unleashed by Henry's weakness pits Englishman against Englishman, neighbor against neighbor, family member against family member. The most famous set piece scene in the play, II.v, shows the effects on ordinary people of the struggles of their social superiors. While King Henry sits on a molehill away from the battle being waged in his name at Towton, he observes, first, a son who bears on stage the body of a man he has slain whom he then discovers to be his father; then, a father who bears the body of a man he has slain whom he then discovers to be his son.

While taking the form of an allegorical tableau in which the nameless sons and fathers act out in schematic form the dangers of civil war to family ties, the scene is also realistic in its account of exactly how such "unnatural" events came to pass. As the son says, viewing his dead father's face: "O heavy times, begetting such events!/ From London by the King was I press'd forth;/ My father, being the Earl of Warwick's man,/ Came on the part of York, press'd by his master;/ And I, who at his hands receiv'd my life,/ Have by my hands of life bereaved him" (II.v.63–8). The "English" are now a divided people, and contending factions are impressing common men into different armies. The patriarchal principle is betrayed at every level as divisions in the state sever the biological ties binding father to son. There is no single and undisputed head of the kingdom, and the man with the most immediate lineal claim to the throne has disinherited his own son. The repercussions are felt all the way down to the bottom of the social hierarchy.

Perhaps the most surprising disruption of family bonds, however, occurs not among the Lancastrians, where Henry's weakness is at least predictable, but among the Yorkists, where the ties between father and sons, brother and brother, seemed particularly strong both in *Henry VI, Part II* and in the opening acts of *Part III*. In *Part II*, York seemed to gain part of his strength from the fact that he had an impressive array of warlike sons to back his undertakings. At the battle of St Albans, York's son Richard, in particular, plays a crucial role in the Yorkist victory. In the folio version of the text Richard's defeat of Somerset under the sign of the Castle Inn follows closely after his father's defeat of Old Clifford. This placement suggests that that the actions of the father are echoed in the actions of the son, that the lineal links between them are strong and apparent.[1] The opening scene of *Henry VI, Part III* at once recalls the triumph of the Yorkist family, father and sons, at the Battle of St Albans with which the former play ended. One son, Edward, boasts that he slew or seriously wounded the Duke of Buckingham, and he brandishes a sword with the duke's blood on it. Richard, however, tops his brother's feat, for what he brandishes is the Duke of Somerset's head. To which sight his father replies: "Richard hath best deserv'd of all my sons" (I.i.17).

The closeness between Richard, Duke of York, and his sons continues. In the play's first scene, they support his bid for the throne in the Parliament House; they urge him to break his subsequent vow to permit Henry to reign in peace in exchange for York's assumption of his crown at his death; and they fight impressively for him at the Battle of Wakefield when Margaret surprises them with her army of northern lords. Just before his capture at Wakefield, York speaks movingly about his sons: "My sons, God knows what hath bechanced them;/ But this I know, they have demean'd themselves/ Like men born to renown by life or death" (I.iv.6–8). The bonds tying this father to his sons recall the bonds between Talbot and his son in *Part I*. Although a chaste wife was necessary to the production of these sons, she never appears on stage in either case. Rather, the fathers and sons seem to exist autonomously, busy in the reproduction of a masculine culture of war and of family honor. As York's sons wait to learn if their father has escaped the Battle of Wakefield alive, Richard praises his father as his father had praised his sons.

> I saw him in the battle range about,
> And watch'd him how he singled Clifford forth.
> Methought he bore him in the thickest troop
> As doth a lion in a herd of neat,
> Or as a bear, encompass'd round with dogs,
> Who having pinch'd a few and made them cry,
> The rest stand all aloof and bark at him.
> So far'd our father with his enemies,
> So fled his enemies my warlike father;
> Methinks 'tis prize enough to be his son.
>
> (II.i.11–20)

It is immediately thereafter that Richard and Edward see the miraculous vision in the sky of three perfect suns that "join, embrace, and seem to kiss,/ As if they vow'd some league inviolable" (II.i.29–30). This vision, with its obvious play on *sons* and *suns*, seems to foretell the impregnable unity of these "sons of brave Plantagenet" (II.i.35), and Edward, the oldest, vows to put the emblem of three shining suns on his shield.

It is the more surprising, then, that these sons of York do not continue in amity throughout the play. In fact, before it is over, Clarence will fight on the Lancastrian side against his brother Edward, and Richard will plot to undermine both brothers. And although Edward by the end of the play has a son to carry on the lineage of his grandfather, Richard, Duke of York, that son's life is ominously shadowed by his uncle Richard's hatred. Given the infant to kiss in the play's last scene, Richard says: "And that I love the tree from whence thou sprang'st,/ Witness the loving kiss I give the fruit" (V.vii.31–2). The tree, of course, is the family tree so often depicted, visually, in genealogies of noble families or of England's monarchs (see Plate 4). Outwardly, Richard pays homage to the newest fruit of that tree, but in an aside to the audience he says: "To say the truth, so Judas kiss'd his master,/ And cried 'All hail!' when as he meant all harm" (V.vii.33–4). Judas, the disciple who betrayed Christ, becomes the ominous model for Richard's actions.

It is important to think about how the play dramatizes this disintegration of the Yorkist family. In Shakespeare's sources, of course, Richard did turn against his brothers, and Shakespeare

Plate 4 Title page from Edward Hall, *The Union of the Two Noble and Illustre Famelies of Lancastre & Yorke* (1550). Representing Henry VIII and his dynastic predecessors as roses growing on a bush, it naturalizes the king's patrilineal authority as a true branch of the royal tree that had produced the red roses of Lancaster (left side of the picture), the white roses of York (right side), and the mixed rose that was the emblem of their union in the Tudor dynasty.

Source: Reproduced by permission of the Furness Collection, Department of Special Collections, Van Pelt-Dietrich Library, University of Pennsylvania

could not entirely alter received history. But what is striking is the way in which the betrayal of male bonds is dramatically linked to scenes involving women or the mention of men's affection for women. When Edward declares that he will bear three sons on his shield, Richard flippantly responds, "Nay, bear three daughters; by your leave I speak it,/ You love the breeder better than the male" (II.i.41–2). Punning on "bear," Richard suggests his brother should carry emblems of three women on his shield and should sire daughters, so much does he prefer women ("breeders") to men. This seems like an unimportant remark, if somewhat out of place in the midst of a scene in which the fate of their father is as yet unknown, but it is Richard's first aspersion on the manliness of his brother, the first sign of a possible breach between them. To be a breeder of women was considered a less perfect act of generation than to be a breeder of men. Richard is twitting his brother with just such a possibility as well as referrring to his inclination to sensuality.

Coppélia Kahn has argued that in the early history plays, "liaisons with women are invariably disastrous because they subvert or destroy more valued alliances between men" (Kahn 1981: 55). In this play, as in the others, this generalization proves true. The Yorkist family seems invincible while united under their powerful father and when separated from the world of women, particularly when compared to the shambles into which the Lancastrian family has fallen. But the Yorkists also begin to disintegrate when the bonds between the brothers are disrupted by Edward's irrational passion for the widow, Lady Elizabeth Grey. Their courtship scene is situated right in the middle of the play, III.ii, when Edward is exulting in his triumph over Margaret's forces and his seizure of the throne. Although Lady Grey has only come to ask for recovery of lands seized during the recent civil wars, the king holds her in conversation for a very long time. As he does, his brothers, Gloucester and Clarence, jestingly comment from the side of the stage on their brother's more-than-casual interest in this petitioner. The staging speaks volumes about the new power dynamics that are evolving at Edward's court. Edward is now the king, the central figure, but instead of being flanked with wise counselors and especially by his warlike brothers, they are pushed to the margins. It is a woman who holds his attention, and a woman, moreover, who has neither high rank nor great wealth to recommend her as a king's bride.

The sensuality that impels Edward to choose Lady Grey as his queen ironically likens him to his great foe, King Henry, who to the anguish of his wisest counselors had determined to marry the foreign-born and impoverished Margaret of Anjou. As Henry was represented as in part undone by his marriage, so is Edward's marriage his chief point of vulnerability. Its first consequence is to set his brother Richard definitively against him. Again, dramatic placement is telling. After Richard has watched his brother and Lady Grey talk, he remains on stage to deliver his great soliloquy of ambition, acknowledging his desire for the crown and describing the Machiavellian tricks he will use to destroy those, including his brothers, who stand in his way.

> I'll drown more sailors than the mermaid shall,
> I'll slay more gazers than the basilisk,
> I'll play the orator as well as Nestor,
> Deceive more slily than Ulysses could,
> And like a Sinon, take another Troy.
> I can add colors to the chameleon,
> Change shapes with Proteus for advantages,
> And set the murtherous Machevil to school.
> Can I do this, and cannot get a crown?
> Tut, were it farther off, I'll pluck it down.
>
> (III.ii. 186–95)

Richard here commits himself to the theatrical pursuit of power with no sense of loyalty to the brothers or to the family tree from which he came. What he acquires, he will acquire on his own, by his own force of will and by his ability to hide his real intentions under a series of carefully stage-managed roles. While it is true that Edward's wooing of Lady Grey is not the only cause of Richard's decision to pursue the crown, it is the immediately precipitating event, the one that makes him articulate his individual ambition, his alienation from his brothers, and his own frustration at not, because of his deformed body, being himself a likely lover.

Edward's wooing of Lady Grey is, however, the only cause of another crucial break in the circle of male alliances that has heretofore supported the Yorkist cause. Warwick, in Margaret's words the "proud setter-up and puller-down of kings" (III.iii.157), defects from his allegiance to Edward when he learns that Edward has married, making a mockery of Warwick's mission to woo

Lady Bona, the French king's sister, for Edward. "Shame on himself! for my desert is honor;/ And to repair my honor lost for him,/ I here renounce him and return to Henry" (III.iii.192–4). Warwick goes so far in cementing this renewed tie to the Lancastrians as to give his eldest daughter in marriage to Prince Edward. Warwick's change of allegiance is just one more instance of the collapse of bonds of fealty and kinship among men, and it is motivated by Edward's over-valuing a sexually desirable woman, rather than making the dynastic marriage of convenience represented by the nearly silent figure of the French king's sister. Onstage while 255 lines of dialogue are spoken, the Lady Bona herself speaks just 7, the first of which is to tell Lewis that in regard to Edward's marriage proposal, "Your grant, or your denial, shall be mine" (III.iii.130). This is a woman, who although she will urge Lewis to revenge her honor, represents the compliant womanhood and the traditional dynastic alliance Edward "should" have chosen. His insistent pursuit of Lady Grey, and eventually his marriage to her, are represented as the catalyst that separates him not only from his treacherous, self-seeking brother, Richard, but also from his chief champion, Warwick, and from his formerly loyal brother, Clarence, who publically criticizes Edward's marriage choice and expresses disgust that Edward is making profitable marriage matches for all the new queen's poor relations. Showing his solidarity with Warwick, Clarence seeks Warwick's second daughter for his own bride and joins King Henry's forces.

Henry VI, Part III, then, is spectacularly marked by the dissolution of every kind of male bond. Fathers disinherit sons; sons slay fathers and fathers sons; brothers turn against one another; dukes and earls who have sworn fealty to one monarch switch their allegiance to another. Such behavior makes perfectly understandable the actions of the simple gamekeepers who capture King Henry when he returns in disguise from Scotland to "greet mine own land with my wishful sight" (III.i.14). Upbraided by Henry for breaking their oath of loyalty to him, they answer pragmatically, "we were subjects but while you were king" (III.i.81). Although Henry castigates these lowly subjects for the sin of oath-breaking, it is his own action of disinheriting his son that has transformed kingship from a sacred inheritance to a transferable property (Hattaway 1993: 14). In such circumstances, allegiance properly belongs not to a single, true, and essential king, but to whatever person happens to possess the crown. This the gamekeepers instinctively seem to realize.

Considered in the larger context of this nearly universal disintegration of male bonds, the place of Margaret in *Part III* becomes clearer. Although she acts in the name of her son's lineal right to the throne, her actions also show how truly she understands that that right will have to be enforced by arms and money. She spends the play, in fact, obtaining both and commanding her troops in the field. But the extraordinary venom directed against Margaret within the play, and the gratuitous cruelty with which Shakespeare invests her character, reveal both her convenience as a scapegoat for the chaos around her and also the theatrical capital that could be made by staging the cultural fantasy of the monstrous Amazonian woman. Although the play quite clearly shows the hollowness of patriarchal fictions, it nonetheless manages to make Margaret the central villain. She is a target of remarkable invective. Richard of Gloucester accuses her of "hav[ing] stol'n the breech from Lancaster" (V.v.24); and Richard of York claims she behaves "like an Amazonian trull" (I.iv.114), that she has a "tiger's heart wrapp'd in a woman's hide" (I.iv.137), and that she is more inhuman than "tigers of Hyrcania" (I.iv.155). Some of these images turn Margaret into a beast; others stress her usurpation of male prerogatives; others play on contemporary myths about Amazons, warlike women with origins in Scythia who supposedly cut off a breast so that they could better use bows and arrows and who lived in all-female groups, using men only for reproductive purposes. Margaret, striding into battle, orchestrating the knighting of her son (II.ii.58–60), silencing her husband if he will not give defiance to his enemies (II.ii.118), and instilling courage in her soldiers by her rhetoric (V.iv.1–38), is a figure who evokes what we might call "Amazon anxiety."

Shakespeare plays up her monstrous qualities. The scene in which her cruelty is most on display – I.iv in which she torments York before his death – is largely Shakespeare's invention. In Hall's chronicle account of York's death, Clifford cuts off the head of the dead York, crowns that head with a paper crown, and presents it on a pole to Margaret. Shakespeare transforms his source to create the violent encounter between the still-living but defeated York and Margaret, Clifford, and Northumberland (Sen Gupta 1964: 81). Margaret is the key figure in contriving her great antagonist's humiliation and torture, first having York stand on a molehill; then inviting him to wipe his tears with a napkin dipped in the blood of his murdered son, and then having him crowned with a paper crown. It is this series of actions that elicits from York his great string of invectives against Margaret, and it is these actions that cause even Margaret's ally, Northumberland, to weep in sympathy with York's suffering. As he says: "Beshrew me, but his passions moves me so/ That hardly can I check my eyes from tears" (I.iv.150–1), and a moment later, "Had he been slaughterman to all my kin,/ I should not for my life but weep with him,/ To see how inly sorrow gripes his soul" (I.iv.169–71). To which Margaret replies, "What, weeping-ripe, my Lord Northumberland?/ Think but upon the wrong he did us all,/ And that will quickly dry thy melting tears" (I.iv.172–4). The presence of Northumberland as a weeping spectator to Margaret's atrocities invites the audience to recognize the extent of her violation of proper femininity.

That this *Grand Guignol* theater had its intended effect of riveting an audience's attention, giving it a villain it could love to hate, is attested to by the fact that York's line about Margaret – "O tiger's heart wrapp'd in a woman's hide!" (I.iv.137) – is, as we saw in Part I, the subject of the earliest printed reference to Shakespeare: Robert Greene's remark about "an upstart Crow, beautified with our feathers, that with his *Tygers hart wrapt in a Players hyde*, supposes he is as well able to bombast out a blanke verse as the best of you: and beeing an absolute *Johannes fac totum*, is in his sure conceit the onley Shakes-scene in a country" (Greene 1592, in Chambers 1923: 4: 241–2). Greene, a university-trained writer, is clearly angry at Shakespeare, who had no such training, either because Shakespeare had borrowed from Greene's work or imitated his style ("beautified with our feathers") or had simply pushed himself forward too successfully as an actor and playwright. Describing Shakespeare as an "upstart Crow," Greene clearly finds something presumptuous in his behavior. It is a testament to Shakespeare's success, however, that Greene singles him out for parody, and it is telling that the line he quotes is from York's denunciation of Margaret. It suggests that this was a scene, and a rhetorical style, that were memorable. It is also fascinating that Greene uses this line the way he does, as a description of Shakespeare and not simply as an example of his rival's high-flown rhetoric. The line in its theatrical context denigrates Margaret for her unnatural and unwomanly behavior; in Greene's polemical context it denigrates Shakespeare for unnatural ambition. Both are implicitly castigated for "forgetting their places," Margaret for forgetting her proper gender role, Shakespeare for forgetting deference to his supposed betters in wit and education. It is a nice irony that the first mention we have from any of Shakespeare's contemporaries about his theatrical work should equate him, if only fleetingly, with Margaret at her moment of greatest hubris and cruelty.

The only figure in the play to rival Margaret as a figure of the monstrous is Richard, Duke of Gloucester. It is as if in this play the failure of patriarchy produces two sorts of anomalies: the Amazonian woman and the deformed Machiavellian man. The striking thing that sets Richard apart from all the others who break bonds in this play is that he alone seems never to need to replace them, nor does he mourn their loss. Warwick moves from one set of allegiances to another; so does Clarence; the nameless father kills his son, and the son his father, but when they discover what they have done, both are overcome with grief. Margaret never forfeits her bond with her son; and even the feckless Henry acknowledges that disinheriting his son is an "unnatural" act (I.i.193) and continues to sigh for the boy afterwards (I.i.191). The disintegration of bonds in the play signals the collapse of a patriarchal edifice, but not the end of longing for those, or other, bonds. Richard is the only exception. His final soliloquy reveals the full extent of his exceptional isolation:

> Then since the heavens have shap'd my body so,
> Let hell make crook'd my mind to answer it.
> I have no brother, I am like no brother;
> And this word "love," which greybeards call divine,
> Be resident in men like one another,
> And not in me: I am myself alone.
>
> (V.vi. 78–83)

Modern psychological readings find the source of Richard's anger and outrageous deeds in his deformity. Certainly that deformity has been part of Richard's characterization from his first introduction in *Henry VI, Part II*. Clifford calls Richard a "heap of wrath, foul indigested lump,/As crooked in thy manners as thy shape!" (*Henry VI, II*: V.i.157–8). And when Margaret is tormenting York before his death she asks him: "Where are your mess of sons to back you now,/ The wanton Edward, and the lusty

George?/ And where's that valiant crook-back prodigy,/ Dicky, your boy, that with his grumbling voice/ Was wont to cheer his dad in mutinies?" (*Henry VI, III*: I.iv.73–7). But the discourse of deformity becomes part of Richard's own self-characterization and a defining aspect of his dramatization only after he breaks away from his brothers after watching Edward court Lady Grey. It is during the long soliloquy following Edward's wooing scene that Richard first speaks of his arm being shrunken "like a wither'd shrub," "an envious mountain on [his] back" and his legs "of an unequal size" (III.ii.156–9). Significantly, the intensified rhetoric about Richard's monstrous body follows immediately upon his declaration of a curse on his brother – "Would he were wasted, marrow, bones, and all,/ That from his loins no hopeful branch may spring" (III.ii.125–6) – and upon his clear declaration that nothing, not even the living bodies of his relations, will keep him from the throne.[2] In short, Richard's bodily deformity is presented as the outward sign of his unnatural nature as much as it is presented as its cause. He becomes defined by the fact of his monstrous body when he severs himself from all human ties, but not before. Rising from the collapse of the patriarchal world around him, claiming to outdo the murderous foreigner, Machiavelli, in evil (III.ii.193), Richard stands alone. In the world of this play, with its emphasis on the tragedy of shattered social bonds, such a figure can be seen only as evil, alien, and unnatural.

If Richard and his deformity are viewed in this way, what is interesting for the gender politics of this play is how differently he and Margaret, as figures of the monstrous and the unnatural, are treated at the conclusion of this play and in the next. Margaret ends *Part III* defeated. Finally captured with her son by the Yorkist faction, she has to watch the young prince stabbed by Edward, Gloucester, and Clarence. This action seems to place her in the feminine subject position which she has so long rejected. Helpless to prevent Edward's death, she swoons at its enactment and is restored only to pour out a heartrending speech of lamentation and accusation:

> Butchers and villains! bloody cannibals!
> How sweet a plant have you untimely cropp'd!
> You have no children, butchers; if you had,
> The thought of them would have stirr'd up remorse,

But if you ever chance to have a child,
Look in his youth to have him so cut off
As, deathsmen, you have rid this sweet young prince!
(V.v.61–7)

There is, of course, irony in the fact that the Margaret who taunted York with his young son Rutland's blood should be outraged at her own son's murder. But what is perhaps most significant is that the tigerish queen is here so completely disempowered and so firmly repositioned in a feminine subject position. Swooning, lamenting, begging for death at her captors' hands, but unable to taunt them into doing the deed, Margaret is finally taken from the stage. When she comes back, unhistorically, in *Richard III*, it will not be as the Amazonian warrior, but as one of a group of suffering women who play no major role in the action except to call on heaven to rain vengeance on Richard's head.

By contrast, Richard is about to become the hero, admittedly a villainous hero, of one of Shakespeare's first tragedies. For all Margaret's theatrical vigor in *Part II* and *Part III*, she is not there allowed the seductive power of the soliloquy, as both Richard of York and Richard of Gloucester are. In the ensuing play, Gloucester gets most of the soliloquies, and his self-conscious theatricality makes him the center of dramatic attention in a way that foreshadows the intense focus on the unique male subject in Shakespeare's later tragedies. From Richard's monstrous deformity, then, emerges the tragic hero, the crookback's unnatural isolation gradually transmuted into a valued uniqueness. But the denouement of Margaret's stage existence is the transformation of her powerful sexuality and her Amazonian strength into the anger of an embittered, desexualized crone. In the second tetralogy, no female figure will have her power or her prominence; warrior women will be replaced by domesticated wives.

The end of *Henry VI, Part III* oddly anticipates the later focus on the family as a locus for affection and on the creation of a domestic space separate from the public realm, but it does so in a manner that undermines Edward's royal authority. As Barbara Hodgdon has observed, the recreation of a family unit at the play's end imposes a fragile comic ending on a play of relentless cruelty and destruction (Hodgdon 1991: 75). The family reconstituted at the end of this play is nothing like the dynastic, male-centered families previously headed by Lord Talbot or by Richard, Duke of York.

Rather, what the uxorious Edward has created is a family centered on the husband's affection for his wife and child, not on his command over a patriline. This marriage has already nearly cost Edward his throne, so little did or does it conform to expectations for dynastic unions; and so little does Edward seem in control of his affections. Not a proper dynastic marriage, Edward's is not a private matter, either, safely separate from and subordinated to, his role in the public realm. Quite the opposite is true, in fact. Edward's love for Elizabeth Grey quite clearly has taken precedence over his concern for his kingdom, and in the last scene it blinds him to the danger standing at his elbow in the person of his brother. Addressing his wife and son familiarly as Bess and Ned, Edward seems devoted solely to his domestic pleasures and to the "stately triumphs, mirthful comic shows" (V.vii.43) that constitute the pleasures of his court. The husband's enthrallment with his loving wife here proves as much a danger to his masculinity and his public power as did the more overt challenges to patriarchal authority posed by demonized, ambitious, and warlike women, such as Joan of Arc, Margaret of Anjou, and Eleanor Cobham. In the Henry VI plays, there is always the anxiety that women, whether lovingly submissive or aggressively independent, will undo the patriarchal edifice and, with it, an always endangered masculinity.

8

RICHARD III

Although the First Folio classifies *Richard III* with Shakespeare's other English histories, the title pages of the quartos suggest generic difference. In the case of *Henry VI, Part II*, the title page of the 1594 quarto version indicates both the episodic chronicle structure of the play and its historical subject: "The First part of the Contention betwixt the two famous Houses of Yorke and Lancaster, with the death of the good Duke Humphrey: And the banishment and death of the Duke of *Suffolke*, and the Tragicall end of the proud Cardinall of *Winchester*, with the notable Rebellion of *Iacke Cade: And the Duke of Yorkes first claime unto the Crowne*." The quarto title page of *Richard III*, by contrast, designates at once its self-consciously dramatic form as a tragedy, its origins as a script for theatrical performance, and its strongly centered focus on the male protagonist: "The Tragedy of Richard the third, Containing, His treacherous Plots against his brother Clarence: the pittiefull murther of his iunocent nephewes: his tyrannicall usurpation: with the whole course of his detested life, and most deserved death. As it hath beene lately Acted by the Right honourable the Lord Chamberlaine his servants."

In Shakespeare's time, the story of Richard III was repeatedly identified as tragic. Edward Hall had entitled his account of Richard's reign "The Tragical Doynges of Kynge Richard The Thirde." Richard's story (along with those of Clarence, Hastings, Buckingham, and Jane Shore) was identified as a tragedy in *A Mirror for Magistrates*. Thomas Legge's Latin play *Richardus Tertius*, performed at Cambridge in 1579, is identified in contemporary texts as an exemplary tragedy, singled out by Sir John Harington and Thomas Heywood to illustrate the beneficial effects of tragic drama and by Francis Meres in his list of "famous tragedies." Yet another play about Richard, anonymously published in 1594 and entitled "The True Tragedy of Richard III," begins with a dialogue between Truth and Poetrie that identifies "Tragedia" as a player in the coming action and the subject of the play as a "Tragedie" (sig. A3r).

The following discussion examines the ways the reconstruction of history as tragedy in *Richard III* transvalued the representations of women on Shakespeare's stage and transformed the gendered relationship between actors and audience in the playhouse. We should begin, however, by acknowledging that the distinction between history and tragedy was by no means clear in the period. The protagonists of tragedy, like those of history, were understood to be characters of high rank. Moreover, in the Renaissance as in antiquity, plays identified as tragedies frequently took their subjects from history (Lindenberger 1975: 72–8; Aristotle *c.* 334–330 BC: IX, XIII in Adams 1992: 53–4, 55; de Vega 1609 in Gilbert 1962: 543). Shakespeare himself is a good case in point: of the eleven plays designated as tragedies in the First Folio, all but *Romeo and Juliet* and *Othello* have historical subjects.

Despite the many similarities between the subjects of the two genres, contemporary descriptions of the ways they affected their audiences were gendered in strikingly different terms. Although antitheatrical invective typically attacked all theatrical performance as effeminating, the English history play offered a significant exception (Rackin 1990: 111–16). Commemorating the valiant deeds of heroic forefathers and celebrating the masculine virtues of courage, honor, and patriotism, the theatrical representation of English historical subjects could actually help to reclaim the endangered masculinity of the men in the theater audience.

Tragedy, on the other hand, was likely to inspire womanly emotions in its spectators. According to Stephen Gosson, "The beholding of troubles and miserable slaughters that are in Tragedies, drive us to immoderate sorrow, heavines, womanish weeping and mourning, whereby we become lovers of dumpes, and lamentation, both enemies to fortitude" (Gosson 1582, in Chambers 1923: 3: 215).[1] The claim that tragedy produced womanly softness in its spectators was not confined to antitheatrical discourse. Sir Philip Sidney recounts a story from Plutarch in which the performance of a tragedy "drewe aboundance of teares" from the eyes of a tyrant "who, without all pitty, had murthered infinite nombers, and some of his owne blood" (Sidney

1595, in Smith 1904: 1: 177–8). Arguing for the salutary effects of tragedy, Sidney does not identify them as effeminating. The terms of his argument, however, suggest just that. He claims, for instance, that tragedy "openeth the greatest wounds, and sheweth forth the Ulcers that are covered with Tissue." As Gail Paster has demonstrated, men's bodies opened and wounded were gendered feminine (Paster 1993: 64–112); and the ulcer image directly parallels the terms in which Hamlet will address his guilty mother: "Lay not that flattering unction to your soul,/ That not your trespass but my madness speaks; /It will but skin and film the ulcerous place,/Whiles rank corruption, mining all within,/ Infects unseen" (III.iv.145–9).

Women, in fact, were especially prominent in descriptions of the effects of tragedies on early modern audiences. In a 1620 recollection of a performance of *The Spanish Tragedy*, for instance, "Ladyes in the boxes" are said to have "Kept time with sighes and teares to [the player's] sad accents." As Richard Levin points out, the numerous contemporary accounts that describe "women weeping in the theatre" suggest a perception "that women had a special sensitivity to, and perhaps a special preference for, pathetic plots and situations" (Levin 1989: 170–1).

In *An Apologie for Actors*, Thomas Heywood recounts three anecdotes to illustrate the beneficial effects of tragedies on their auditors. Two of them center on women who had murdered their husbands. In the first, "a townes-woman (till then of good estimation and report)" watching a play about a woman who had committed a similar crime "suddenly skritched and cryd out Oh my husband, my husband! I see the ghost of my husband fiercely threatning and menacing me" and subsequently confessed her crime to the people about her in the audience. In the second, the particulars of the tragic plot are somewhat different, but they have exactly the same effect on the wicked woman: during the performance of a play in which a laborer, envied by his fellow workers for his diligence, is murdered by having a nail driven into his temples, "a woman of great gravity" becomes "strangely amazed" and "with a distracted & troubled braine oft sighed out these words: Oh my husband, my husband!":

> The play, without further interruption, proceeded; the woman was to her owne house conducted, without any apparant suspition, every one coniecturing as their fancies led them. In this agony she some few dayes languished, and

on a time, as certaine of her well disposed neighbours came to comfort her, one amongst the rest being Church-warden, to him the Sexton posts, to tell him of a strange thing happening him in the ripping up of a grave: see here (quoth he) what I have found, and shewes them a faire skull, with a great nayle pierst quite through the braine-pan, but we cannot coniecture to whom it should belong, nor how long it hath laine in the earth, the grave being confused, and the flesh consumed. At the report of this accident, the woman, out of the trouble of her afflicted conscience, discovered a former murder. For 12 yeares ago, by driving that nayle into that skull, being the head of her husband, she had trecherously slaine him. This being publickly confest, she was arraigned, condemned, adiudged, and burned.

(Heywood 1612: sigs. G1^v, G2^v)

Heywood's lurid examples represent an extreme case. The plays he describes belong to the subgenre of domestic tragedy, an innovative dramatic form that moved down the social scale and into the home to find its subjects in a domestic space where female characters could and did play central roles (Dolan 1994). Not all of the female spectators of tragedy were imagined as "guilty creatures sitting at a play," and not all of the spectators of tragedy were imagined as women. Nonetheless, the spectators were repeatedly and consistently described in contemporary accounts as moved to emotions and responses (compassion, remorse, pity, tears) that were understood as feminine. This conception of the effects of tragedy as feminizing, although not always explicitly stated, is remarkably consistent: it appears in arguments for and against the theater, in the prologues and epilogues to plays, in accounts of actual experience as well as in prescriptive directions.

The Induction to *A Warning for Fair Women* (1599) begins with the stage direction, "*Enter at one doore, Hystorie with Drum and Ensigne: Tragedie at another, in her one hand a whip, in the other a knife.*" During the ensuing dispute with Comedie and Hystorie, Tragedie's feminine gender receives repeated emphasis. She is addressed by the others as "mistris buskins" and "my Ladie *Tragedie,*" and she describes the kind of performance she requires as one that will produce feminine emotions in the audience:

I must have passions that must move the soule,
Make the heart heave, and throb within the bosome,

103

Extorting teares out of the strictest eyes,
. . . Untill I rap the sences from their course
(*Warning* 1975: sigs A2ᵛ, A3ʳ)

Over half a century later, Margaret Cavendish, the Duchess of Newcastle, described the effects of Shakespeare's tragedies in similar terms:

> in his Tragick Vein, he Presents Passions so Naturally, and Misfortunes so Probably, as he Peirces the Souls of his Readers with such a True Sense and Feeling thereof, that it Forces Tears through their Eyes
> (Cavendish 1664, in Evans *et al.* 1974: 1847)

In direct contrast to Nashe's celebration of the history play, which imagines an audience of men inspired by the representation of a heroic masculine world to emulate the manly virtues of the forefathers, tragedy is repeatedly described as appealing to women as well as men; and its appeal to men is repeatedly described as directed towards their feminine sympathies, softening hard hearts, piercing guilty souls with remorse, ravishing the entire audience with the feminine passions of pity and fear, and forcing them to weep.

A similar gendered difference characterized the subjects of the two genres. On the stage as in the audience, the exemplary subjects of tragedy – "Gods and Goddesses, Kynges and Queenes" (Webbe 1586, in Smith 1904: 249) – were understood to include women as well as men. Because history sought to commemorate the past, typically reconstituted as a nostalgically idealized world of the fathers, women and sexuality occupied only marginal roles. Both tragedy and comedy, however, assigned important roles to women and marriage. In comedy, conflicts between older and newer social dispensations are characteristically resolved in marriage; in tragedy, they often constitute the hero's predicament, which is defined at least partly in terms of his relationship to women. This is true not only in plays like *Romeo and Juliet*, *Othello*, and *Antony and Cleopatra*, which center on romantic relationships, but also in virtually every tragedy in the Shakespearean canon, with the possible exceptions of *Julius Caesar* and *Timon of Athens*.

As we have seen, in his early history plays Shakespeare often opposed the troubling realities of cultural change by projecting a better world in the past – the remembered world of Henry V's conquest of France, for example, or the idealized world of Talbot's military endeavors. Shakespeare's tragedies, by contrast, play out those cultural contradictions in the struggles of an individual heroic figure destroyed by the irreconcilable conflicts they produced. The ambivalent place of women in early modern England and the instability of the gender ideologies that attempted to contain them were part of the contradictory material which his tragic dramas attempted to master (Rose 1988; Callaghan 1989). The reconstruction of history as tragedy in *Richard III* is accompanied by a remarkable transformation in the representation and placement of female characters. Paradoxically, even as the female characters are ennobled, they are also disempowered. On the one hand, women are much more sympathetically portrayed than in the Henry VI plays. On the other, they lose the vividly individualized voices and the dangerous theatrical power that made characters like Joan and Margaret potent threats to the masculine project of English history-making. Robert Weimann's distinction between *locus* and *platea* can be used to chart both the elevation of the female characters and their containment. Weimann associates the *locus* with the upstage site of mimetic illusion, "aloofness from the audience, and representational closure" which privileges the authority of the objects represented, the *platea* with the forestage where actors addressed their audiences, a liminal space where the authority of the represented narrative could be challenged by calling attention to the immediate theatrical occasion with all its subversive potential (Weimann 1978: 73–85, 224–6; 1988: 409–10). Although not always or necessarily literalized in specific locations on the physical stage, the different acting styles and different relationships between actor and audience that Weimann associates with *locus* and *platea* provide a useful basis for understanding the transformation of women's roles in *Richard III*. Ennobled, the female characters move into the privileged *locus* of hegemonic representation, but this move also subsumes them into the patriarchal project of that representation and distances them from the present theater audience.

Many of the female characters in Shakespeare's English history plays are distinguished by foreign nationality or low social origin. Joan of course has both, but it is worth remembering that all the female characters in *Henry VI, Part I* are French and that Margaret's French origins receive repeated emphasis in the subsequent Henry VI plays. In the second tetralogy, there will be the tavern women in the Henry IV plays, Mortimer's Welsh bride in *Henry IV, Part I*, and three more French women in *Henry V*. Many of these women are also distinguished from the English male protagonists by linguistic differences – in the first tetralogy by Joan's earthy, colloquial language and in the second by Mistress Quickly's malapropisms and the foreign languages spoken by the Welsh and French women (even when their male parents speak perfectly good English). These marks of national and class difference set these women apart from the noble English men who are the dramas' most privileged figures. In direct antithesis, all of the female characters in *Richard III* are highborn English women who speak in the undifferentiated, formal blank verse that constitutes the standard language of the playscript. Recruited to the service of the hegemonic project of the plot, the accession of Henry VII to the English throne, the women are also subsumed in its hegemonic discourse. As Nicholas Brooke has observed, "the flexibility of private speech" in this play is almost entirely "confined to Richard" (Brooke 1984:108). Even Margaret, the most powerful of Richard's female antagonists, speaks in the generalized rhetorical terms that constitute the normative language of the play.

Assuming their tragic roles as pitiable victims, female characters are no longer represented as dangerous, demonic Others. Instead, they conform to the stereotypical representation of female characters, especially bereaved mothers, in the drama of the period as "a symbolic focus of pity" rather than as individual figures "involved in an action through [their] own motive and volition" (McLuskie 1989: 136 and chapter 6 *passim*). The subversive theatrical energy of the peasant Joan is replaced by the pathos of suffering English queens. Margaret, the adulterous wife and bloodthirsty warrior of the Henry VI plays, is transformed into a bereaved and suffering prophet of divine vengeance for the crimes of the past. In the Henry VI plays, the female characters are defined as opponents to the masculine project of English history-making. In *Richard III*, all of the women support the desired conclusion of the historical plot, the foundation of the Tudor dynasty.

Although the overarching goal of the dramatic action in *Richard III* (as in all of Shakespeare's English histories and a number of his tragedies as well) is the maintenance of a legitimate royal succession, in this play, unlike the earlier histories, it is the male protagonist who opposes the patriarchal project. The threats to patrilineal succession represented in the *Henry VI* plays by Joan's bastardy and sexual promiscuity and Margaret's adultery are replaced by Richard's murders and his deceitful effort to deny the legitimacy of his brother's innocent children, the rightful heirs to the throne he usurps, and even of Edward himself. In *Richard III*, the subversive power associated with female characters in the earlier plays is demystified, and all the power of agency and transgression is appropriated by the male protagonist. The threat of adultery is no longer real, and the character who threatens to displace legitimate heirs is not an adulterous woman, but the slanderous man, Richard, who brings the charge. Witchcraft, the quintessential representation of the dangerous power of women, is similarly reduced from a genuine threat to a transparent slander. Both Joan in *Henry VI, Part I* and Eleanor Cobham in *Henry VI, Part II* summon demons to the stage. In *Richard III*, however, there are only Richard's unsupported and obviously false charges against Queen Elizabeth and Jane Shore.

Joan in *Henry VI, Part I* is the prototype for the marginal and criminal status of the women in the Henry VI plays and also for their subversive, theatrical energy. Her inexplicable military power, first explained as deriving from the Blessed Virgin, is finally defined as witchcraft and punished with burning. Her very subversiveness, however, paradoxically authorizes her dramatic power. As both Catherine Belsey and Karen Newman have observed, the custom of requiring witches to confess from the scaffold "paradoxically also offered women a place from which to speak in public with a hitherto unimagined authority which was not diminished by the fact that it was demonic." These public occasions were also theatrical. As both critics note, "the crowds at trials and executions" were frequently described as "beholders" or "the audience," and "Pamphleteers often describe[d] the scene of execution explicitly as a play" (Newman 1991: 67; Belsey 1985b: 190–1).

Two episodes, one near the beginning of *Richard III* and one near its end, illustrate the way the powerful role of demonic other, occupied by women in the Henry VI plays, is now transferred to Richard. The longer of these is the second, the encounter near the end of Act IV between Richard and Queen Elizabeth, where Shakespeare altered his historical source in order to ennoble the character of the widowed queen. As Barbara Hodgdon observes,

Shakespeare "displaces those attributes the chronicler ascribes to the Queen onto Richard" (Hodgdon 1991: 109–10). In Hall's version, Queen Elizabeth exemplifies female "inconstancie," first promising her daughter Elizabeth (or, in the event of Elizabeth's death, her next daughter, the Lady Cecile) to Richmond (Hall 1548: 391), then, persuaded by promises of "promocions innumerable and benefites," agreeing to Richard's demands:

> putting in oblivion the murther of her innocente children, the infamy and dishonoure spoken by the kynge her husbande, the lyvynge in avoutrie leyed to her charge, the bastardyng of her daughters, forgettyng also ye feithfull promes & open othe made to the countesse of Richmond mother to ye erle Henry, blynded by avaricious affeccion and seduced by flatterynge wordes, first delivered into kyng Richards handes her. v. daughters as Lambes once agayne committed to the custody of the ravenous wolfe.
>
> (Hall 1548: 406)

Shakespeare's widowed queen, unlike Hall's, keeps faith with Richmond and adamantly refuses Richard's urgings to forget past wrongs. Insistently recalling the fate of her murdered children, she charges, "No doubt the murd'rous knife was dull and blunt/ Till it was whetted on thy stone-hard heart/To revel in the entrails of my lambs" (IV.iv.227–9). Shakespeare thus appropriates for Elizabeth's use against Richard the very arguments, and even the terms, by which the authoritative narrative voice in Hall's chronicle condemns her action.

In Shakespeare's representation, it is Richard and not Elizabeth – or any of the women – who becomes the sole object of condemnation. The women are deprived of theatrical power and agency, both of which are appropriated by Richard, along with their demonic roles. The audience is never allowed to see Elizabeth deciding to bestow her daughter on Richmond. All we get is Stanley's laconic report that "the Queen hath heartily consented/He [Richmond] should espouse Elizabeth her daughter" (IV.v.7–8); and a number of critics have accepted Richard's judgment at the end of their encounter that the queen is a "relenting fool, and shallow, changing woman" (IV.iv.431; Hammond 1981: 296). Like the other women in *Richard III*, Elizabeth serves as a kind of ventriloquist's dummy. She gives forceful and eloquent voice to Richard's crimes, but her own motives can remain ambiguous because they are finally irrelevant to the outcome of the plot. What is important is that Richmond marries her daughter; whether or when the queen gives her consent is of so little consequence that it is never clearly specified in Shakespeare's script.

The earlier incident is much more brief, a telling moment in Act I when Richard literally appropriates the demonic power of a woman's voice. Margaret of Anjou, sent at the end of *Henry VI, Part III* back to France (where her historical prototype died in 1482), returns unhistorically in *Richard III* like a voice from the dead to recall the crimes of the past and pour out curses on her old enemies. In I.iii, she comes on stage as an eavesdropper who punctuates the dialogue with bitter comments delivered to the audience, unheard by the other characters. Finally, she moves forward to dominate the stage with a great outpouring of curses and denunciations, directed at each of the other characters in turn. When she comes to Richard, however, he interrupts the stream of malediction to turn Margaret's curses back upon herself. "O, let me make the period to my curse!" she complains. "Tis done by me," he replies, "and ends in 'Margaret'" (I.iii.237–8).

This exchange dramatizes what will be a major source of Richard's theatrical power. Late in Act III, Buckingham advises Richard to "play the maid's part ... and take" the crown (III.vii.51), but the woman's part has been included in the master showman's repertory from the very beginning. Characterized throughout in terms of warlike masculinity and aggressive misogyny, Richard also commands the female power of erotic seduction. It is interesting that Ian McKellen, who recently played the part of Richard to great acclaim, is openly gay. The dominant sexual ideology of our time equates masculinity with male heterosexuality, but McKellen's virtuoso performance in the part of Richard destabilizes this equation, bringing out what is implicit in Shakespeare's text, namely, that masculinity and femininity are performatively secured and are neither determined by a sexed body nor reducible to the performance of any particular sexual acts. In Shakespeare's play, Richard's monopoly of both male and female sexual energy is vividly portrayed in his seduction of Anne. The turning point comes when Richard lends her his sword and lays his breast "naked" for her penetration (I.ii.177). Overwhelmed by Richard's aggressive passivity, Anne's resistance quickly collapses, whereupon Richard seals his sexual conquest by enclosing her finger with his ring. "Look how my ring encompasseth thy finger," he says. "Even so thy breast encloseth my poor heart" (I.ii.203–4). Owner of both the sword and the naked breast, both penetrated ring and penetrating heart, Richard has become, as Rebecca Bushnell observes, "both the man who possesses and the woman who submits" (Bushnell 1990: 124).

The power that Richard takes from women to curse and seduce is not his only power. He is also able to transcend the frame of historical representation, to address the audience directly without the knowledge of the other characters, and to exude the theatrical energy that serves to monopolize the audience's attention. The structure of Richard's exchange with Margaret is also the structure of the early scenes in the play: it is always Richard who has the last word – along with the first. Each scene is punctuated by soliloquies in which Richard addresses the audience, predicting the action to come, responding to the action just past, flaunting his witty wickedness, gloating at the other characters' weakness and ignorance, and seducing the fascinated auditors into complicity with his diabolical schemes. It is a power we glimpsed in his father's soliloquies as early as *Henry VI, Part II*.

The association between the transgressive, the demonic, and the theatrical is consistently used to characterize Richard. It is, in fact, associated with his story from its beginning in More's *History of King Richard the thirde* (*c.* 1513–18), written about thirty years after Richard's death, the source for the versions Shakespeare found in Hall and Holinshed (Hammond 1981: 77–8). In Shakespeare's representation, as in his sources, Richard's wickedness is repeatedly and explicitly associated with his characterization as an actor. These associations were established even in *Henry VI, Part III* when just before his murder by Richard, Henry asks, "What scene of death hath Roscius now to act?" (V.vi.10). Earlier in the play, Richard's long soliloquy (discussed in the chapter on *Henry VI, Part III*) describes his villainy in the same terms that Renaissance writers often used to describe actors:

> Why, I can smile, and murther whiles I smile,
> And cry "Content" to that which grieves my heart,
> And wet my cheeks with artificial tears,
> And frame my face to all occasions.
> . . . .

110

I can add colors to the chameleon,
Change shapes with Proteus for advantages,
And set the murtherous Machevil to school.
          (*Henry VI, III*: III.ii.182–93)[2]

In *Richard III* Richard's identity as a master performer becomes the structural principle of the dramatic action. Not only the central character in the *locus* of historical representation, Richard also monopolizes the *platea* of direct address to the audience: as the only Shakespearean character to begin a play in soliloquy, he plays the roles of "chorus and presenter" as well as dramatic protagonist (Leggatt 1988: 32; Weimann 1978: 159–60). The early scenes of the play are punctuated by asides and soliloquies in which Richard announces his chosen dramatic role ("to prove a villain"), shares his wicked plots with the audience before stepping back into the frame of representation to execute them upon the other characters, and then returns to the *platea* to gloat about the efficacy of his performance.

By defining his villainy as theatrical *tour de force*, Richard invites the audience to suspend their moral judgment and evaluate his actions simply as theatrical performances. Significantly, the most striking instance of this maneuver occurs in the soliloquy at the end of the scene when he seduces Anne. "Was ever woman in this humor woo'd?" he asks the audience. "Was ever woman in this humor won?":

What? I that kill'd her husband and his father,
To take her in her heart's extremest hate,
With curses in her mouth, tears in her eyes,
The bleeding witness of my hatred by,
Having God, her conscience, and these bars against me,
. . . .
Hath she forgot already that brave prince,
Edward, her lord, whom I, some three months since,
Stabb'd in my angry mood at Tewksbury?
. . . .
And will she yet abase her eyes on me,
That cropp'd the golden prime of this sweet prince
And made her widow to a woeful bed?
                                        (I.ii.227–48)

This soliloquy, which ends the scene, goes on for thirty-seven lines, reminding the audience of the historical wrongs that should have made Anne reject his suit, flaunting the theatrical power that made her forget the past. Here, and throughout the first act of the play, Richard performs a similar seduction upon the audience. For the audience as for Anne, the seduction requires the suspension of moral judgment and the erasure of historical memory, since Shakespeare's contemporaries would have entered his theater well aware of the demonic role that Richard had been assigned in Tudor historiography; but the sheer theatrical energy of Richard's performance supersedes the moral weight of the hegemonic narrative.

The conflation of the historical seduction represented on stage with the theatrical seduction of the present audience, of the character Richard with the actor who played his part, and of the feminine character he seduces on stage with an audience inter- pellated as feminine is implicit in two well-known anecdotes associated with the play from the beginning of the seventeenth century. In March, 1602, John Manningham recorded in his diary an account of a "citizen" in the audience "upon a tyme when Burbidge played Rich. 3." who "greue soe farr in liking with him, that before shee went from the play shee appointed him to come that night unto hir by the name of Ri: the 3" (Evans 1974: 1836). Another anecdote, not explicitly sexual, also attests the identi- fication of Richard with the actor who played his part. Bishop Richard Corbet, a friend of Ben Jonson, described a visit to the site of the Battle of Bosworth Field in which his host, "when he would have said, King Richard dyed,/And call'd – A horse! a horse! – he, Burbidge cry'de" (1807: 194).

Both of these anecdotes point to a subtle but significant dif- ference between conceptions of tragedy and history, a difference which helps to explain both the ennobling and the disempowering of the female characters in *Richard III*. Contemporary descriptions of the history play genre focus on the historical objects of repres- entation. Celebrating "our domesticke histories," Thomas Hey- wood asks,

> What English Prince should hee behold the true portrature of that famous King *Edward* the third, foraging France, taking so great a King captive in his owne country, quartering the English Lyons with the French Flower-delyce, and would not bee suddenly Inflam'd with so royall a spectacle, being made apt and fit for the like atchievement. So of *Henry* the fift.
>
> (Heywood 1612: 1: sig. B4^r)

Thomas Nashe, as we noted in Part I, makes essentially the same claims for the theatrical performance of English history. For Nashe as for Heywood, the value of the history play is identified with the value of the objects of historical representation such as "brave *Talbot* (the terror of the French)." However, Nashe then imagines Talbot's pleasure had he known that "hee should triumphe againe on the Stage, and have his bones newe embalmed with the teares of ten thousand spectators at least (at severall times) who, in the Tragedian that represents his person, imagine they behold him fresh bleeding" (Nashe 1592, in Chambers 1923: 4: 238–9). The thought of the weeping spectators leads inexorably to the thought of the "Tragedian." The present actor who elicits the spectators' feminine tears suddenly displaces the historical character who constitutes the object of masculine emulation.

Conceived as historical drama, the play features the objects of representation. Conceived as tragedy, it features the theatrical power of the actor. In either case, the role of the protagonist is reserved for a male character, but so long as that protagonist is identified, like Heywood's Edward III or Nashe's (and Shakespeare's) Talbot, with the *locus* of historical representation, the transgressive power of theatrical performance can be mobilized by a woman like Joan (or a subversive, effeminate man like Falstaff) to call in question the foregrounded action. Once the protagonist assumes the role of tragic hero, however, he can also dominate the *platea* (although that *platea* continues to be occupied by subversive figures such as Lear's fool, as well). Not only the character privileged in the represented action, the tragic hero is also the actor privileged in theatrical performance. When Richard speaks to the audience, the *platea* begins to assume the function it would have in plays like *Hamlet* and *Macbeth* as the site of the soliloquies where the masculine subject of tragedy was to be constructed.[3]

The movement in *Richard III* from historical chronicle to tragical history is also a movement into modernity. Tragedy, as Catherine Belsey has shown, was deeply involved with the emergent conception of an autonomous masculine identity defined in performance (Belsey 1985b). Shakespeare's early history plays were doubly associated with the past, not only with the traditional heroes of the historical chronicles they represent, but also with an older conception of masculine identity rooted in patrilineal inheritance. As a dramatic genre, moreover, tragedy represented the wave of the future, while the vogue of the history play was remarkably short-lived, beginning in the 1580s and ending soon after the accession of James I (Levy 1967: 233; Rackin 1990: 30–2). Placed within a tragic frame, Richard III represents a demonized form of modern masculinity. He eschews all kinship ties; he relies on his theatrical skills and his seductive charm to attain his ends. But the play can only reach its proper ideological resolution if the demonic Richard is replaced on the throne by a figure who embodies successful compromise between modernity and tradition, between performance and genealogy as warrants for his rule. In this play, that figure is Richmond, a clever actor who has five men wearing his coats at Bosworth Field (an action that reveals that kingship is in part only a role) but who can also lay claim to divine and genealogical authority to justify the outcome of his successful performance in this crucial battle.

As an examination of Richmond's role will further clarify, the Shakespearean history play, both transitional and transient, was shaped by the same process of rapid cultural transformation that quickly produced its obsolescence as a dramatic genre. Especially in the second tetralogy, Shakespeare's histories incorporate many of the emerging elements in the culture around them. Collectively they contain at least two potentially contradictory versions of national and personal identity. They rationalize new conceptions of royal authority and masculine identity by reference to old models of patrilineal inheritance, amalgamating medieval cultural structures of dynastic succession with emergent concepts of personal achievement and private property. In so doing, they anticipate the new concept of feudalism that Richard Halpern describes as James I's "major innovation on the absolutist claims of the Tudors" the conception of the crown as a piece of property inherited by the king. As Halpern explains,

> [The older] theory relies on a divine conception of *political* authority, which is mystically passed from the body of the ruling king to his successor; it regards the monarch as the political representative of God and therefore invests the office of kingship with certain unique qualities. The [emergent] "feudal" theory, by contrast, envisions not a mysterious transmission of power but a legal transmission of property, with the king as little more than a particularly privileged landlord. Political authority derives not from

divine sanction but from the prerogatives of property ownership, and is conterminous with it.

(Halpern 1991: 222)

One way to view *Richard III* is in terms of the contradiction
between these two models of royal authority. The play depicts the
end of the old Plantagenet dynasty and its replacement by the
House of Tudor; its project is to bring together and ratify the
property rights that Richmond acquired by his victory at Bosworth field with the warrant of God's grace, expressed throughout
the play by prophecies, dreams, and curses, and the patriarchal
legitimacy that he appropriates by his marriage to Elizabeth.

In the Henry VI plays, marriage is represented as dangerous
and destructive to men. *Richard III*, on the other hand, reaches its
happy resolution in the marriage between Richmond and Elizabeth, the foundation of the Tudor dynasty. In so doing, it looks
forward to Shakespeare's representation of Henry V, where the
successful courtship of Katherine is presented as the culminating
event of Henry's triumphant reign. The resolutions of those plots
in marriage literalize the scripture from Proverbs, widely quoted
in contemporary marriage handbooks and sermons, "A good wife
is the crown of her husband" (Newman 1991: 15). Like a newly
prosperous commoner who acquired a coat of arms in order to
authorize his new wealth in genealogical fictions of hereditary
entitlement, both kings authorize their possession of the lands
they have won in military conquest by marrying women who can
secure that land to their heirs by genealogical authority.

Although both marriages are historical facts, their deployment
in Shakespeare's plays is a product of dramatic selection. Their
location as the satisfying theatrical culminations of the represented stories also satisfies the ideological imperatives of an
emergent capitalist economy and an emergent nation state that
increasingly employed the mystified image of a patriarchal family
to authorize masculine privilege and rationalize monarchial
power.[4] The hero the Chorus calls the "mirror of all Christian
kings" (II.Cho.6), Shakespeare's Henry V is also a prototype for
the emergent ideal of modern masculinity, a gender identity that
can only be established in the performance of heterosexual conquest. *Richard III* in many ways anticipates the gender ideologies
of the later play. The association of royal authority with
the authority of a married man looks ahead to the emergent

construction of the masculine ideal as paterfamilias. In keeping with this ideal, all the female characters in *Richard III* are related by blood or marriage to English kings and are defined by their familial relationships – as wife, as prospective wife, as mother, as widow. Unlike the Henry VI plays, where both Joan and Margaret appeared on stage in masculine battledress and led armies on fields of battle, the female characters in *Richard III* are confined to domestic roles and domestic settings. This domestication of women represents a movement into modernity; it adumbrates the rising barriers that were to confine respectable women within the household, defined as a separate, private sphere. The movement into modernity reaches its culmination in the speech in which Richmond seals his victory at Bosworth Field by announcing his intention to marry Elizabeth of York. It is only by appropriating Elizabeth's genealogical authority as the last survivor of the House of York that Richmond can authorize himself as king and author-ize the legitimacy of the Tudor dynasty, only by becoming a paterfamilias that he can secure his new identity as king. Eliza-beth, moreover, literalizes the legal status of a married woman as a *feme covert*,[5] reduced to a disembodied name, a place-marker for the genealogical authority that Richmond needs to authorize the Tudor dynasty.

The female characters who do appear in the play are also recruited to Richmond's project; and like Elizabeth, they are also sacrificed to it. Richmond's victory, in fact, re-enacts in benevolent form Richard's earlier appropriation of the feminine. Just as the play begins with Richard's appropriation of Margaret's power of subversive speech, it ends with Richmond's appropriation of the moral authority of bereaved and suffering women to authorize his victory. To serve that purpose, the female characters must lose their individuality and become an undifferentiated chorus of ritual lamentation, curse, and prophecy that enunciates the play's providential agenda. Recounting the crimes of the past, they speak as "poor mortal-living ghost[s]" (IV.iv.26). Like the literal ghosts who appear on the night before the Battle of Bosworth Field, they announce the obliteration of patrilineal genealogy and invoke the higher authority of Divine Providence to validate Richmond's accession (Hodgdon 1991: 114).

In praying for Richmond's victory, the ghosts of Richard's victims speak for the entire nation, which is now identified as a helpless, suffering woman. This identification is reiterated in

Richmond's final speech: "Abate the edge of traitors, gracious Lord," he prays, "That would reduce these bloody days again,/ And make poor England weep in streams of blood!" (V.v.35–7). The suffering victim of Richard's bloody tyranny, England is also the cherished object of Richmond's compassionate concern. Both here and in his oration before the battle, Richmond characterizes himself as a loving, protective paterfamilias, and he also promises his soldiers the rewards that go with that role:

> If you do fight in safeguard of your wives,
> Your wives shall welcome home the conquerors;
> If you do free your children from the sword,
> Your children's children quits it in your age.
>   (V.iii. 259–62)

Richard, by contrast, resorts to jingoistic appeals to masculine honor and misogynist charges that Richmond is a "milksop" (V.iii.325) and his soldiers "bastard Britains [i.e. Bretons], whom our fathers/ Have in their own land beaten, bobb'd, and thump'd." "If we be conquered," he says, "let men conquer us" (V.iii.333–4, 332).

Richard is still a powerfully seductive actor, but by this point in the play he is thoroughly discredited as a monarchial figure. The audience can now reject his aggressively masculine rhetoric and respond instead as Richmond's "loving countrymen" (V.iii.237) who desire to "sleep in peace" (V.iii.256). But although the audience is invited to accept Richmond's appeal to their "feminine" desires for peace and prosperity, the scene withholds actual images of female royal or theatrical authority. No women actors, of course, were on the stage, and no women characters appear in this scene. When Richmond invites the audience to join him in a prayer that the descendents of his union with Elizabeth will "Enrich the time to come with smooth-fac'd peace,/ With smiling plenty, and fair prosperous days" (V.v.33–4), he is invoking, as the descendent of this pair, the female monarch, Elizabeth I, who ruled England when Shakespeare was writing *Richard III*, and is praising the peace and prosperity she had brought to England. But just as the Elizabeth Richmond marries never appears on stage, the Elizabeth he foretells is never mentioned by name or even identified as a woman.

Assuming the role of benevolent paterfamilias, Richmond constructs himself in direct antithesis to the solitary individualism of the tragic hero he supplants, the murderer of the young princes, the character who defined himself from the beginning by his contempt for women and his separation from the loving bonds of kinship. Nonetheless, the play ends as it begins, with a male character speaking from the *platea* empowered by his appropriation of the woman's part and his performative self-construction as the object of a feminized audience's desire.[6]

9

KING JOHN

Although there is no conclusive evidence for the date of *King John*'s first production (estimates range from 1591 to 1598), many scholars place it between the two tetralogies. It is tempting to accept that suggestion, because the play seems in many ways to have been conceived as an antithesis to – or perhaps a reaction against – *Richard III*. Of all Shakespeare's Elizabethan histories, *Richard III* is the one that brings the action closest to the present, and of all of them, it is most fully invested in the official Tudor version of England's medieval past, which claimed that only with the marriage of Henry Tudor and Elizabeth of York was England saved from a devastating civil war that had been God's punishment for the deposition of a legitimate king, Richard II. Looking backward to the preceding plays and forward to the Elizabethan present, *Richard III* retrospectively imposes a tidy ending on the first tetralogy: old crimes are punished, every chicken comes home to roost, and the moral account books are neatly balanced to provide a providential warrant for the accession of Henry VII. Separated from the temporal and genealogical chain that unites the two tetralogies, *King John* moves farthest back into the past, and the entire action seems designed to foreground every kind of moral and political and historiographic ambiguity. The providential justice that determines the outcome in *Richard III* is nowhere to be seen, and every attempt to resolve the action or make sense of it is immediately frustrated by the moral ambiguities of an episodic plot where success and failure ride on the shifting winds of chance. Whatever its date of composition, *King John* exposes the ideological faultlines that threatened to undermine the genealogical narratives that could make the marriage of Henry Tudor and Elizabeth of York seem a secure resolution to the civil strife

119

which preceded it, the turning of brother against brother, father against son. If the play was produced between the two tetralogies, that may help to explain why the story of the loss and recuperation of royal authority and national integrity that ended so neatly in *Richard III* had to be restaged, but with much more difficulty and in a different way, in the second tetralogy.

In the plays of first tetralogy, female characters fall neatly into gendered groups. Although Joan is a peasant and the Countess of Auvergne and Margaret of Anjou are aristocrats, all three are united in nationality and in their roles as enemies to the English, male protagonists' struggle to preserve the legacy of Henry V. In *Henry VI, Part II*, Margaret and Eleanor are bitter enemies, but Shakespeare characterizes them in similar terms and uses them for similar purposes: self-willed and ambitious, both women defy their husbands' authority and threaten the peace of the realm, exposing the weakness of patriarchal authority in an increasingly disordered world. In *Richard III*, Margaret is a vengeful Lancastrian widow and Elizabeth a Yorkist queen, but before the play ends they too are united with each other and with the Duchess of York in a chorus of distinctively female lamentation – all victimized and bereaved, all gifted with the power to prophesy and curse and articulate the will of Providence.

The *Henry VI* plays depict a world where male right is threatened by female wrong; in the wicked world ruled by Richard III, the women line up on the side of heaven and the Earl of Richmond. But no such simple moral equations are possible in *King John*. Its female characters will not reduce to a single class or category. Like the ambiguous ethos of the play itself, the female characters here are deeply divided, both in action and in characterization. Elinor is a soldier queen, a tough, Machiavellian dowager; Constance an outraged, lamenting mother; Blanch a compliant, helpless victim. Elinor and Constance back rival claimants for the English throne, and they wrangle openly on stage, adroitly subverting each other's claims and arguments (II.i.120–94). Constance and Blanch are both depicted as suffering victims, but neither can be consoled without wronging the other, and when they kneel together before the Dolphin (III.i.308–10) they do so to plead for opposite decisions.

In a well-ordered patriarchal world, women are silent or invisible. First as daughters, then as wives, they are subject to male control, and men speak and act on their behalf. But in *King John*, the fathers and husbands are dead, reduced to the status of names in history books, and the mothers survive on Shakespeare's stage to dispute the fathers' wills and threaten their patriarchal legacies. Elinor and Constance interrupt the parley between the two kings to accuse each other of adultery, each other's sons of bastardy (II.i.120–33). Elinor impugns her grandson's birth in order to deny him the patriarchal right she knows is his (I.i.39–43). Constance, in the name of that right, impugns the legitimacy of her husband, subverting the patriarchal lineage that authorizes her son's claim to the throne. She proposes an alternate, female genealogical chain, deriving from Elinor and conveying a heritage of sin and suffering: "Thy sins are visited in this poor child,/The canon of the law is laid on him,/Being but the second generation/Removed from thy sin - conceiving womb" (II.i.179–82). And she refuses to hold her tongue, despite the men's commands. As Juliet Dusinberre points out, it "is clear from reading the play – and Deborah Warner's 1988 production reinforced this impression – . . . that up till the end of Act III the dramatic action is dominated by the women characters, and this is a cause of extreme embarrassment to the men on stage" (Dusinberre 1990: 40).

Speaking with strong, irreverent voices, these women claim a place in the historical narrative and challenge the myths of patriarchal authority that the men invoke to justify their actions. When John answers the French threat with the conventional boast, "Our strong possession and our right for us," Elinor wittily and irreverently reminds him, "Your strong possession much more than your right,/Or else it must go wrong with you and me" (I.i.39–41). When Pandulph claims that Constance lacks the "law and warrant" that give him, the papal legate, the authority to curse John, Constance replies by challenging the law itself:

> when law can do no right,
> Let it be lawful that law bar no wrong;
> Law cannot give my child his kingdom here,
> For he that holds his kingdom holds the law;
> Therefore since law itself is perfect wrong,
> How can the law forbid my tongue to curse?
> (III.i.185–90)

In *King John*, Shakespeare subjects masculine voices to skeptical feminine interrogation, and the history he represents becomes problematic, an arena for contending interests to compete and for unauthorized voices to be heard and to challenge the voices of patriarchal authority.

Like Margaret and Joan, the disorderly women in the first tetralogy, women in *King John* usurp masculine prerogatives. Elinor announces in the opening scene that she is "a soldier" (I.i.150), and her role is no anomaly in a play where "ladies and pale-visag'd maids/ Like Amazons come tripping after drums," changing "their thimbles into armed gauntlets . . . their needl's to lances, and their gentle hearts/To fierce and bloody inclination" (V.ii.154–8). Unlike Talbot, who found Joan's presence on the battlefield unnatural, the men in *King John* seem to accept the fact of warrior women, even though the presence of women seems to lead to gender blurring. The English soldiers, for example, are said to have both "ladies' faces" and "fierce dragons' spleens" (II.i.68). When the Earl of Salisbury weeps, the Dolphin declares that he values those "manly drops" above the "lady's tears" that have melted his heart in the past (V.ii.47–9). Both contenders for the English crown – the bold and warlike John no less than his infant rival – find their authority compromised by subjection to the domination of powerful, vociferous mothers, and the King of France bows to the threats of a mother church. Unwilling to break his truce with John lest they "make . . . unconstant children" of themselves (III.i.243), he finally agrees to do both after Pandulph threatens that "the Church, our mother, [will] breathe her curse,/A mother's curse, on her revolting son" (III.i.256–7).

Blanch is the only woman in the play who is cast in the traditional feminine mold. Imported into the plot (as John, apparently, imports her into France) only for her ill–fated marriage to the Dolphin, she is placed in the archetypically feminine role of a medium of exchange between men. Blanch is perfectly docile: "My uncle's will in this respect [i.e. the marriage] is mine./ If he see aught in you that makes him like,/ That any thing he sees, which moves his liking,/ I can with ease translate it to my will" (II.i.510–13). With no will or agenda of her own, Blanch is ready to be used as an instrument of kinship arrangements, political alliance, and patriarchal succession. Perhaps taking his cue from the name of the historical character, Shakespeare depicts his Blanch as a blank page awaiting the inscription of masculine texts. To the Dolphin, Blanch is a "table" where his own image is "drawn" (II.i.503). To the two kings, she is the medium in which they will write their peace treaty. And to all three men, she represents a site for the inscription of a patriarchal historical narrative.

Exercising a traditional patriarchal right by marrying his son to the blank and docile Blanch, the French king makes his strongest claim to leave a mark on history: "The yearly course that brings this day about," he declares, "Shall never see it but a holy day" (III.i.81–2). Like Elizabeth of York in *Richard III* and Katherine of France in *Henry V*, Blanch will serve as the inert female material of masculine history-making. But in *King John*, that female material also includes the recalcitrant and self-willed Elinor and Constance. Rejecting the French king's effort at prospective history-making, Constance demands,

> What hath this day deserv'd? what hath it done,
> That it in golden letters should be set
> Among the high tides in the calendar?
> Nay, rather turn this day out of the week,
>
> (III.i.84–7)

And Constance's own appeal to the heavens – "Let not the hours of this ungodly day/Wear out the [day] in peace; but ere sunset,/ Set armed discord 'twixt these perjur'd kings!" (III.i.109–11) – seems to be answered. Refusing to allow the marriage a place in the historical record, Constance rejects the news of it as a "tale" "misspoke, misheard" (III.i.4–5) and later demands to have the day on which it took place removed from the calendar. Denying the men's story and demanding the literal erasure of the date, she speaks for the forces that make the writing of patriarchal history impossible in the world of this play.

Inverted by a world turned upside down, the traditional bases for order and unity become in *King John* sources of disorder and conflict. The bonds that unite mother and child serve to divide Elinor and Constance. The marriage of Blanch to the Dolphin, which momentarily promises to unite the rival forces after their inconclusive battle for Angiers, is immediately contravened by the intervention of the papal legate, Pandulph, a spokesman for a religious power as ambiguous as every other source of authority in this play; and Pandulph's intervention becomes a source of further conflict when the Dolphin uses it as an excuse to claim the English throne. Blanch, the conventional compliant woman, allows herself to be used as an instrument of kinship arrangements, political alliance, and patriarchal succession. But Constance's immediate, outraged rejection of the news of Blanch's marriage as a "tale" "misspoke, misheard" and her hyperbolic demand to have the day on which it took place removed from the calendar remind an audience that the political alliance the marriage is designed to effect would still leave Constance and Arthur and the hereditary rights they claim unincorporated and unappeased and that this marriage will have no impact upon history.

Failing in her traditional feminine role as a medium to unite the warring kings, Blanch becomes the embodiment of their divisions. Niece to the English king, wife to the French Dolphin, she pleads desperately for the peace her marriage was designed to secure. Having failed in her plea, she cries,

> Which is the side that I must go withal?
> I am with both, each army hath a hand,
> And in their rage, I having hold of both,
> They whirl asunder and dismember me.
>
> (III. i. 327–30)

This image of dismemberment makes Blanch the human embodiment of the many divisions that characterize this play – of the divisions among the female characters, of the division of the English throne between John's possession and Arthur's right, and especially of the divided allegiances that perplex the audience as they struggle with the ethical and political ambivalences that make *King John* the most disturbing of all Shakespeare's English histories. Geography and aggressive masculinity favor John against a youthful rival supported by foreign powers, and John's defiance of the papal legate – "from the mouth of England/ . . . no Italian priest/ Shall tithe or toll in our dominions" (III.i.152–4) – must have evoked a sympathetic response from Shakespeare's audience; but John's claim to the crown is fatally compromised by his lack of genealogical authority.

Even the authority of history is compromised. In this play, it is not John but the King of France who values history and wants to write it. Philip appeals to historical genealogy to support Arthur's claim, describing him as a "little abstract" of what "died in" Arthur's father, which "the hand of time/Shall draw . . . into as huge a volume" (II.i.101–3). He swears that he will put John down "Or add a royal number to the dead,/ Gracing the scroll that tells of this war's loss/ With slaughter coupled to the name of kings" (II.i.347–9). But the historical scroll he foresees will never be written, for Philip, no less than his English enemy, lives in a world where the historical project is stalled in contradiction. No actions are conclusive, neither the wills of fathers, nor the marriages of children, nor the French king's repeated efforts at prospective history-making. John himself seems to have the last word on the subject on the one occasion – just before his death – that he associates himself with an historical text: the text he imagines is as fragile and mutable as he now sees his own life to be: "a scribbled form, drawn with a pen/ Upon a parchment," shrinking up against the fire that will destroy it (V.vii.32–4).

The image of the burning parchment completes Shakespeare's picture of John's estrangement from the tradition of Tudor historiography. Tudor accounts of John's reign tended to emphasize his quarrel with the Pope, collapsing the distance between John's world and their own to depict John as a heroic prototype of Henry VIII, a patriotic English king defying the foreign power of the papacy. Compared to his predecessors, Shakespeare makes very little use of the anti-papal material, and his John is a much less sympathetic figure than theirs. Constructed in terms of difference and distance, Shakespeare's amoral portrait of John resists the patriotic appropriations of humanist historiography. Even in the twentieth century, the play has been called the "most unhistorical" of Shakespeare's English histories (Honigmann 1967: xxxi). John envisions his history as a fragile manuscript, the kind of text produced in his own time, not as the enduring monument that Renaissance humanists tried to create in the printed books they produced. Moreover, when John envisions the manuscript shrinking up in flames, he anticipates what would happen when the monasteries were destroyed in the time of Henry VIII, who becomes, in this construction, not the heir and fulfillment of John's historical legacy, but its destroyer.

King John has been called an "incoherent patchwork" where "the action is wandering and uncertain" (Honigmann: xxxi). This incoherence is moral as well as structural, and it relates closely to the crisis in patriarchal authority the play depicts. In *King John*, Shakespeare leaves his audience, like the Bastard, "amaz'd" and lost "among the thorns and dangers" of an incomprehensible world (IV.iii.140–1), where every source of authority fails and legitimacy is reduced to a legal fiction. For the characters within the play, there is no clear royal authority. For the audience watching it, there is no unblemished cause and no unquestioned authority to claim their allegiance. None of these dilemmas is resolved until the end of the play when John's death ends the crisis of patriarchal authority and the Bastard adopts the idiom of historical faith and patriotic jingoism. The accession of Prince Henry, we are promised, will "set a form upon that indigest/ Which he [John] hath left so shapeless and so rude" (V.vii.26–7). It is significant that before this reconstruction can take place, the women's voices must be stilled (Vaughan 1989). Blanch is removed from the stage, reduced to a genealogical pretext for the Dolphin's claim to the English throne. Elinor and Constance die, offstage and unhistorically. Their deaths three days apart are reported in a single speech of six lines (IV.ii.119–24) as if to suggest the containment of these bitter enemies within a single, gender-determined category, their reduction from vociferous actors to the silent objects of male narration. As Juliet Dusinberre has astutely observed, "the play goes to pieces once the women leave the stage, or once the boys leave it. . . . and it never recovers the energy associated with the new world of the Bastard and the new generation: the boys. Or, in our terms, and certainly in Elizabethan terms, the women" (Dusinberre 1990: 51–2).

As long as the women live and speak, they set the subversive keynote for the other characters. John and the French king trade charges of usurpation (II.i.118–20), matching the women's mutual charges of adultery. Pandulph shares their distrustful vision of political process, embracing *realpolitik* with a cynicism that matches their own. The Bastard shares their iconoclastic idiom, satirizing the heroic language that "talks as familiarly of roaring lions/ As maids of thirteen do of puppy-dogs," and linking it to the patriarchal authority it claims to represent when he protests, "I was never so bethump'd with words/ Since I first call'd my brother's father dad" (II.i.459–67).

King John not only demystifies the past it represents; the Bastard's ironic soliloquies on the ways of "worshipful society" (I.i.184–216) and "Commodity, the bias of the world" (II.i.561–98) extend the critique to the time of the present theater audience; and the subversive vision implicit in the represented action also reaches back into its own prehistory to undermine the heroic image of Cordelion. Like *Henry VI, Part I, King John* looks back to a dead, heroic king, but while the legacy of Henry V was opposed and endangered in the world his infant son inherited but could not rule, it remained an intact and clearly defined, if increasingly remote, ideal. In *King John*, the legacy of the great Cordelion is problematized and dispersed. The audience sees his lion's skin adorning the back of the dishonorable Archduke of Austria, "little valiant, great in villainy,/ ... ever strong upon the stronger side" (III.i.116–17), and the same scene that describes his "honor – giving hand" bestowing knighthood upon Robert Faulconbridge (I.i.53) also reveals that he dishonored Faulconbridge by seducing his wife. Cordelion has left no clear successor. His only biological son is a bastard. His heir by law of primogeniture is his nephew Arthur. The Bastard has "a trick of Cordelion's face" and "the accent of his tongue" (I.i.85–6), but Arthur, a dispossessed and defenseless child, has his lineal right to the throne. And John, who has neither, sits upon that throne.

The dispersion of Cordelion's legacy among three defective heirs makes it impossible even to know who is the rightful king of England, and it gives rise to the crucial issue in *King John* – the problem of legitimacy. As Herbert Lindenberger has pointed out, "The action of historical drama is more precisely a struggle for legitimacy than a struggle for power as such. Dramas that depict a hereditary throne generally present sharply divergent readings of genealogies to justify the rights of various contenders for the throne" (Lindenberger 1975: 160). Genealogical anxiety haunts Shakespeare's Lancastrian kings, and genealogical arguments rationalize the rebellions that plague them. *Richard III* follows what Robert Ornstein has called the "time-honored custom for usurpers to bastardize those they overthrew" (Ornstein 1972: 26n) when he orders Buckingham to "infer [i.e. assert] the bastardy of Edward's children" (III.v.75); and imputations of bastardy provide potent weapons in all the plays. In *Henry VI, Part I*, for instance, even the threat of being thought a bastard helps to persuade Burgundy to change sides in the middle of a war (*Henry VI, Part I*: III.iii.60–1).

Although legitimacy is always an issue in Shakespeare's history plays, it is nowhere else so central as it is in *King John*. Failures of authority – problems of legitimacy – take a variety of forms in and around *King John*. For the characters within the play, these range from specific, literal accusations of bastardy (brought against Arthur and John as well as Philip Faulconbridge) to the general absence of any clear royal authority. For the audience watching the play, there is no unquestionably legitimate cause to claim their allegiance. For scholarly editors, the play has a problematic text and a clouded authorial genealogy. Not only does it include an abundance of fictional material not found in the historiographic sources; in addition, there is no way to know whether Shakespeare is the original author of that fictional material, since much of it is also found in a roughly contemporary play, *The Troublesome Raigne of Iohn King of England* (1591). No one has been able to determine which play was written first (although, of course, many arguments have been advanced on both sides of the question).

The entire action hangs on an unanswerable (and finally unanswered) question: "who is the legitimate heir of Cordelion?"; and the presiding spirit of this play is not the king who gives it its name but the human embodiment of every kind of illegitimacy – the Bastard. The most powerful and dramatically compelling of the characters, the Bastard is also the one to whom John assigns "the ordering of this present time" (V.i.77), and the one to whom Shakespeare gives the last word in the play. The Bastard's literal illegitimacy characterizes the status of the king (who relies on "strong possession" rather than "right" for his throne), the problems the play explores, and the curious nature of Shakespeare's creation. The Bastard has no real place in history, neither in the chain of patriarchal succession, where he can never inherit his father's throne, nor in the historical record Shakespeare found in Holinshed. He dominates a play which is unique among Shakespeare's English histories for its own lack of historical authority. *King John* has the flimsiest of relationships to its historiographic sources, compressing and marginalizing John's dispute with Rome and the revolt of his nobles and centering instead on a historically insignificant character invented for the sixteenth – century stage.

Despite efforts to identify a historical prototype for the Bastard, the only undisputed historical source for the character is a single sentence in Holinshed on "Philip bastard sonne to king Richard, to whom his father had given the castell and honor of Coinacke, [who] killed the vicount of Limoges, in revenge of his fathers death" (1587: 2: 278). If the *Troublesome Raigne* was a source for Shakespeare's play, the Bastard has a dramatic source there, but whichever version came first, the Bastard's origins are theatrical. His role is empowered, like that of Falstaff in the Henry IV plays, not by any historical authority, but by the sheer theatrical energy of his characterization.

The fact that the Bastard is characterized in positive terms represents an important stage in the history plays' negotiations between historical authority and theatrical power. In the first tetralogy, bastardy is typically an attribute of unsympathetic characters, and theatricality is associated with subversion. The Bastard's most obvious theatrical predecessors – Joan, Jack Cade, and Richard III – are the most animated and distinctive characters in their respective plays, but they are all cast as antagonists to true royalty and the English state. The Bastard shares their vividly individualized speech, their theatrical energy, their irreverence and contempt for traditional pieties; but, unlike them, he is a loyal subject to English royalty, and an enthusiastic spokesman for English patriotism. As such, he prefigures the renegotiation of the relationship between historical authority and theatrical power that will take place in the second tetralogy. In the earlier plays, the emblematic flatness of the characters who act in the name of God and country and the uniformity of their language contrast with the vivid particularity of those who oppose providential order to pursue their own agendas. In the figure of the Bastard, the binary scheme that opposes theatrical character to historical plot breaks down, producing a character as riven by contradiction as the play he dominates. Moreover, as Peter Womack has suggested, that a bastard is the play's most vivid spokesman for "England" and its most jingoistically patriotic figure anticipates the gradual process by which the idea of the nation became distinguishable from the idea of the monarch (Womack 1992: 116–26). Significantly, it is during the crisis of royal legitimacy enacted in this play that an unauthorized spokesman such as the Bastard Faulconbridge can emerge both to speak for England and to become the most theatrically attractive figure in the play.

Despite the theatricality of the Bastard's characterization, the character himself is profoundly contemptuous of theatrical display and enthusiastic in his loyalty to the English crown and nation. He denounces the citizens of Angiers who watch the battle between rival kings for possession of their city by comparing them to a base-born audience "in a theatre" who "gape and point / At . . . industrious scenes and acts of death" performed by their betters (II.i.373–6). He speaks reverently of "the lineal state and glory of the land" (V.vii.102) and he ends the play by swearing his "faithful services/ And true subjection everlastingly" (104–5) to the new king and proclaiming the jingoistic moral:

This England never did, nor never shall,
Lie at the proud foot of a conqueror,
But when it first did help to wound itself.

. . . .

Nought shall make us rue
If England to itself do rest but true.

(V.vii.112–18)

As many critics have noted, these speeches seem inconsistent with the Bastard's earlier characterization, for just as his vivid dramatic presence implicitly betrays his origins in the theater he despises, the explicit representation within the play of his origin in bastardy inscribes him, along with the women, in the register of illicit sexuality that subverts the "lineal state and glory of the land" to which he gives his allegiance.

These contradictions come to a head in the curious episode, which serves to introduce the Bastard, that takes up most of the first act in *King John* and exposes, like nothing else in any of Shakespeare's histories, the arbitrary and conjectural nature of patriarchal succession and the suppressed centrality of women to it. The Bastard – here called Philip Faulconbridge – and his younger brother Robert come before the king to dispute the Faulconbridge legacy, Robert claiming that his older brother is not really their father's son and should not inherit the Faulconbridge lands and title. The Faulconbridge quarrel, like the war between Arthur and John over the English throne, hinges on ambiguities and ruptures in the relationship between legal and biological inheritance. In both families – that of the king and that of the Faulconbridges – the patriarchal succession has been interrupted. John has taken the throne that belongs by law of primogeniture to Arthur, a fact that Shakespeare emphasizes by suppressing Holinshed's record of Richard I's bequest of the throne to John, by inventing Elinor's unequivocal assertion that John's claim is based on "strong possession much more than . . . right," and even by implying that Arthur is Cordelion's son (as he does by ambiguous wording in II.i.2, when France describes Cordelion as the "great forerunner" of Arthur's "blood" and again in II.i.177, when Constance tells Elinor that Arthur is her "eldest son's son").

Like the controversy over the crown, the Faulconbridge controversy involves a disputed will and rival claimants to patriarchal succession, and both quarrels involve the mothers – but not the fathers – of the contending heirs. John's mother, Elinor, and Arthur's mother, Constance, play important roles in the historical contest between their sons, but neither is the chief actor. The fictional Faulconbridge quarrel, on the other hand, centers on a woman, for Lady Faulconbridge's infidelity has created the nightmare situation that haunts the patriarchal imagination – a son not of her husband's getting destined to inherit her husband's lands and title. The Faulconbridge episode makes explicit the ideological fault line that lies beneath the stridency of patriarchal claims and repressions – the repressed knowledge of women's power to subvert men's genealogical continuity and their genealogical claims.

John's attempt to arbitrate the Faulconbridge quarrel exposes a deep contradiction in patriarchal law. "Sirrah," he says to Robert, "your brother is legitimate":

> Your father's wife did after wedlock bear him;
> And if she did play false, the fault was hers,
> Which fault lies on the hazards of all husbands
> That marry wives. Tell me, how if my brother,
> Who, as you say, took pains to get this son,
> Had of your father claim'd this son for his?
> In sooth, good friend, your father might have kept
> This calf, bred from his cow, from all the world;
> In sooth he might; then if he were my brother's,
> My brother might not claim him; nor your father,
> Being none of his, refuse him. This concludes:
> My mother's son did get your father's heir;
> Your father's heir must have your father's land.
>
> (I.i.116–29)

According to the laws of patriarchy as expounded by John (and according to good English law in Shakespeare's time), a wife, like a cow, is mere chattel, the possession of her husband. All her actions, even an act so radical as betrayal of the marriage bond, are powerless to affect her son's name, possession, legal status, or identity. Only the man's entitlement has significance under law. Any child she bears is his, even if he is not the biological father. Thus, the very absoluteness of patriarchal right provides for its own subversion, since women can in actuality, though not in law, disrupt and subvert male genealogy.

By admitting that the relationship between father and son is finally no more than a legal fiction, John attacks the very basis of patriarchal thought. Relying on "strong possession" rather than "right" for his throne (I.i.40), John opposes the patriarchal authority that would legitimate Arthur. Having himself crowned a second time, he denies the permanence and efficacy of the ritual that made him king (IV.ii.1–34). Everything, even the unique ceremony by which monarchial authority is passed down in temporal succession from one male ruler to the next, now becomes repeatable and reversible. When the French king describes Arthur as a "little abstract" of the "volume" that "died in" Arthur's father, (II.i.101–3), he grounds the historical record in nature. But John's verdict on the Faulconbridge controversy demythologizes that record, depriving it of the natural status implied by the French king's metaphor of man as volume and boy as abstract and exposing it as a social construct designed to shore up the flimsy and always necessarily putative connections between fathers and sons.

Elinor is the first to guess the Bastard's true paternity, for she can read the wordless text of his physical nature:

> He hath a trick of Cordelion's face;
> The accent of his tongue affecteth him.
> Do you not read some tokens of my son
> In the large composition of this man?
> (I.i.85–8)

But without Lady Faulconbridge's testimony, the Bastard's paternity would remain conjectural, and his name and title would belie the biological truth of the paternity they purported to represent. It takes one woman to guess the truth and another to verify it. In Holinshed, Cordelion recognizes his bastard son, giving him "the castell and honor of Coinacke." In the *Troublesome Raigne*, the Bastard guesses his true paternity even before he asks his mother. In fact, he gets the news from Nature herself: "Methinks I hear a hollow echo sound," he says,

> That *Philip* is the son unto a King:
> The whistling leaves upon the trembling trees,
> Whistle in concert I am *Richard's* son;
> The bubbling murmur of the water's fall,
> Records *Phillipus Regis filius*;

132

Birds in their flight make music with their wings,
Filling the air with glory of my birth;
Birds, bubbles, leaves and mountains, echo, all
Ring in mine ears, that I am *Richard's* son.
                    (*Troublesome Raigne* 1591: Part I: i.242–51)

Only in Shakespeare is he required to receive his paternity from the hands of women.

Lady Faulconbridge is an unhistorical character, but she is the only one who knows the truth about the Bastard's paternity. The Bastard's words are significant: "But for the certain knowledge of that truth/ I put you o'er to heaven and to my mother" (I.i.61–2). The Bastard's ironic coupling of his adulterous mother with heaven as the only sources of the elusive truth of paternity suggests an affinity between them as keepers of a knowledge never directly accessible to men. In *King John* Shakespeare goes as far as he will ever go in making women, women's skeptical voices, and women's truth central to the history he staged, leaving his sources behind and venturing into the realm of the unwritten and the conjectural, and into the inaccessible domain (the no man's land) where the secrets of paternity are kept.

Part III

GENDER AND NATION

Anticipations of modernity in the second tetralogy

10

RICHARD II

From a feminist standpoint, one of the most striking features of the second tetralogy is the restriction of women's roles. We have already seen how the formidable power of the women warriors in the Henry VI plays and *King John* was replaced in *Richard III* by the pathetic laments of mourning widows and bereaved mothers. In the second tetralogy, women's roles are further constricted. There are fewer female characters; they have less time on stage and less to say when they get there. Moreover, virtually all the women we see in these plays are enclosed in domestic settings and confined to domestic roles. The only exceptions to the wholesale domestication of female characters are the disreputable, comic women at the Eastcheap Tavern: Mistress Quickly, the hostess; and Doll Tearsheet, the prostitute.

Even foreign women are domesticated. The dangerous, demonic otherness and vivid, subversive speech of Joan La Pucelle are replaced by the appealing, feminine helplessness and the broken English of the French princess in *Henry V*. The women warriors of the earlier plays are no longer seen on stage. Their only vestige is the fleeting reference at the beginning of *Henry IV, Part I* to the "beastly shameless transformation" performed by Welsh women upon the bodies of the English soldiers killed in the Battle of Holmedon (I.i.44). The atrocity is performed offstage and never explicitly described (the only Welsh woman who appears on stage is a weeping wife). Even the terms in which the women's savagery is reported at the English court – as an act "as may not be/ Without much shame retold or spoken of" (I.i.45–6) – mark its erasure from the scene of English history.

In the plays of the second tetralogy, as in *Richard III*, female sexuality no longer threatens to disrupt legitimate authority. When Bullingbrook charges in *Richard II* that Bushy and Green "have in manner with [their] sinful hours/ Made a divorce betwixt his queen and him, /Broke the possession of a royal bed" (III.i.11–13), the sexual culprits are the king and his male favorites: it is not even clear that any women are involved.[1] The only reference to the queen's sexuality is purely metaphorical – the "unborn sorrow, ripe in fortune's womb" her feminine intuition detects (II.ii.10). The sorrow, moreover, is a fully legitimate conception: caused by a premonition of her husband's impending fall, it is implicitly designated as the offspring of her lawful marriage. The other women in the play – the Duchess of Gloucester and the Duchess of York – are too old to pose a sexual threat. The Duke and Duchess of York, in fact, make this point explicit. In V.ii the duchess reminds her husband that her "teeming date" is "drunk up with time" (91); and in V.iii, York opposes her attempt to plead for her son's life by reminding her how preposterous it would be if her "old dugs" should "once more a traitor rear" (90).

Barbara Hodgdon's observation about *Henry IV, Part I* – that the play is "unlike Shakespeare's earlier histories, where conflict centers on genealogical descent in a struggle for the crown's rightful ownership" (1991: 155) – is applicable to the entire second tetralogy and to *Henry VIII* as well. In *Richard II* York gives his allegiance to Bullingbrook despite his knowledge that Richard is the legitimate heir of Edward III. Because patrilineal inheritance is no longer sufficient to guarantee patriarchal authority, female sexual transgression no longer threatens to subvert it. The issues of bastardy and adultery arise only briefly and only in Act V, when the action degenerates from the historical tragedy of Richard's fall to the farcical domestic quarrel between the Duke and Duchess of York about their son. Terrified by her husband's threat to report Aumerle's treason to the new king, the duchess assumes, wrongly, that he is motivated by doubts about his son's paternity:

> But now I know thy mind, thou dost suspect
> That I have been disloyal to thy bed,
> And that he is a bastard, not thy son.
> Sweet York, sweet husband, be not of that mind,
> He is as like thee as a man may be
> Not like to me, or any of my kin.
>
> (V.ii.104–9)

Neither York nor the audience has any reason to doubt what the duchess says. In fact, her anxious suspicion that York doubts his son's paternity is expressed in terms that render it ludicrous. Instead of empowering the duchess as a sexual threat to the authority of her husband and the legitimacy of her son, her reference to the possibility of her adultery is designed to elicit dismissive laughter.

Here, as in *Richard III*, the constriction of women's roles represents a movement into modernity, the division of labor and the cultural restrictions that accompanied the production of the household as a private place, separated from the public arenas of economic and political endeavor.[2] To move from the first tetralogy to the second is to move backward to the time of Richard II, but it is also to move forward from a story of warring feudal families to one of the consolidation of the English nation under the power of a great king. In the first tetralogy, virtue and military power like Talbot's are inherited along with the patrilineal titles of nobility; in the second, they are the personal assets that enable the son of an enterprising upstart like Henry Bullingbrook to achieve the status of the mirror of all Christian kings and the aspiring men in the theater audience to earn their places in the commonwealth.

In *Richard II* the contradictions between those two models of personal and royal legitimacy are personalized in the opposition between Richard and Bullingbrook; but they are also framed as abstract issues, the subjects for repeated debate by male characters in the play, the motives and rationalizations for their acts and decisions. The dynastic loyalties that motivate much of the action in the first tetralogy typically make political action the product of filial devotion, but in *Richard II* the private affective bonds that unite fathers and sons are opposed to and superseded by the demands of political principle and civic duty. Gaunt agrees to the banishment of his own son because, as he tells King Richard, "You urg'd me as a judge" and not "like a father" (I.iii.237–8). The Duke of York, discovering that his son has joined a conspiracy to kill the new king, Henry IV, pleads that his son *not* be pardoned because, he explains, "If thou do pardon, whosoever pray,/More sins for this forgiveness prosper may./ This fest'red joint cut off, the rest rest sound,/This let alone will all the rest confound" (V. iii.83–6). Even the instructions the gardener gives his helpers take the form of a lesson in political theory:

Go thou, and like an executioner
Cut off the heads of [too] fast growing sprays,
That look too lofty in our commonwealth:
All must be even in our government.

(III.iv.33–36)

The concern for the commonwealth that unites the lowly gardeners with their betters at court also separates men from women. All of the female characters in *Richard II* come from the top of the social and political hierarchy, but their interests are delimited by the private affective bonds of family loyalty, and the women are entirely preoccupied by concerns for their male relations. These concerns differ significantly from the strong genealogical ties that bind fathers to sons in the Henry VI plays. Those ties, while they often include an affective dimension, as in Talbot's concern for his son, also have a public political and economic dimension: the defense and consolidation of dynastic power and its transmission from one generation to the next. Gaunt shares the Duchess of Gloucester's grief for her murdered husband, who was his own brother, but when the duchess tries to persuade him to avenge Gloucester's death, Gaunt refuses because his loyalty to the principle of divine right takes precedence over his personal loyalty to his brother: Richard, he explains, is God's "deputy," and "I may never lift/An angry arm against His minister" (I.ii. 38–41). The same gendered difference distinguishes the gardener and his helper from the queen. The common men lament Richard's bad government and its effects upon the commonwealth as well as his downfall; the royal woman responds to the news as a personal catastrophe for herself and her husband. Intensified to the point of caricature, the opposition between masculine political considerations and feminine affective loyalty is reiterated in Act V when the Duke and Duchess of York wrangle over whether their son should be punished or pardoned for his part in the conspiracy to assassinate the new king.

Like the bereaved and grieving women in *Richard III*, the Duchess of Gloucester and the queen in *Richard II* dramatize the private emotional costs of the men's public, political conflicts; and, like the women in *Richard III*, they are powerless to affect the outcome of those conflicts. When Gaunt refuses to avenge her husband's murder, the Duchess of Gloucester leaves the stage to die of grief. The queen does not even learn that Richard is to be deposed until she eavesdrops on the gardeners' conversation. When Bullingbrook pardons Aumerle, the Duchess of York becomes the only woman in the play who manages to influence the action, but her farcical wrangling with her husband also reinforces the separation between the public, political concerns of men and the private, affective loyalties of women. The bickering between the duke and duchess – and with it the lowering of the dramatic register – begins in V.ii when York struggles frantically to get his boots so he can ride off to warn the king about Aumerle's participation in a conspiracy to assassinate him, while the duchess, equally frantic, struggles to prevent him. In the following scene the domestic quarrel resumes in the royal presence, and this time the humor is explicitly identified with the inappropriateness of the duchess's intervention. Her demand to be admitted to the royal presence initiates a telling remark from the new king: "Speak with me, pity me, open the door!," she cries, "A beggar begs that never begg'd before." In a comment probably meant to be addressed to the audience, the king responds, "Our scene is alt'red from a serious thing,/And now changed to "The Beggar and the King" (V.iii.77–80), signalling that the historical "Tragedy of Richard II" is being interrupted by the low comic farce of "The Beggar and the King." Significantly, it is the woman who is blamed for initiating both the generic lowering of the drama and the social lowering of the action (Hodgdon 1991: 139). The solemn dignity of the court (and of the history play) has no place for domestic quarrels or the shrill-voiced supplications of an anxious mother.

The gendering of excessive emotion as feminine has unsettling effects on the gender position – and the authority – of Richard II, perhaps the most emotive of all Shakespeare's kings. While masculinity and femininity are never the exclusive properties of male and female persons, aspects of English culture in the late sixteenth and early seventeenth centuries made the performative and constructed nature of gender difference disturbingly visible. In the theaters, boys played women's roles and many kinds of social distinctions were indicated by a semiotics of dress and gesture. On the throne, there was a female monarch who claimed masculine authority by referring to herself as a "prince" (Marcus 1988: 60). In the streets of London, women paraded in masculine dress (Harrison 1587: 147). An increasingly urbanized and performative culture destabilized traditional status distinctions, including the distinctions between men and women (Newman 1991:

123), and produced a wide variety of anxious attempts to re-establish them. For the literate, increasing concern with the need to observe masculine and feminine roles was expressed in satiric writing that made the "womanish" man and the "mannish" woman stock objects of invective. In villages, failure to abide by the codes of gendered behavior was punished by court prosecutions of scolds and witches and community shaming rituals such as charivaris (Underdown 1985: 127).

All these efforts to enforce gender difference can be seen as responses to an emergent culture of personal achievement. If a man's place in the social hierarchy had to be achieved and secured by his own efforts, any claims to authority required that both social status and gender status had to be sustained in performance. In *Richard II*, the king's patrilineal authority is vitiated by his womanish tears and his effeminate behavior: he has no taste for foreign wars, he talks when he should act, and he wastes his kingdom's treasure by indulging in excessive luxuries. Bullingbrook, who has no hereditary right to the crown, acquires it by the successful performance of masculine virtues.

Many critics have remarked that the conflict between Richard and Bullingbrook is framed as a conflict between two models of royal authority, Richard associated with a nostalgic image of medieval royalty, grounded in heredity and expressed in ceremonial ritual, Bullingbrook with the emergence of an authority achieved by personal performance and expressed in the politically motivated theatrical self-presentation of a modern ruler. What is less frequently noted is how thoroughly the binary opposition personalized in the conflict between Bullingbrook and Richard is implicated in an early modern ideology of "masculine" and "feminine" (see Plates 5 and 6). Deborah Warner's 1995 production of the play, which starred Fiona Shaw as Richard, exploited this gendered opposition to brilliant dramatic effect. Shaw, in the words of one reviewer, "simply played Richard as a woman" (Berkowitz 1996: 9). Although Shakespeare does not literalize the gendered opposition between the two antagonists, his Bullingbrook, like Warner's, plays the "man" to Richard's "woman." A master of military and political strategy, Bullingbrook is shown in company with a noble father, and he alludes to the existence of an "unthrifty" son (V.iii.1); but we hear nothing of his wife or mother, and he is never represented in association with women. Richard, by contrast, has a wife but no son. Although our own gender ideology privileges male heterosexual passion as an expression of virility, this was not yet the case in Shakespeare's time. Richard is characterized as "effeminate," but this does not mean that he is "homosexual": indeed, the terms "homosexual" and "heterosexual," along with the conceptions of gendered personal identity they denote, are post-Shakespearean inventions (Bray 1988: 13–32; Bredbeck 1991: 3–30; Goldberg 1992: 1–26; Rackin 1992: 37–52). Richard is effeminate because he prefers words to deeds, has no taste for battle, and is addicted to luxurious pleasures. His rapid fluctuations from overweening confidence to the depth of despair (III.ii) recall early modern misogynist denunciations of feminine instability (Ferris 1981), but even his virtues are represented in feminine terms: York's sympathetic description of Richard's behavior in adversity – his "gentle sorrow" and "His face still combating with tears and smiles,/ The badges of his grief and patience" (V.ii.31–3) – draws on the same discourse of suffering feminine virtue as the description of Lear's Cordelia smiling and crying at once as "patience and sorrow [strove]/ Who should express her goodliest" (IV.iii.16–17). Bullingbrook speaks few words but raises a large army. Richard is a master of poetic eloquence, unsurpassed in what Mowbray calls "a woman's war . . . of . . . tongues" (I.i.48–9), but he surrenders to Bullingbrook without waging a single battle. His viceroy is the superannuated York, who appears "weak with age," "with signs of war about his aged neck" (II.ii.83, 74); confronted by Bullingbrook's military challenge, York immediately capitulates, declaring that he will "remain as neuter" (II.iii.159).

The gendered opposition between Richard and Bullingbrook takes much of its force from the predicament of the English aristocracy at the time the play was produced. The noblemen who support Bullingbrook's rebellion are motivated by what they perceive as monarchial threats to their traditional power and authority, threats which are explicitly identified as emasculation when Ross charges that Richard's appropriation of Bullingbrook's inheritance has left him "bereft and gelded of his patrimony" (II.i.237). As Richard Halpern points out, "the aristocracy felt emasculated by conversion from a militarized to a consuming class." This anxiety was heightened during Elizabeth's reign by the presence of a female monarch and by the queen's transformation of the medieval culture of aristocratic honor from martial service to courtly display (Halpern 1991: 245). Richard's

Plate 5 This contemporary portrait of Richard II (*c.* 1395), now in Westminster Abbey, emphasizes the king's youth and feminine beauty.
Source: Reproduced by permission of the Dean and Chapter of Westminster

Plate 6 This effigy of Henry IV in Canterbury Cathedral offers a striking contrast to the portrait of Richard in Plate 5.
Source: Reproduced by permission of the National Portrait Gallery, London

possession of the throne, like Elizabeth's, is authorized by the old warrant of patrilineal inheritance, but his loss of it is defined in terms of the new anxieties that Halpern describes.

Richard's father, York recalls, "Did win what he did spend, and

145

spent not that/ Which his triumphant father's hand had won" (II.i.180–1). Richard, by contrast, has "basely yielded upon compromise/ That which his noble ancestors achiev'd with blows" (II.i.253–4) and wasted the land's wealth in luxurious pleasures and courtly extravagance. Holinshed's *Chronicles*, Shakespeare's main historical source for the play, also represents Richard as indulging in unprecedented personal extravagance at the expense of the commonwealth:

> He kept the greatest port, and mainteined the most plentifull house that ever any king in England did either before his time or since . . . In his kitchen there were three hundred servitors, and everie other office was furnished after the like rate. Of ladies, chamberers, and landerers, there were above three hundred at the least. And in gorgious and costlie apparell they exceeded all measure, not one of them that kept within the bounds of his degree. Yeomen and groomes were clothed in silkes, with cloth of graine and skarlet, over sumptuous ye may be sure for their estates. And this vanitie was not onelie used in the court in those daies, but also other people abroad in the towns and countries, had their garments cut far otherwise than had beene accustomed before his daies, with imbroderies, rich furres, and goldsmiths worke, and everie daie there was devising of new fashions, to the great hinderance and decaie of the common-welth.

> (Holinshed 1587: 2: 868)

In Holinshed's account, as in Shakespeare's, Richard's extravagance is both a fabulous image of lost splendor and a socially disruptive innovation. Like Elizabethan pageantry, it appeals to nostalgia and to an appetite for gorgeous display, but the new-fangled "vanities" Holinshed describes also evoke the anxieties that were associated with an increasingly unstable social hierarchy. Shakespeare makes those anxieties explicit when he associates Richard's appetite for the vanity of luxurious new fashions with the figure of the "Italianated Englishman" who was a familiar object of satire in the sixteenth, but not the fourteenth, century (Ure 1961: 48–9n). York explains that Richard cannot hear his venerable uncles' good advice because his ear is stopped by

> Report of fashions in proud Italy,
> Whose manners still our tardy, apish nation
> Limps after in base imitation.

Where doth the world thrust forth a vanity –
So it be new, there's no respect how vile –
That is not quickly buzz'd into his ears?

(II.i.21–6)

Like the absentee landlords of Shakespeare's own time who betrayed the old feudal traditions of obligation to enclose their property and exploit it for money to spend on lavish displays at court, Richard's taste for effeminate luxury forces him to degrade his office from king to "landlord" (II.i.113).

Confronted by rapid cultural change, Shakespeare's contemporaries often idealized the past as a time of stable values and national glory, when social status was firmly rooted in patrilineal inheritance and expressed in chivalric virtue. In Shakespeare's representation of Richard II, however, the schematic oppositions between an idealized masculine past and a degraded effeminate present give way to expose the cultural contradictions that lay at the heart of Elizabethan nostalgia for the medieval past. In Richard's characterization – as in the case of Elizabeth herself – the polluting forces of effeminate modernity are embodied in the same person who represents the patrilineal royal authority they threaten to subvert.

Despite (or perhaps because of) its association with the cult of Elizabeth, the nostalgic ideal of a glorious English past was overwhelmingly masculine. Just as Elizabeth's male courtiers paid tribute to their queen with elaborate reconstructions of medieval tournaments, Edmund Spenser used archaic language and the conventions of chivalric romance to celebrate Elizabeth, but the form of Spenser's narrative minimizes her power. Although the Faerie Queene is the nominal center of Spenser's poem, she is actually confined to its margins. As Richard Helgerson points out, she "never appears in the poem and exercises only the loosest and most intermittent control over its action" (1992: 48). A similar paradox informs John of Gaunt's nostalgic projection of the England that Richard has betrayed. For although Gaunt's ideal England is a "nurse," a "teeming womb of royal kings" (II.i.51), none of its inhabitants are women. A "fortress" surrounded by a sea which serves it as a "moat," a "royal throne of kings" who are "renowned ... for Christian service and true chivalry," the object of Gaunt's nostalgic longing is inhabited exclusively by a "happy breed of men" (II.i.40–54), and the deeds that prove its worth are their heroic battles.

Gaunt invokes an ideal past in order to rebuke a degenerate present – the degraded world of an effeminate king who wastes the land's wealth and honor on luxurious pleasures rather than augmenting them in manly wars against the French. The antithesis he constructs between a warlike, masculine historical world and a degenerate, effeminate present employs exactly the strategy that Thomas Nashe described as the virtue of the history play – the representation of a "valiant" world of English "forefathers" as a "rebuke" to "these degenerate effeminate dayes of ours." Written in the time of Elizabeth – a queen frequently compared to Richard II – Shakespeare's English histories appealed to a similar nostalgia for a masculine, historical world projected in idealized opposition to the present realities of female power and authority.[3] In the second tetralogy, however, this gendered opposition between past and present is increasingly disrupted and deconstructed.

In the earlier plays, performative masculinity is demonic. Richard III, in fact, is its prime exemplar. By the end of the second tetralogy, however, performance will provide the basis for the legitimate royal authority that Henry V achieves despite what he explicitly acknowledges as "the fault/ My father made in compassing the crown" (*Henry V*: IV.i.293–4). In *Richard II*, as in *King John*, both forms of authority are compromised. The older model of royal authority based on patrilineal succession (which had produced a female monarch in Elizabeth I) is represented in the person of an effeminate, theatrical king, who is nonetheless the legitimate heir to the throne. The emergent masculine ideals of personal merit and performance are associated with the usurper, who is empowered by the support of the overwhelming majority of his countrymen.

Although Bullingbrook explains his unauthorized return from banishment in terms of the feudal logic of hereditary entitlement, claiming that he does so only to secure his patrilineal legacy as Duke of Lancaster, he quickly redefines it as service to the "commonwealth" (II.iii.166–7). In Shakespeare's account, as in Holinshed, Bullingbrook has the overwhelming support of the people. Describing Bullingbrook's departure for exile, Holinshed reports, "A woonder it was to see what number of people ran after him in everie towne and street where he came, before he tooke the sea, lamenting and bewailing his departure, as who would saie, that when he departed, the onelie shield, defense and comfort

148

of the commonwealth was vaded and gone" (1587: 2: 848). Shakespeare's Richard reports the same event with anxious contempt: we "Observ'd his courtship to the common people," he says, "what reverence he did throw away on slaves,/ Wooing poor craftsmen with the craft of smiles . . . Off goes his bonnet to an oyster-wench/ A brace of draymen bid God speed him well,/And had the tribute of his supple knee" (I.iv.24–33). Holinshed notes that Bullingbrook's rebellion had "the helpe and assistance (almost) of all the whole realme" (1587: 2: 855), and Shakespeare repeatedly alludes to the universal dissatisfaction with Richard's government and support for Bullingbrook (II.i. 246–88; III.ii.112–19).

In the context of a public theater, these allusions work to empower Bullingbrook and discredit Richard. Shakespeare's descriptions of Richard's offenses against both "the commons" and "the nobles" (II.i.246–8) and of the crowds that take up arms in support of the rebellion ("white-beards," "boys, with women's voices," "distaff-women," "both young and old" [III.ii.112–19]) emphasize their inclusiveness, and they could stand equally well for a description of the heterogeneous audience in the playhouse. The theatrical milieu tended to support the emergent form of authority, in which a king, like a player, had to depend on the favorable responses of the people for whom he performed. Moreover, Richard's contempt for his humble subjects is not likely to have endeared him to their counterparts in Shakespeare's audience.

Hereditary legitimacy, projected in the first tetralogy as a lost ideal represented by the name of Henry V, is now compromised in the person of its leading representative. When the play begins, Richard is already guilty of a crime against the royal blood, the murder of the Duke of Gloucester, his uncle. Contrasting Richard and his father, York defines that crime as a separation from the patrilineal line: "His hands were guilty of no kinred blood,/ But bloody with the enemies of his kin" (II.i.182–3), a recurrent charge in the first two acts of the play. The Duchess of Gloucester recalls Richard's murder of her husband in the same terms, as the spilling of a "vial full of Edward's sacred blood" (I.ii.17). Richard continues to undermine the patrilineal principle upon which his own authority depends when he disinherits Bullingbrook. As York explains,

Is not Gaunt dead? and doth not Herford live?
Was not Gaunt just? and is not Harry true?
Did not the one deserve to have an heir?
Is not his heir a well-deserving son?
Take Herford's rights away, and take from Time
His charters and his customary rights;
Let not to-morrow then ensue to-day;
Be not thyself; for how art thou a king
But by fair sequence and succession?

(II.i.191–9)

Bullingbrook makes the same argument: "If that my cousin king be King in England,/It must be granted I am Duke of Lancaster" (II.iii.123–4).

In Gaunt's nostalgic projection of medieval England as a "royal throne of kings," there is a seamless union between English patriotism and loyalty to the king, but Richard's offenses set them in oppositon to each other. The wars between York and Lancaster in the Henry VI plays are motivated by competing claims to genealogical authority, but the conflict in *Richard II* is framed in terms that recall the ideological conflicts in early modern England between an emergent national consciousness and the Tudor and Stuart monarchs' efforts to rationalize, defend, and extend royal authority. To Bullingbrook, as to the gardeners, England is a "commonwealth" (II.iii.166). To Richard it is simply his personal property, to be used as he desires for his own benefit. The dialogue in the early scenes is laced with patriotic sentiment, which is mobilized in opposition to Richard. Gaunt charges that the "blessed plot" England "Is now leas'd out . . ./ Like to a tenement [i.e. land held by a tenant] or pelting [i.e. paltry] farm" (II.i.59–60). The banishment of Mowbray and Bullingbrook elicits moving affirmations of national identity, but always with the implication that Richard is to blame for violating the bond between faithful subjects and mother England. Mowbray protests that he has deserved better at Richard's hands than to be exiled for life: "The language I have learnt these forty years,/ My native English, now I must forgo. . . . What is thy sentence [then] but speechless death,/ Which robs my tongue from breathing native breath?" (I.iii.159–73). As Richard Helgerson has observed, "a kingdom whose boundaries are determined by the language of its inhabitants is no longer a kingdom in the purely dynastic sense" (1992:

2). The ringing couplets with which Bullingbrook departs for his own exile also invoke an emergent sense of national identity grounded in the place of his nativity:

> Then England's ground, farewell, sweet soil, adieu:
> My mother, and my nurse, that bears me yet!
> Where e'er I wander, boast of this I can,
> Though banish'd, yet a true-born Englishman.
>
> (I.iii.306–9)

Bullingbrook defines his relationship to the land in the same terms that John of Gaunt uses when he describes "This blessed plot, this earth, this realm, this England" as "This nurse, this teeming womb of royal kings" (II.i.50–1); but for Bullingbrook the "sweet soil" is the "mother" and "nurse" of every "true-born Englishman." To the Richard of the first two acts, it is his personal property and a source of ready cash: "We are enforc'd to farm our royal realm [i.e. sell the profits from future taxes],/ The revenue whereof shall furnish us/ For our affairs in hand" (I.iv.45–7). Moreover, even when Richard speaks lovingly of the English land, the terms he uses construct a gendered contrast that favors Bullingbrook. When Richard returns from Ireland, he "weep[s] for joy" and salutes the "dear earth ... as a long-parted mother with her child" (III.ii.4–8). The rhyme words in Bullingbrook's final couplet – "boast of this I can" and "a true-born Englishman" – emphasize his masculinity as well as his Englishness. Richard's language effeminizes him as a mother and infantilizes the land as his child. And unlike Bullingbrook, he does not identify the earth as English; in fact, although Richard has by far the greatest number of lines in the play, he speaks the words "England" or "English" only five times in the entire script (I.iv.35; II.i.220; III.iii.97, 100; IV.i.264) and almost always perfunctorily.

Richard II destabilizes the schematic oppositions between past and present, male and female, patrilineal authority and its subversion, English patriotism and foreign threat that defined the meaning of the dramatic conflicts in the first tetralogy. It also destabilizes the binary opposition between theatrical power and historical authority, and in so doing begins the renegotiation of their relationship that will be a major project in the succeeding plays. The rhetorical impact of Richard's theatricality, like that of Richard III, is ambivalent. On the one hand, both characters are associated by their theatricality with the feminine and with the loss of integrity in an increasingly complicated contemporary world. On the other hand, both are empowered by their theatricality, because of its inevitable attraction for a theater audience. What is new in *Richard II* is the association of theatrical power with legitimate royal authority.

The contest between Richard and Bullingbrook, in fact, is specifically framed as a contention between rival actors. As early as Act I, Richard anxiously describes the success of Bullingbrook's theatrical self-presentation to the London citizens:

> How he did seem to dive into their hearts
> With humble and familiar courtesy,
> What reverence he did throw away on slaves,
> Wooing poor craftsmen with the craft of smiles
> And patient underbearing of his fortune,
> As 'twere to banish their affects with him.
> Off goes his bonnet to an oyster-wench,
> A brace of draymen bid God speed him well,
> And had the tribute of his supple knee,
> With "Thanks, my countrymen, my loving friends,"
> As were our England in reversion his,
> And he our subjects' next degree in hope.
>
> (I.iv.25–36)

Publicly acting like a king, Bullingbrook finally becomes one, and in Act V York explicitly compares the Londoners' enthusiastic reception of the newly crowned Henry IV to the response of a theater audience to a "well-graced actor," their contempt for Richard to the indifference of playgoers to an inferior performer:

> As in a theatre the eyes of men,
> After a well-graced actor leaves the stage,
> Are idly bent on him that enters next,
> Thinking his prattle to be tedious,
> Even so, or with much more contempt, men's eyes
> Did scowl on gentle Richard.
>
> (V.ii.23–8)

It is significant, however, that although Bullingbrook's theatrical power is described, it is never shown. Instead of seeing these scenes, the audience in Shakespeare's playhouse is told about them – and told, moreover, by characters who do not share the London crowds' enthusiasm for Bullingbrook's performance.

The reports of Bullingbrook's spectacular success in staging himself in the streets of London anticipate the politically motivated theatricality of Tudor and Stuart monarchs, but Richard's self-dramatization on Shakespeare's stage anticipates the theatrical appeal of Shakespeare's later tragic heroes. The quarto title page of *Richard II*, like that of *Richard III*, identifies the play as a tragedy, and Richard II, even more than his dramatic predecessor, prefigures the heroes of Shakespeare's later tragedies. Like a true tragic hero, he gives long and eloquent expression to his feelings and motivations. Unlike Bullingbrook's theatricality, which is described as an effective political strategy, Richard's is presented as a powerful expression of personal subjectivity.

Bullingbrook has very little to say on stage beyond what is required to advance the plot, and his motives are notoriously inscrutable, provoking many fruitless critical debates as to when or whether he decided to seize the crown. Richard's personality is a major issue in the play; but not Bullingbrook's. There is only one place, in fact, where the dramatic action seems designed to portray Bullingbrook's character – the dialogue in Act I when John of Gaunt advises his son to sweeten his exile by imagining himself at court: "Suppose the singing birds musicians," Gaunt says, "The grass whereon thou tread'st the presence strow'd,/ The flowers fair ladies, and thy steps no more/ Than a delightful measure or a dance" (I.iii.288–91). Discounting both the effeminate pleasures of the court and the feminine pleasures of the imagination, Bullingbrook replies,

> O, who can hold a fire in his hand
> By thinking on the frosty Caucasus?
> Or cloy the hungry edge of appetite
> By bare imagination of a feast?
> Or wallow naked in December snow
> By thinking on fantastic summer's heat?
> (I.iii.294–9)

Bullingbrook's "bare imagination" provides a striking, gendered contrast to the fertility of Richard's. Confined, in Act V, to a solitary prison cell, Richard launches into a sixty-six-line soliloquy. "My brain I'll prove the female to my soul," he says, "My soul the father, and these two beget/ A generation of still-breeding thoughts" to "people this little world,/ In humors like the people of this world. . . . Thus play I in one person many people"

(V.v.6–10, 31). The androgynous fertility of Richard's imagination and his ability to play multiple roles associate him with playwright and actor (McMillin 1984: 46). Although Bullingbrook knows how to stage himself to the people for political advantage, his manly rejection of "fantasy" associates him with the antitheatrical writers who decried the deceptive fictions of the stage. It also reiterates his association with the forces of modernity, for as James Calderwood has observed, the opposition between Richard and Bullingbrook is also an opposition between two ideals of language, one "medieval, sacramental, and poetic" and the other "modern, utilitarian, and scientific" (Calderwood 1971: 162).

Richard imagines himself as a figure in a medieval tableau, his mortal life as "a little scene,/ To monarchize . . . and kill with looks," abruptly ended when the personified figure of Death pierces "his castle wall" with "a little pin" (III.ii.164–70). In the deposition scene, he compares himself to the crucified Christ, and he turns on the assembled audience with an indictment that recalls speeches delivered by actors who portrayed Christ in medieval mystery plays, reminding the spectators that "all of you that stand and look upon me/ . . . Though some of you, with Pilate, wash your hands,/ Showing an outward pity, yet you Pilates/ Have here deliver'd me to my sour cross,/ And water cannot wash away your sin" (IV.i.237–42). Once Bullingbrook takes the throne, theatrical display assumes the modern forms of royal procession and commercial performance. York alludes to both when he describes the new king's triumphant entry into London with Richard at his heels.

Associating royal authority with theatrical display, York's simile signals the modernity of the world of Henry IV. Paradoxically, however, the performance in Shakespeare's own commercial playhouse seems designed to elicit a response opposite to the one York describes, for although Bullingbrook wins in the represented action, the play that depicts his triumph came to Shakespeare's audience, not as the celebration of the accession of Henry IV, but as "The Tragedy of Richard II." Although Richard's feminine self-indulgence and histrionic narcissism disqualify him for political action, Richard and not Bullingbrook was the "well-graced actor" in Shakespeare's theater: no acting company would give the smaller and less demanding role of Bullingbrook to its best actor and deny him the chance to play the leading role of Richard.

Even in the deposition scene, where the represented action depicts Bullingbrook's acquisition of Richard's power, Richard dominates the stage. He deposes himself and makes long and eloquent speeches about his complicated emotional responses to the action. The other actors are restricted for the most part to single lines or even half-lines. Richard calls for a looking-glass, and it instantly appears (IV.i.275). Taking the glass and contemplating his own image, he meditates aloud for sixteen lines about his face. The instrument of feminine vanity becomes the means of theatrical empowerment, for it demands that all eyes in the playhouse, including Richard's own, will be fixed on Richard's face. Then, in a remarkable *coup de théâtre*, he dashes the glass against the floor and turns to Bullingbrook with his conclusion: "Mark, silent king, the moral of this sport,/ How soon my sorrow hath destroy'd my face" (IV.i.290–1). The silent, practical new king attempts to arrest the theatrical display with a terse rebuttal that draws on the familiar Elizabethan association between shadows and actors: "The shadow of your sorrow hath destroy'd/ The shadow of your face." But Richard is much too quick-witted and voluble to be silenced by this literal-minded reply. He takes off for another twelve lines, making metaphors about shadows and ironically thanking Bullingbrook for "not only [giving him] cause to wail but [teaching him] the way/ How to lament the cause" (IV.i.300–2). In the represented historical action, Bullingbrook has taken the crown of England from Richard, but he is still compelled to play straight man to Richard's agile wit on Shakespeare's stage.

The new king plays straight man again in Act V, when the Duke and Duchess of York force him to participate in their domestic quarrel over the fate of their son. Replacing the gorgeous pageantry of Richard's late medieval court with the vulgar domestic farce of a suddenly modern world, this episode reproduces in a lower register the loss of patriarchal authority that has already taken place in the main action of the play. The entire scene, in fact, seems calculated to exhibit the new king's lack of inherent authority and to degrade him by association with the low concerns of ordinary subjects. To do so, it turns from the political to the domestic realm, naturalizing Henry's lack of patriarchal authority in the image of the troubled family that will be a *leitmotif* in both parts of *Henry IV*. At the very beginning of the scene, before York enters, the king complains about his "unthrifty" son – absent from the court for three months and rumored to be consorting with dissolute companions in London. Both the king's inability to control his son and his use of the term "unthrifty" associate him with York, who uses the same monetary language when he refuses the king's offer to pardon Aumerle. If he accepts it, he says, Aumerle "shall spend mine honor with his shame,/As thriftless sons their scraping fathers' gold" (V.iii.68–9). Refiguring the offer of royal largesse as a degrading commercial transaction in which aristocratic honor is transformed into money to be spent, York's amplification of the image of the thriftless son degrades both himself and the new king by association with the money-grubbing, miserly father of a spendthrift son, a stock character with a disquieting resemblance to an ambitious Elizabethan merchant.

The most explicit marks of the men's debasement, however, are the work of the duchess. Both York and Henry are diminished by their inability to silence the woman and their ultimate capitulation to her demands, and degraded by their participation in the indecorous scene she stages. When York first enters, the king speaks to him in blank verse and the language of royal decorum, but once the duchess enters, she inducts him into the debased idiom of domestic wrangling. He answers her unceremonious demand for admission to the royal presence – "What ho, my liege! for God's sake let me in" – without rhyming. "What shrill-[voic'd] suppliant makes this eager cry?," he asks. But the duchess's response – "A woman, and thy aunt, great King, 'tis I" – signals his incorporation in the domestic farce; identifying herself as the king's aunt, she also rhymes her answer to his question. The king's next speech – four lines that consist of two self-contained couplets – signals his entry into the low discourse of domestic comedy (V.iii.74–82).

Richard also has a domestic scene in Act V, but his is anything but comic. Apparently designed to contrast with the farcical wrangling between the Duke and Duchess of York, the elegiac parting between Richard and his queen is steeped in nostalgic pathos. Like the other scenes in Act V, its purpose is retrospectively to ratify Richard's authority and discredit that of Henry IV. Despite this nostalgic purpose, however, the means are modern, for the difference between legitimate and illegitimate kings is no longer defined by differences in patrilineal authority, but instead by their personal character and performance, by the allegiance of humble subjects, and by their roles as husbands. Richard has always surpassed his rival in the extravagance of his theatricality, but in Act V, he is also shown as the recipient of a humble subject's heartfelt devotion when the groom visits his prison (V.v.67–97). Most important, however, is the contrast between the Duchess of York's comic victory over her husband and the new king and the noble pathos of the parting between Richard and his loving queen.

The importance of the women's roles in Act V is attested by the fact that both are unhistorical. York's first wife, Isabel of Castille, had died in 1393, six years earlier; but although the Duchess of York at the time of Richard's deposition and Aumerle's treachery was actually Aumerle's stepmother, Shakespeare insists on the biological connection. His duchess reproaches her husband, "Hadst thou groan'd for him/ As I have done, thou wouldst be more pitiful" (V.ii.102–3). York, in turn, rejects her desperate efforts to save her son by asking, "Thou frantic woman, what dost thou make here?/ Shall thy old dugs once more a traitor rear?" (V.iii.89–90). Richard's wife at the time of his deposition, also named Isabel, was a ten-year-old child, the daughter of the King of France, whom Richard had married when she was seven in order to secure a truce with her father (Saccio 1977: 22). Shakespeare transforms the child into a mature woman and the dynastic marriage into a loving affective union in order to provide a retrospective ratification for Richard's patriarchal authority, now grounded in the matrimonial authority of a husband rather than the royal patrimony that Richard lost when he betrayed the legacy of his forefathers (see II.i.163–85). Neither the usurpers' insistence on sending the queen back to France nor the tearful parting between husband and wife has any basis in Holinshed, who reported that after Richard's death Henry attempted, against the will of the French, to keep the child and her dowry in England and marry her to the Prince of Wales (Holinshed 1587: 3: 16–18).

Shakespeare's mature queen is nameless to the end and power-less to affect the historical action, but she provides the mystical warrant for Richard's legitimacy. Her grief, like that of the women in *Richard III*, endows her with a prophetic power that is specific-ally identified as feminine. She has premonitions of disaster, which she describes as an "unborn sorrow, ripe in fortune's womb" (II.ii.10), and when Green brings her the news that Bulling-brook has returned to England, she calls him "the midwife to my woe" (II.ii.62). At the end of the play, Richard entrusts the queen with the task of telling his story:

In winter's tedious nights sit by the fire
With good old folks and let them tell [thee] tales
Of woeful ages long ago betid:
And ere thou bid good night, to quite their griefs,
Tell thou the lamentable tale of me,
And send the hearers weeping to their beds.
For why, the senseless brands will sympathize
The heavy accent of thy moving tongue,
And in compassion weep the fire out,
And some will mourn in ashes, some coal-black,
For the deposing of a rightful king.

(V.i.40–50)

Imagining his story as a nostalgic tale "of woeful ages long ago betid" told by a fire on a winter night, Richard consigns his history to the female genre of domestic oral narrative.[4] Enjoining the queen to tell it, he depends on the "moving tongue" of a woman and the compassionate responses of her auditors to provide the posthumous ratification of his legitimacy as "a rightful king."

Like the women in *Richard III*, the queen has been a focus for pathetic sentiment from the beginning. As Scott McMillin points out, she "speaks at length in only three scenes" and "in each of them she weeps – tears are her leading characteristic" (McMillin 1984: 42). It is not until the moment of their parting, however, that the sympathy she evokes is extended to Richard. In the earlier scenes where she appeared, she grieved for her husband, but always in isolation from him, and there was nothing to counter Bullingbrook's accusation that the nameless sins of Richard's courtiers had somehow "Made a divorce betwixt his queen and him,/ Broke the possession of a royal bed,/ And stain'd the beauty of a fair queen's cheeks/ With tears drawn from her eyes by your foul wrongs" (III.i.12–15). In Act V, by contrast, the queen's tears come from the prospect of separation from the husband who is now identified as her "true-love," and the "divorce" between them is the work of the usurpers.

In both cases, the accusation of royal divorce is a political charge, empowered by the mystification of patriarchal marriage as a paradigm of political order. Hall used it to authorize the Tudor dynasty when he entitled his history of all the kings from Henry IV to Henry VIII "The Union of the Two Noble and Illustre Famelies of Lancastre & Yorke" and explained that "the union of

man and woman in the holy sacrament of matrimony" symbolized political peace and unity.[5] Naturalizing royal authority in the
image of a patriarchal family, both Elizabeth and James repeatedly
likened their relationships to England to that of a husband to his
wife. But the husband–sovereign analogy also worked in the
opposite direction, to justify the authority of every husband by
reference to the mystified image of sovereignty. At the end of *The
Taming of the Shrew,* for instance, Kate rationalizes her submission
by declaring that a husband is his wife's "sovereign" and comparing her duty to him to "Such duty as the subject owes the
prince" (V.ii.147, 155). The troubled families in Act V of *Richard
II,* like the imagery of troubled families that appears in both parts
of *Henry IV,* imply an analogy between the failure of royal
authority in Bullingbrook's kingdom and the failure of patriarchal
authority in the families of ordinary subjects. Richard II makes the
same connection when he accuses Bullingbrook's men: "Doubly
divorc'd! Bad men, you violate/ A twofold marriage – 'twixt my
crown and me,/ And then betwixt me and my married wife"
V.i.71–3). The accusation, like the queen's wifely devotion, displaces an emergent basis for masculine authority backward in
time to the Middle Ages and upward in status to the royal family
when it naturalizes Richard's status as king by equating it with
his status as husband. Although Richard has a clear, hereditary
right to the English throne, he loses it by squandering his patrimony. He regains it in retrospect by his possession of a devoted,
domesticated wife.

11

THE HENRY IV PLAYS

In the last moments of his life, Richard follows his loving queen's injunction to emulate the royal lion, who thrusts out his paw in noble resistance at the moment of his death (V.i.29–34). Behaving, for once, like the warrior kings who were his ancestors, he kills two of his assassins with his own hands, and he uses his dying breath to reassert his status as king and to reclaim the land as his kingdom: "Exton, thy fierce hand/ Hath with the King's blood stain'd the King's own land" (V.v.109–10). In the Henry IV plays, England is no longer a kingdom, but an aggregate of heterogeneous people and places. Geographical space replaces allegiance to monarchial authority as the defining principle of Englishness, but England is not yet a unified nation, for it is divided by endless civil wars.

Shakespeare's history plays are primarily monarchial in orientation. Other history plays, such as Heywood's *Edward IV* (c. 1599), focus a great deal of attention on the city of London, its citizen classes, and its mercantile culture. Shakespeare, by and large, does not. Rather than focusing on the city of London and the relations between the king and the city, his history plays foreground struggles between English kings and foreign monarchs and between English kings and the heads of the country's great feudal families. But there is a subterranean tension, especially in the second tetralogy, between the idea of a borderless state centered on the body of the monarch and a chorographic focus on the land and people of England, including the city of London, as defining the nation. This tension is implied even in *Richard II*, of all Shakespeare's English histories the play most insistently focused on the monarch; but in the Henry IV plays it becomes fully manifest in the social heterogeneity of the characters and the geographical heterogeneity of the settings. No longer confined to the elevated domain of court and battlefield, the world of Henry IV includes a variety of vividly detailed contemporary settings, ranging, like a disordered chorographic "perambulation," from Shallow's bucolic Gloucestershire, to an innyard on the road to London, to Falstaff's bustling, urban Eastcheap.

The coronation procession at the end of *Henry IV, Part II* returns to the chronicles to impose in retrospect a teleological order on the plot of the two plays, culminating in patrilineal succession. A show of state, the coronation procession stages the restoration of the hierarchical, patriarchal order that has been disrupted both by the preceding action and in its representation. As Lawrence Manley explains, a state procession constructed "a model of society . . . segmented in graduated degrees" that "form a syntagmatic chain . . . leading upward toward . . . elite patriarchal leadership" (1983: 360). Up to this point, however, the dramatic structure of the two plays has constructed a model of a fragmented society. The linear, causal plot of *Richard II*, centered on the king, is replaced by a proliferation of subplots tenuously connected by the spatial principles of analogy, parody, juxtaposition and contrast. Structured by the spatial form of chorography, the subplots interrupt the chronicle narrative of diachronic royal succession for a synchronic perambulation of the landscape, moving from royal council chamber and battlefield to borderland and alehouse and country orchard.[1] The displacement of chronicle by chorography in the Henry IV plays transforms the temporality of the narrative from past to present, not only because chorography was a newer form of historiographic representation but also because chronicle, by its very nature, is set in the past tense, while chorographical descriptions, although they typically began with the history of a place, focused on contemporary life rather than the ancient past. Shakespeare's anachronistic, contemporary Eastcheap, like his anachronistic representation of Shallow's country home in Gloucestershire, recalls the present temporality of chorographic description.

No longer the center of dramatic action, the king also lacks both patrilineal right and providential warrant. His desire to recuperate the sacramental authority of a medieval crusader king by leading a pilgrimage to Jerusalem is endlessly deferred and finally discredited as a mask for a secular domestic political agenda – "To lead out many to the Holy Land,/ Lest rest and lying still might make them look/ Too near unto my state" (*Henry IV*, II: IV.v. 210–12). The model of a self-made theatrical man, Henry conceives his reign as a drama and theatrical performance as the basis of royal authority. In *Part I* he lectures his son on the arts of calculated public self-presentation, without which, he says, "Opinion, that did help me to the crown/ Had still kept loyal to possession,/ And left me in reputeless banishment,/ A fellow of no mark nor likelihood" (III.ii.42–4). By the end of *Part II*, the king acknowledges the failure of his performance, but he still uses theatrical language to describe it: his entire reign, he says, has been "but as a scene/Acting" an "argument" of usurpation and domestic disorder (IV.v.197–8). Hal, he now recognizes, will put on a better show.

Hal's promise as heir apparent is based, from the beginning of *Henry IV, Part I*, on his superior performative power, but although performance provides a necessary basis for royal authority, it is not represented as sufficient. As Barbara Hodgdon has observed, the spectacle of many men marching in the king's coats at Shrewsbury "recirculates the question of the true king's identity, the central issue behind the Hotspur–Northumberland rebellion" (1991: 158) This practice had ample historical precedent (Holinshed, in fact, records the presence of decoys "apparelled in the kings sute" at Shrewsbury), but its foregrounding in Shakespeare's representation of the battle draws on antitheatrical sentiment to offer an implicit critique of Henry's reliance upon theatrical performance to secure his authority. For although costume and performance are indeed sufficient to make a king in a theatrical production, their proliferation here is staged in a way to remind an audience that off the stage costume is not everything: who is wearing the coat really does make a difference. As Douglas says in *Part I*, after killing Blunt, "A borrowed title hast thou bought too dear . . . I will kill all his coats . . ./ Until I meet the King" (V.iii.23–8).

Dynastic authority is even more explicitly discredited by its association with the forces of rebellion and national disunity. The alliance between the rebel leaders is cemented by the traditional bonds of dynastic alliances (Mortimer is married to Glendower's daughter, Hotspur to Mortimer's sister), and they rationalize their rebellion in terms of patrilineal right, since Mortimer is the lineal heir to Richard II. But the rebel cause is discredited, not only or even chiefly because it defies the authority of the monarch, but because it threatens to dismember the body of the land, a threat that is graphically illustrated when the rebel leaders haggle over the map of Britain and agree finally to have the river Trent turned from its natural course in the interest of their "bargain" (*Henry IV, I*: III.i.137).

Patrimonial inheritance no longer legitimates royal authority, but in this play, unlike *Richard III* and *Richard II*, neither does matrimony. There are no women at Henry's court and only two brief references to Henry's queen, both, significantly, in the form of irreverent jokes at the Eastcheap Tavern. The first is when Hal is informed that a nobleman has come from the court with a message from his father. Hal's flippant response – "Give him as much as will make him a royal man, and send him back again to my mother" (II.iv.290–1) – defies the authority of his father, expresses his disrespect for nobility and conflates the names of hereditary entitlement with the names of coins. The second comes in the form of theatrical parody when Falstaff assumes the role of king in the play extempore. Expert in theatrical performance, Falstaff evokes delighted exclamations from Mistress Quickly, but he immediately redefines her response to cast her in the stereotypical role of his weeping queen, thus providing himself with a token of royal authority that Henry never manages to achieve (II.iv.391–4). The same association between a king's authority and that of a husband – along with a reminder that Henry never manages to achieve either – provides the basis for the Archbishop of York's description of the king's inability to govern: the land, he says, is like "an offensive wife/ That hath enrag'd him on to offer strokes,/ As he is striking, holds his infant up/ And hangs resolv'd correction in the arm/ That was uprear'd to execution" (*Henry IV, II*, IV.i.208–12). Significantly, the Archbishop's metaphor is the only place in the text where Henry himself is cast in the role of a husband.

As Barbara Hodgdon notes, in *Part I* "only the rebel leaders – Hotspur and Lord Mortimer – have wives" (1991: 155); but in both cases the wives pose a threat to their husbands' public success. Hotspur, for example, must leave his wife because, as he explains, "This is no world/ To play with mammets and to tilt with lips" (II.iii.91–2). When there is a kingdom to be won, the sexual warfare of the bedroom can only be a distraction. Mortimer stays home with his wife, but the home he stays in is hers, and it is located in the alien world of Wales; once Mortimer decides to stay there he loses his claim to royal authority and his place in English history. Here, as in the Henry VI plays, a man's desire for his wife is represented as a source of potential danger and disempowerment.

The heterogeneous, decentered world of the Henry IV plays includes marginal spaces where female characters regain some of the subversive power they had in the first tetralogy. Here, as in *Richard III* and *Richard II*, women are excluded from court and battlefield, but they play dominant roles in Eastcheap and Wales.[2] Both Eastcheap and Wales are separated from the central scenes of English historical representation, and both, like the commercial theaters in Shakespeare's England, are represented as sexualized domains of idleness and play. The location of the female characters in Eastcheap and Wales also recalls the places that real women occupied in the public theaters; for although English women never appeared on stage, they did appear in the playhouses as paying customers, and French and Italian companies, which included women, did occasionally perform in England (Orgel 1989: 9 and 28, n. 2).

Mistress Quickly's tavern in Eastcheap is a plebeian, comic, theatrical – and strikingly contemporary – place that mirrors the disorderly push and shove of the playhouse itself. The women in the tavern are theatergoers, entrepreneurs, and purveyors of commercial sex. Their portraits are unexpectedly modern. The name of Quickly's tavern is not specified in the text, but its traditional identification as the Boar's Head is suggested in *Henry IV, Part II* (II.ii.146–7), and it seems appropriate in a number of ways. One critic has made the intriguing suggestion the name was a spoonerism for "whore's bed" (Black 1979: 167). Historically associated with Sir John Fastolfe, Falstaff's real-life namesake, the Boar's Head was also the name of at least six real taverns in Shakespeare's London, one of them used for a theater (Hemingway 1936: 124–5; Chambers 1923: 2: 443–5). Shakespeare's anachronistically modern tavern is both a playhouse and a bawdy house (see Plate 7). Frequented, like the playhouse, by a disorderly, socially heterogeneous crowd, it is also the scene of playacting. Falstaff pretends to be Hal; Hal pretends to be Falstaff; and both degrade the dignity of royalty by playing the part of the reigning king. The pleasures of the Boar's Head are illicit, and they are also dangerous. The disreputable crowd the tavern attracts is given to every sort of transgression, from drunkenness and brawling to thieving and prostitution. Here, as in the antitheatrical tracts, the dangers of the playhouse are most prominently represented by women and sexuality. Like the prostitutes who looked for customers in the theater audiences, Doll Tearsheet infects her customers with venereal disease; and at the end of *Henry IV, Part II*, when Doll and the hostess are arrested, we learn that "there hath been a man or two kill'd about her" (V.iv.5–6). Whether "her" means Doll or the hostess and whether "about" means "concerning" or "near," clearly the women are a source of danger. A. R. Humphreys, the editor of the Arden edition, glosses this line with a quotation from Dekker's *Honest Whore*: "O how many thus . . . have let out/ Their soules in Brothell houses . . . and dyed/ Just at their Harlots foot" (III.iii.77–80).

Although the tavern is clearly marked as a feminized, theatrical space, the most memorable inhabitant of that space – and of the Henry IV plays generally – is not the hostess, or any other woman, but Falstaff. Physically a man and a womanizer, Falstaff is nonetheless characterized in feminine terms (Traub 1992: 50–70). In *The Merry Wives of Windsor*, one of the punishments for his sexual pursuit of Mistress Ford is a beating in women's clothes, which recalls the rough punishments meted out in early modern English villages to uxorious men who failed to conform to the

Plate 7 Tavern scene from Peter Rollos' *Le Centre de l'amour* (1680).
Source: Reproduced by permission of the Spencer Collection, The New York Public Library, Astor, Lenox and Tilden Foundations

conventions of patriarchal marriage (Underdown 1985). Falstaff's contempt for honor and military valor, his incompetence on the battlefield, his inconstancy, his lies, his gross corpulence, and his sensual self-indulgence all imply effeminacy within the system of analogies that separated spirit from body, aristocrat from plebeian, and man from woman in early modern England (Rackin 1992).[3] Contemplating what he thinks is Falstaff's corpse at the end of the battle of Shrewsbury, Hal asks, "What, old acquaintance! could not all this flesh/ Keep in a little life?" (*Henry IV, I*: V.iv.102–3). Falstaff himself, in a usage that would have been clearly intelligible to Shakespeare's audience, refers to his fat belly as a "womb" (*Henry IV, II*: IV.iii.22: "My womb, my womb, my womb undoes me"); and he compares himself to a "sow that hath overwhelm'd all her litter but one" (I.ii.11–12).

Like Richard III and Richard II, Falstaff is both empowered and discredited by his appropriation of the woman's part, especially by its theatricality. However, Falstaff's "female" theatricality, unlike theirs, is inscribed in the degraded register of comedy. Hal appropriates Falstaff's theatrical power for his own use, as indeed he must, since the power of theatrical performance is a requisite for royal authority in the modernized world of the second tetralogy (Howard 1994: 139–53). However, just as Hal's robbery of the Gadshill robbers serves to distance him from the taint of criminality that attends the initial theft and just as his victory over Hotspur at Shrewsbury appropriates the dead rebel's honor without the personal and political defects that attend it, this appropriation, sanitized by Hal's final rejection of Falstaff, produces a theatrical power purged of its feminine pollution.

Falstaff, like the queen in *Richard II* and Katherine in *Henry V*, is thus ultimately conscripted into the hegemonic project of affirming the authority of a true king. Nonetheless, throughout most of the Henry IV plays he exercises a subversive theatrical power and performs a subversive role in the represented action, both of which are articulated in his threat to "beat [Hal] out of [his] kingdom with a dagger of lath" (*Henry IV, I*: II.iv.136–7). Like Joan in *Henry VI, Part I*, Falstaff discredits the aristocratic shibboleths of martial valor and chivalric honor; like Margaret, he threatens to dominate and effeminate the heir to the English throne, for the fat knight is not only feminized; he also threatens the virility of other men. *Henry IV, Part I* ends with the spectacle of Falstaff mutilating Hotspur's corpse (V.iv.128). Wounding the dead hero's thigh, he reenacts the female threat to manhood and military honor symbolized in the opening scene by a report that the women of Wales have inflicted some unspeakably shameful mutilation on the corpses of English soldiers (I.i.43–6).

The parallel between the two veiled references to castration suggests an analogical relationship between the world of Eastcheap and that of Wales, both associated with the loss of masculine honor. Analogy, however, is not identity. Although both settings are clearly marked as comic and theatrical and thus as opposed to history, the low comic scenes in the Boar's Head Tavern recall the disorderly scene of present theatrical performance, while the scene in Wales, with its emphasis on magic and romantic love and its exotic setting, recalls the Shakespearean genre of romantic comedy. The women in the tavern are too familiar to enter history, too much like the disorderly women in the theater audience. The woman in Wales, by contrast, is marked as an exotic creature from another world, like the French and Italian actresses who occasionally appeared on the English stage, or the heroine of a narrative romance or romantic comedy.

Or, perhaps, like Queen Elizabeth herself. In this connection, the epilogue to *Henry IV, Part II* is revealing. In the preceding scene, the representation of the great historical moment when the wild Prince Hal of popular legend takes his historical place as Henry V, no female characters are present. The epilogue is rarely performed today, perhaps because it problematizes the closing representation of patriarchal historical order. The epilogue is set apart from the prior action in the folio text of the play, where it is printed on a separate page, marked off by colophon devices. As Barbara Hodgdon points out, "other Epilogues are not so separated, in either Quarto or Folio texts" (Hodgdon 1991: 285, n. 73). Some critics have suggested that the banished Falstaff – or the actor who played his part – returned to speak the epilogue (Hodgdon 1991: 181–2); but whoever its speaker, the epilogue serves to reconstitute the preceding action – and the action to come – as comic entertainment. It promises the restoration of Falstaff, and of female characters – to "continue the story, with Sir John in it, and make you merry with fair Katherine of France" (27–9); and it contains two additional references to women. One recalls the world of Eastcheap as it acknowledges the presence of women – and of sexual transactions between men and women – in the theater audience: "All the gentlewomen here have forgiven me," he says, and "if the gentlemen will not, then the gentlemen do not agree with the gentlewomen, which was never seen in such an assembly" (22–5). The other acknowledges the presence of a woman on the English throne, kneeling "to pray for the Queen" (17).

This is the only reference to Elizabeth in the history plays Shakespeare wrote during her lifetime, but the ideological contradiction she embodied hovers just beyond the horizon of the historical world they project. The presence of a woman on the English throne, like the matter of Wales, haunts the borders of Shakespeare's Lancastrian histories. Both evoked powerful, and related, anxieties for a patriarchal culture ruled by a female monarch who traced her hereditary right to a Welsh grandfather who had turned to the dim mists of Welsh antiquity to buttress his tenuous genealogical authority, incorporating the red dragon of Cadwallader in the royal arms and giving his eldest son the name of Arthur. Wales was both a necessary origin for Tudor monarchial legitimacy and a place of dangerous difference. The Welsh troops, mentioned but never seen, mark the transmission of royal power in *Richard II* when they desert Richard's army, "gone to Bullingbrook, dispers'd and fled" (III.ii.74). Throughout the two parts of *Henry IV*, the audience is reminded of Hal's title as Prince of Wales, and even in *Henry V*, the king's Welsh origins are a subject of repeated emphasis. Nonetheless, the only history play in which Shakespeare actually takes the audience to the wild country just beyond the English border is *Henry IV, Part I*.

An alien world of witchcraft and magic, of mysterious music, and also of unspeakable atrocity that horrifies the English imagination, Shakespeare's Wales is inscribed in the same register that defined the dangerous power of women. In addition to the liminal location at England's geographical border that makes Wales a constant military threat and the liminal attributes that make it psychologically disturbing, Wales is also the place where the hereditary heir to the throne is sequestered.[4] This is the case not only in *Henry IV, Part I* but also in *Cymbeline*, a much later play which is also based on Holinshed and also centers on issues of English national identity. A land of miracles and music and also of mortal danger, the Wales in *Cymbeline* is also the place where the true heirs to the British throne (disguised with the historically resonant names of Polydore and Cadwal) are hidden from sight of the court.

The double association of Wales with savagery and with female power had a precedent as ancient as Geoffrey of Monmouth's *Historia Regum Britanniae*, which records that the name *Welsh* derives "either from their leader Gualo, or from their Queen Galaes, or else from their being so barbarous" (Geoffrey of Monmouth *c*. 1136: 284). It also had a contemporary context in anxieties about English colonists who married native women and became assimilated to the culture of the savage places they had been sent to domesticate.[5] As Christopher Highley points out, Mortimer's "capitulation to Glendower replays the process of 'going native' whereby English colonists in Ireland were assimilated to Gaelic society" (Highley 1990: 97), a process that Spenser identified in his *View of the Present State of Ireland* (1596) as "degendering" and exemplified by, among others, "the great Mortimer, who forgetting how great he was once in England, or English at all, is now become the most barbarous of them all" (quoted in Highley, 97).

At the beginning of *Henry IV, Part I*, the Earl of Westmerland comes to the English court with bad news from a Welsh battlefield: Mortimer's army has been defeated in battle, Mortimer captured by Owen Glendower, a thousand of his soldiers killed. Westmerland also reports that after the battle, the Welsh women committed some "beastly shameless transformation" upon the bodies of the dead English soldiers – an act, he says, "as may not be/ Without much shame retold or spoken of" (I.i.43–6). Refusing to describe the act, Shakespeare follows Holinshed, who anxiously reported, "The shamefull villanie used by the Welshwomen towards the dead carcasses, was such, as honest eares would be ashamed to heare, and continent toongs to speake thereof" (1587: III: 20). In Shakespeare's historical source as in his play, Wales is identified as the scene of emasculation and female power – and also as the site of a repression in the English historical narrative.

Told in the English court, Shakespeare's account of the Welsh women reproduces Holinshed's anxious repressions, but the unspeakable threat of castration returns and proliferates throughout the play. It surfaces in Kate's playful threat to break Hotspur's "little finger" (II.iii.87) and in Falstaff's desecration of Hotspur's corpse. Most insistently, however, the threat of emasculation returns in Act III, when Shakespeare moves beyond the boundary of English historical narration to stage a scene in Wales. Westmerland's horrified report of Welsh barbarism is replaced by the glamour of Glendower's poetry and his daughter's singing, the castrating savages of the battlefield with the seductive allure of the lady in the castle. What makes this replacement interesting is that Glendower's daughter is also associated with the Welsh women who intruded on the masculine space of the battlefield to deprive the English soldiers of their manhood and honor. Unwilling to part with her amorous companion, she resolves, ominously, that "She'll be a soldier too, she'll to the wars" (III.i.193). Like the weeping queens in *Richard II* and *Richard III*, Glendower's daughter is a devoted wife, bathed in tears at the prospect of her husband's departure for battle. Like the women in the Boar's Head Tavern, however, she resists domestication. The inhabitant of a marginal place, she speaks a language that announces her otherness, and she embodies a dangerous sexuality that disables the man who succumbs to its temptation.

Holinshed's passing reference to Mortimer's marriage refuses to specify Mortimer's motivation, but it identifies the union in traditional medieval terms, as a contract between men designed to secure a treaty: "Edmund Mortimer earle of March, prisoner with Owen Glendouer, whether for irksomnesse of cruell captiuitie, or feare of death, or for what other cause, it is vncerteine, agreed to take part with Owen, against the king of England, and tooke to wife the daughter of the said Owen" (Holinshed 1587: 3: 21). In Shakespeare's play, however, Mortimer is motivated – and emasculated – by sexual passion for his wife. Although Shakespeare emphasizes Mortimer's lineal claim to the English throne, we see him agreeing to a treaty that will divide the land, and we hear him identify that division as "gelding" the portion that will be left for him (III.i.109). His manhood lost to female enchantment, Shakespeare's Mortimer prefers what he calls the "feeling disputation" (III.i.203) of kisses with his wife to military battle in pursuit of his patriarchal right. He is "as slow/ As hot Lord Percy is on fire to go" (III.i.263–4) to join the battle that will decide the future of the English kingdom (Wikander 1986: 14–25).

Shakespeare's Welsh interlude replaces the unspeakable horror of castration with the theatrical performance of seduction. A similar displacement seems to characterize Shakespeare's relation at this point to his historical source. The love scene in Wales has no historical precedent, but its structural position in Act III of the play is similar to that of a passage inserted by Abraham Fleming in the 1587 edition of Holinshed's *Chronicles* (the edition Shakespeare used). Fleming interrupts the account of a later battle to insert a detailed account of the act Holinshed had refused to describe:

> The dead bodies of the Englishmen, being above a thousand lieng upon the ground imbrued in their owne bloud ... did the women of Wales cut off their privities, and put one part thereof into the mouthes of everie dead man, in such sort that the cullions hoong downe to their chins; and not so contented, they did cut off their noses and thrust them into their tailes as they laie on the ground mangled and defaced.
>
> (Holinshed 1587: 3: 20, 34)

Fleming seems delighted with the grisly story, introducing it with numerous references to gory atrocities committed by women against men in classical times, but he also feels constrained to defend his decision to write the problematic material into the English historical record. He notes the precise location in Thomas Walsingham's Latin chronicle where he found it, and he explains,

> though it make the reader to read it, and the hearer to heare it, ashamed: yet bicause it was a thing doone in open sight, and left testified in historie; I see little reason whie it should not be imparted in our mother toong to the knowledge of our owne countrimen, as well as unto strangers in a language unknowne.
>
> (1587: 3: 34)

Fleming's belated account of the atrocities performed by the Welsh women seems to lie behind Shakespeare's deferred Welsh scene. Both interrupt the historical narrative for a belated supplement to Holinshed's account, but Shakespeare transvalues the terms of Fleming's gruesome description. Fleming's account of bloody corpses lying on the ground, their organs of bottom and top horribly transposed, becomes the lady's seductive invitation to Mortimer to lie down upon the "wanton rushes" – his head luxuriously resting in her lap, while she sings "charming [his] blood with pleasing heaviness," a delicious languor like the state "'twixt wake and sleep" (III.i.211–16). The strange tongue from which Fleming translated his gruesome story becomes the sweet babble of the lady's Welsh, a sound that Shakespeare represents by repeated stage directions, *The lady speaks in Welsh.*

Although the lady cannot speak English, she expresses her love in tears, in kisses, and in music. She wishes, her father explains, to sing "the song that please[s]" Mortimer (III.i.213); and even her speech reminds her besotted husband of "ravishing" music "Sung by a fair queen in a summer's bow'r" (III.i.207–8). Music, as Shakespeare's Orsino tells us, was considered the "food of love." Philip Stubbes, well known for his warnings against the dangerous consequences of theater-going, also warned that music could corrupt "good minds, [making] them womanish and inclined to all kinds of Whoredom and mischief" (sig. D4^r, quoted in Austern 1989: 424). In fact, the spectacle of a woman singing was widely regarded in Shakespeare's time as an incitement to lust (Austern 1989; Maguire 1992: 144).

Like the historical record of the Welshwomen's barbarism, and like the French that Katherine speaks in *Henry V*, Glendower's daughter speaks in a language that requires translation. In *The Famous Victories of Henry the Fift* the French princess speaks the same good English as the men. Shakespeare, however, departs from theatrical convention to write the women's lines in foreign tongues, thus excluding them from the linguistic community that includes all the male characters – French and Welsh as well as English – along with his English-speaking audience. The incomprehensible speech that masks the lady's meaning is doubly the language of the Other – the language of England's enemies and also the language of women and of love. The difference, however, is that while Katherine learns English in order to communicate with Henry, Mortimer proposes to learn Welsh. Bewitched and enthralled in Wales, he desires to abandon the King's English, the discourse of patriarchal authority, for the wordless language of love. He looks beyond words to communicate with his lady – "I understand thy looks," he says, "I understand thy kisses, and thou mine" (III.i.198, 202) – and he resolves to learn Welsh, the language of England's barbarous enemies, the incomprehensible discourse of the alien world that lies beyond the bounds of English historical narration.[6] Geographically and dramatically isolated, Shakespeare's representation of Mortimer in Wales interrupts the progress of the English historical plot to depict the dangerous allure of a world that is both feminine and effeminating. The Welsh scenes thus serve a double purpose. They discredit Mortimer's lineal claim to the English throne by aligning him with what in this play is represented as non-English, the territory and language of Wales. At the same time, they demonstrate the degrading uxoriousness that is the dangerous aspect of spousal affection. If in the first tetralogy, women threaten to disrupt the men's genealogical authority by adultery, here they threaten to disable their husbands for the public achievements required by a performative conception of male authority by drawing them to private sensual pleasures.

Significantly, these pleasures are also represented as theatrical. When Glendower calls his daughter "a peevish self-will'd harlotry" (III.i.196), he uses a word that associates her with the women in the Boar's Head Tavern, and also with the playhouse itself. The only other time that word appears in the *Henry IV* plays is in the immediately preceding scene, when Mistress Quickly praises Falstaff's acting: "he doth it as like one of these harlotry players as ever I see!" (II.iv.395–6). The term "harlotry players" makes explicit the association between the dangers (and the pleasures) of sexual indulgence and those of the playhouse which also informs the scene in Glendower's castle. Shakespeare's representation of Mortimer in Wales enacts contemporary beliefs that excessive sensuality would make a man effeminate, but it also recalls the antitheatrical arguments that the theater encouraged idleness and lechery. And it anticipates his representation of Cleopatra's Egypt, another exotic, alien nation where, as Caesar complains, Antony "is not more manlike / Than Cleopatra; nor the queen of Ptolemy / More womanly than he" (I.iv.5–7).[7] Like the Romans' contempt for Cleopatra's feminine wiles and the luxurious idleness of Antony's Egyptian life, the bickering between Hotspur and Glendower recalls the charges that the theater encouraged idleness and lechery, the denunciations that associated dramatic impersonation with sorcery and deception, and the condemnations of the playhouse as Satan's synagogue. Hotspur is impatient at the waste of time in Wales. Glendower identifies himself as a magician; like Prospero, he claims he can "call spirits from the vasty deep" (III.i.52). Hotspur calls Glendower a liar and denounces magic as the work of the devil. Nonetheless, when Glendower declares that he will summon musicians who "hang in the air a thousand leagues from hence" to play for his guests, Shakespeare's text supports Glendower's project – and his claim to magical power – with the stage direction "*The music plays*" (III.i.224, 228). In fact, Shakespeare seems in this scene to be complicit with the Welsh magician. Together they detain – and entertain – their audiences with an idyllic interlude that interrupts the progress of the historical plot.

Endlessly repeated in antitheatrical polemics, the charge that theatrical performance corrupted its audiences with incitements to sexual lust – often accompanied by supporting anecdotes – attests to an attraction as powerful as the anxiety it produced (Cook 1977; Levine 1994). The lush, theatrical scene that depicts Mortimer's Welsh idyll has a similar ambivalence. Replacing historical narrative with dramatic enactment and Westmerland's horrified report with the sensual beauty of Glendower's poetry and his daughter's singing, it moves the audience from the austere English court to an outlandish world of idleness and illicit pleasure. It uses the seductive art – the music – of theatrical performance to represent the dangerous female power that was present in the playhouse and in the world but could never be "retold or spoken of" in the discourse of patriarchal history.

The scene in Wales is a brief interlude in *Henry IV, Part I*. The numerous scenes in Eastcheap, however, threaten to take over both parts of the play. The epilogue to *Henry IV, Part II*, acknowledges their prominence and relies on their appeal for the theater audience to advertise a sequel: "If you be not too much cloy'd with fat meat, our humble author will continue the story, with Sir John in it" (26–8). The quarto title pages for both plays also advertise Falstaff, and the second adds a reference to "swaggering Pistoll" as well. Moreover, even in *Richard II*, there is a passage that looks very much like an advertisement for the tavern scenes in the play to come, when the new king, Henry IV, worries about his wayward son who has been absent from court for three months:

> Inquire at London, 'mongst the taverns there,
> For there, they say, he daily doth frequent,
> With unrestrained loose companions,
> Even such, they say, as stand in narrow lanes
> And beat our watch and rob our passengers,
> Which he, young wanton and effeminate boy,
> Takes on the point of honor to support
> So dissolute a crew.
>
> (V.iii.5–12)

This speech announces in advance two important features of Hal's characterization: the fact that his chosen companions are exactly the sort of people that antitheatrical writers claimed constituted

174

the majority of the audience in the commercial theaters, and the fact that the king regards those associations as symptoms of effeminacy. It also serves as a good advertisement for the Henry IV plays, where all the scandalous behavior the king describes will be enacted on stage for the pleasure of the theater audience.

The tavern is a pivotal locale in the Henry IV plays. For the prince, as for the audience, it offers the attractions as well as the dangers of the playhouse. For Hal, it is the place of liberty and experimentation where he escapes from his princely responsibilities to fleet the time in play-acting, jokes, and revelry. For the audience, it is a place of transgressive entertainment. The Boar's Head, however, is not only a timeless, Saturnalian space, but also the very specific world of contemporary London. In the Boar's Head Tavern, the historical prince meets unhistorical characters who drink anachronistic cups of sack and wear anachronistic ruffs and peach-colored silk stockings (Rackin 1990: 139). Here the realities of sixteenth-century urban life – its theatricality and its commercial vigor – interrupt, impede, and parody a historical narrative detailing the monarchial history of fifteenth-century England.

The fear of social indifferentiation hangs heavy over the heterogeneous world of the Henriad (Osborne 1985). At the inn, a carrier complains, "This house is turn'd upside down since Robin ostler died" (*Henry IV, I*: II.i.10–11). In the countryside, Justice Shallow's servant Davy o'ermasters his master; in the city, Falstaff flouts the authority of the Chief Justice, and Hal assumes the roles of highwayman and then serving-man in an Eastcheap tavern. Hal threatens to betray his patriarchal lineage by making the lawless Falstaff his parent and Ned Poins his brother. Falstaff even accuses Poins of giving it out that Hal will marry Poins's sister (*Henry IV, II*: II.ii.127–9). Shrinking from court and longing for small beer, the prince seems to be out of love with his greatness (*Henry IV, II*: II.ii.6–12). The endings of both Parts of *Henry IV* seem attempts to allay this specter of indifferentiation. At Shrewsbury, Hal differentiates himself from the cowardly Falstaff and emerges as a chivalric hero; at the end of *Part II* Hal embraces first his own father and then the Chief Justice, casting off his false father, Falstaff. Similarly, the prince casts aside his tavern brothers to embrace his blood brothers in a fellowship founded on their assumed difference from both the English lower orders and the French others.

Significantly, no female characters are present in either of these scenes. The last scene in *Part II*, however, is preceded by a brief interlude in which Quickly and Doll Tearsheet are hustled off to prison (V.iv). The scene is only thirty-one lines long, it is unhistorical, and there is no explicit connection between the women's arrest and the transformation of the wild prince Hal into the model King Henry V. The two are connected, however, by the same logic of displacement that entails the representation of the tavern women as criminalized and comic figures upon whom anxieties about social disorder could be conveniently displaced. While Hal's dereliction of duty threatened to make monarchy "common" and to undo all forms of social hierarchy, some of the anxiety occasioned by his behavior is displaced onto the tavern women. Through prostitution, it is suggested, these women erase distinctions between man and man, and Quickly's pervasive malapropisms erase, as well, distinctions between one word and another. Nonetheless, the very act of representing Quickly and Tearsheet as internal threats to the nation, as the criminal underbelly of the commonwealth, opens the door to registering their theatrical vitality and their links to the commercial world where the players plied their own trade. These women may be socially marginal and the roles their prototypes played in their nation's history may be elided, but on the stage, players they most definitely are. Their presence calls attention to the gap between official history and the social domains it must exclude to constitute itself.

In *Henry IV, Part I* and *Part II* Quickly's presence fractures the hermetically sealed world of aristocratic, masculine history to confront London playgoers – both men and women – with a representation of contemporary life in which a woman runs a tavern, both uses and defies the law, exists for a time without a husband, and with her friend Doll Tearsheet probably participates in the sale of sex. This "public" woman hardly conforms to dominant codes of acceptable femininity, and nothing more clearly signals her ideological volatility than the play's ambivalent representation of her status as wife, for a woman's marital status was a crucial component of her identity in early modern England. As *The Lawes Resolutions of Womens Rights*, published in 1632, explicitly states, "all [women] are understood either married, or to be married" (T.E. 1632: sig. B3ᵛ).

A notable exception to the wholesale domestication of female characters that began in *Richard III*, Quickly is not easily assimilated to the institution of marriage. In the course of the Henry IV plays, in fact, her marital status becomes increasingly ambiguous. In *Henry IV, Part I* Quickly is identified as the "wife" of "an honest man" (III.iii.93, 119). Mr Quickly, however, never appears on stage, and the hostess seems to preside by herself over a domain that is clearly connected with lawlessness as well as the freedom of play. It is in her tavern that the prince and Falstaff elude the law after the Gadshill robbery and there that the two of them turn kingship into a role a "harlotry player" might perform (II.iv.395–6). The feminized, theatrical world of the tavern is set in clear opposition to the world of masculine power and duty symbolized by Henry IV and his court. At the Boar's Head, disorder and carnival freedom reign. Even Quickly's deformed speech – her cheerfully rendered malapropisms and double entendres – underscore her social marginality and disorderliness. Not even the King's English – let alone the king's son – is safe in her hands. When Falstaff says of her, "She's neither fish nor flesh, a man knows not where to have her," she replies, "Thou art an unjust man in saying so. Thou or any man knows where to have me, thou knave, thou!" (*Henry IV, I*: III.iii.127–30). Attempting to establish her integrity, Quickly inadvertently announces her sexual availability.

Part II intensifies the sense of lawlessness, anarchy and disease not only in Henry IV's kingdom but also in Nell Quickly's tavern. Now joined on stage by her prostitute friend Doll Tearsheet, Quickly seems to lose her tenuous place in the marriage system. The figure of the prostitute is a potent symbol in this text. As rebellion threatens to fracture the unity of the nation and as Hal's disaffection from the duties of kingship threatens further debasement of the institution of monarchy, the prostitute comes to embody the general breakdown of order and social distinctions. Not the exclusive property of one man, Doll Tearsheet sleeps with many, rendering them interchangeable. And she does so for profit, leaving her partners, it is suggested, bonded in a gruesome fraternity of disease. As Falstaff intones, "We catch of you, Doll, we catch of you" (II.iv.45–6).

Especially intriguing in this text, however, is the way Quickly gradually becomes assimilated into the discourse of prostitution surrounding Doll, and the way Quickly's status as wife becomes increasingly ambiguous. In an example of what we might call the disappearing husband syndrome, Mistress Quickly seems to lose her husband at exactly the time she acquires Doll as a companion. In *Part II* there is no more talk of the hostess's good husband: rather, Quickly insistently pursues Falstaff to make good on his promise to marry her.

> Thou didst swear to me upon a parcel-gilt goblet, sitting in
> my Dolphin chamber, at the round table by a sea-coal fire,
> upon Wednesday in Wheeson week, when the Prince broke
> thy head for liking his father to a singing-man of Windsor,
> thou didst swear to me then, as I was washing thy wound,
> to marry me and make me my lady thy wife.
>
> (II.i.86–92)

The playscript offers no corroborating evidence for the Chief Justice's assumption that Falstaff has "made her [Quickly] serve your uses both in purse and in person" (II.i.115–16). Quickly's own uncertain control of the English tongue and the double entendres that dance through her speech, make determining her degree of sexual activity all the more difficult. To the Chief Justice, she says, "take heed of him! He stabb'd me in mine own house, most beastly, in good faith. 'A cares not what mischief he does, if his weapon be out. He will foin like any devil, he will spare neither man, woman, nor child" (II.i.13–17). It is not quite clear what "weapon" Falstaff has been brandishing. Whatever the "truth" of Quickly's sexual involvement with Falstaff, certainly her close association with Doll Tearsheet colors the audience's perception both of her and of the tavern, now not only a refuge for male criminals and a wayward prince but a place as well for female criminality: prostitution and violence against a man. In the last scene Quickly and Doll are accused of having, with Pistol, beaten a man to death, perhaps an unruly male consumer of Doll's sexual wares (*Henry IV, II*: V.iv.16–17). The women of the tavern are increasingly presented as preying on the commonwealth, endangering its (male) citizens and diverting its wealth from authorized purposes.

Interestingly, the sexualizing and criminalizing of Quickly in *Part II* seems to coincide with an increasing emphasis on her economic well-being. Once one begins to notice them, signs of her economic independence litter the text. Here, as in *Part I*, she has employees, such as the hapless apprentice Francis, under her control. In the first act of *Part II*, she calls in the law to make Falstaff pay his debts to her, an indication that she has been able to lend him money. And he insists she has the means, if she wishes, to supply his present needs as he sets off for war. We now discover that she has plate and tapestries to sell or pawn for more cash (*Henry IV, II*: II.i.140–2), and, if the beadle in V.iv is to be believed, she also has a dozen cushions for the seats in her tavern, one of which has been used to pad Doll Tearsheet's stomach to fake a pregnancy in order to avoid punishment for her various crimes (V.iv.14–15).

The tavern world in *Part II*, rendered as a sexualized scene of female entrepreneurship, becomes the locus for the play's anxiety about a levelling lawlessness. Doll, the sexually independent woman, and Quickly, the economically independent woman, form a threatening combination. They challenge both gender ideology and the system of social stratification distinguishing man from man. Predictably, the punishment meted out to these women is severe. Unlike Falstaff, they are not simply banished from the king's presence; rather, they are sent off to prison to be whipped. As Barbara Hodgdon observes, when Doll and Quickly are arrested in V.iv, "The potential threats Carnival represents are displaced on the play's women," who are now "demonized as corrupt, set aside and excluded from the commonwealth" (1991: 172). It is not clear what place, if any, they will possibly have in the reordered state that is about to follow from Hal's assumption of the throne. Hardly good wives, these women become the detritus of official history.

The closing scenes of *Henry IV, Part II*, which include the imprisonment of Doll and Quickly, look forward to *Henry V*, where the king attempts to construct a renewed sense of national identity and purpose. The success of this project depends in part on casting out of the commonwealth all those who do not assent to the king's logic, a logic that makes the interests of some men – king, aristocrat, and churchman – the interests of all. Men like Bardolph, Nym, and Pistol who put their own material interests ahead of the king's are excluded from the band of brothers. The place of women in the renewed nation is also precarious. While there is a space for Katherine in the marriage arranged between Henry and the French king, the old inhabitants of the tavern fare less well. Criminalized at the end of *Henry IV, Part II*, Quickly remarkably emerges at the beginning of *Henry V* once more a wife – but now she is wed neither to some unseen "good husband" nor

to Falstaff but to the disreputable Pistol. As *his* wife, her entrepreneurial activities threaten to move her ever deeper into illicit
territory. At one point she laments, "we cannot lodge and board
a dozen or fourteen gentlewomen that live honestly by the prick
of their needles but it will be thought we keep a bawdy house
straight" (*Henry V*: II.i.32–5). Perhaps the lady protests too much.
Her comment raises the possibility that she does indeed now keep
a bawdy house and that while her husband is being a horseleech
abroad, she is being one at home. It is therefore not too surprising
when the last thing we hear of Quickly is that she died a whore's
death. Or is it really Doll who dies this death? The humiliated
Pistol says,

> News have I that my Doll is dead i' th' spittle
> Of a malady of France,
> And there my rendezvous is quite cut off.
> (*Henry V*: V.i.81–3)

Textual editors have a variety of ways of explaining the "curious
reference" to Doll Tearsheet which, to quote the Riverside editors,
"properly should be to Mistress Quickly, Pistol's wife" (Evans *et
al.* 1974: 972). But the momentary textual conflation of the two
women–whatever its source – underscores the symbolic conflation
of the two types of "public women," the entrepreneurial tavern
keeper and the prostitute, that has been underway since *Henry IV,
Part II*. Quickly cannot simply be a "good man's" wife, because
her visibility, her volubility, and her economic independence clash
with patriarchal imperatives regarding wifely behavior. Quickly's
remarkably unsteady relationship to the marriage state signals the
gender trouble she embodies. There seems, finally, no way for the
entrepreneurial urban woman to exist in the Shakespearean
history play except on terms of criminality. Quickly exits the play
as a common whore.

In the second tetralogy, the Eastcheap tavern is the only place
where non-aristocratic women enter the Shakespearean history
play, but Quickly's degradation implies that they can do so only
on sexualized and criminalized terms. It is as if the playwright,
gesturing nervously toward the famed independence of the
women of contemporary London can acknowledge their existence
only by transforming that independence into sexual licentiousness
and criminality. And yet, this is only half the story. While the
playwright does criminalize Quickly and Doll, he also endows

them, intentionally or not, with remarkable theatrical vitality. Quickly's speech, in particular, is a source of enormous comic pleasure, and it introduces – along with Pistol's bombastic swagger and the dialects of Jamy, Fluellen, and Macmorris – a sense of the linguistic and social differences that the dominant language of the court cannot eradicate or homogenize.

At the beginning of Act II of *Henry IV, Part II*, for example, Quickly urges two officers of the law, Fang and Snare, to lay hands on the fat knight, Falstaff, and bring him to justice:

I am undone by his going. I warrant you, he's an infinitive thing upon my score. Good Master Fang, hold him sure. Good Master Snare, let him not scape. 'A comes [continuantly] to Pie-Corner (saving your manhoods) to buy a saddle, and he is indited to dinner to the Lubber's Head in Lumbert street, to Master Smooth's the silk-man. I pray you, since my exion is ent'red and my case so openly known to the world, let him be brought in to his answer. A hundred mark is a long one for a poor lone woman to bear, and I have borne, and borne, and borne, and have been fubb'd off, and fubb'd off, and fubb'd off, from this day to that day, that it is a shame to be thought on. There is no honesty in such dealing, unless a woman should be made an ass and a beast, to bear every knave's wrong.
Enter SIR JOHN [FALSTAFF] *and* BARDOLPH *and the Boy* [PAGE]
Yonder he comes, and that arrant malmsey-nose knave, Bardolph, with him. Do your offices, do your offices, Master Fang and Master Snare, do me, do me, do me your offices.

(II.i.23–42)

This is quite a piece of language, so plain and yet so mystifying to those who seek in the King's English a standard of authoritative communication. In Quickly's world there is on the one hand an absolute correspondence between people and the concrete objects and occupations by which they are known. A silk merchant is named Smooth; officers of the law are called Snare and Fang; Falstaff is an infinitive thing upon Quickly's score. Yet as that troubling word, *infinitive*, suggests, there is static in the communicative circuit, a potential doubleness, in a great many of the things Quickly says. When she calls Falstaff an "infinitive" thing upon her score, the playgoer probably silently translates *infinitive* to *infinite*, thus imaging Falstaff as an endless series of chalk

181

markings on a board on which Quickly keeps track of credit extended. But at the same time, the grammatical term *infinitive* is not simply wiped from consciousness; it has its own resonances, pointing exactly to a domain – that of grammar – where Quickly is no master and in which, in fact, she can be read as comically deficient by those who "know better."

The same doubleness subtends the rest of her speech, making its reception unpredictable. Falstaff is *indited* to supper, the domain of hospitality entangled in Quickly's speech with the domain of legal punishment, social fact and Quickly's desire running together indiscriminately. He has been *invited*, but Quickly would like him to be *indicted*. Similarly, even as she calls for the law to vindicate her rights as tavern keeper and virtuous woman, one who will not be "an ass and a beast, to bear every knave's wrong," her iterations, "do me, do me, do me your offices," make her the unintentional solicitor of sexual favors, so that her status as victim seeking legal redress for wrongs done her is made uncertain by the way her speech continually sexualizes her, suggesting that she is a loose woman and so perhaps herself deserving of legal correction rather than assistance. Quickly's malapropisms jam the communicative networks by which the law does its work of making distinctions and hierarchies, separating criminals from honest men and women, whores from wives, winners from losers, legitimate kings from their theatrical imitations.

Quickly's language is, of course, a means of marking her social unimportance and transforming her into an object of fun. In the Henry IV plays and *Henry V*, the distance of various characters from the culture's center of power and importance is marked by their linguistic distance from perfect command of the King's English. Many of those who inhabit Quickly's tavern are marked as outsiders by their deformed speech. Francis has "fewer words than a parrot" (*Henry IV, I*: II.iv.98–9); Pistol's bombastic swagger makes his language incomprehensible even to the other characters in the play. In *Henry IV, Part II*, in fact, Falstaff has to tell him to deliver his news "like a man of this world" (*Henry IV, II*: V.iii.97–8). In *Henry V*, the regionals – Fluellen, Jamy and Mac-morris, sturdy officers in Henry's army – become the butts of a mildly deprecating humor because of their dialects. In *Henry IV, Part I* Hotspur rebukes his wife for using language that makes her sound like "a comfit-maker's wife" who never walks "further than Finsbury" (a London district popular with ordinary citizens):

"Swear me, Kate, like a lady as thou art,/ A good mouth-filling oath, and leave 'in sooth,'/ And such protest of pepper-gingerbread,/ To velvet-guards and Sunday-citizens" (III.i.248, 252–6). In short, linguistic difference is used in the service of social stratification. The women of the tavern enter the national history play on sexualized and criminalized terms, and they also enter by means of a language that infantilizes, others, and culturally disempowers them.

This is not the whole story, however. To become the butts of linguistic humor, figures such as Mistress Quickly have to be brought into the circuits of representation. Mistress Quickly's speech renders her comic, but it also pluralizes the language of the play and denaturalizes the authority and automatic primacy of the speech of dominant groups. The carnivalized rhetoric of Quickly's first-act conversation with the Chief Justice, like Dogberry's malapropisms in *Much Ado About Nothing* and Elbow's in *Measure for Measure*, provides material resistance to the operations of the law and the hegemony of its official language. Before the law, a woman is either a virtuous wife or widow and so worthy of the law's support, or she is a whore and subject to the law's force. Quickly's speech importuning the Chief Justice for aid in apprehending Falstaff makes it difficult to determine just which she is. Eventually the law makes a determination, and both Quickly and Doll are hauled off to prison, but for much of *Henry IV, Part II* the hostess's sexual, legal, and marital status remains wonderfully ambiguous.

It is not necessary, in fact it would be unwise, to impute to Mistress Quickly an oppositional, politicized consciousness. She is a fictional creation written to be a humorous butt. But her speech, in the tradition of carnival foolery, makes available a logic and language that can provide an alternative to the logic and language of dominant groups. In the public theater, with its socially mixed audiences, it is not clear how such speech would have been received. Men who wrote against the theater worried that the stage would foster unruliness and licentiousness among its socially diverse auditors. Certainly the linguistic and social variety in these plays enhances the possibilities for "unauthorized" acts of reception. Toward the end of her time on stage, Quickly makes a speech about the death of Falstaff that suggests the disruptive potential of the alternative world view made available through her troubling language:

Nay sure, he's not in hell; he's in Arthur's bosom, if ever man
went to Arthur's bosom. 'A made a finer end, and went away
and it had been any christom child. 'A parted ev'n just
between twelve and one, ev'n at the turning o'th'tide; for
after I saw him fumble with the sheets, and play with
flowers, and smile upon his finger's end, I knew there was
but one way; for his nose was as sharp as a pen, and 'a
[babbled] of green fields. "How now, Sir John?" quoth I,
"what, man? be a' good cheer." So 'a cried out, "God, God,
God!" three or four times. Now I, to comfort him, bid him 'a
should not think of God; I hop'd there was no need to trouble
himself with any such thoughts yet. So 'a bade me lay more
clothes on his feet. I put my hand into the bed and felt them,
and they were as cold as any stone; then I felt to his knees,
and so up'ard and up'ard, and all was as cold as any stone.

(*Henry V*: II.iii.9–26)

This speech again fractures the logic of authority by which this
jester was banished as a vice. Quickly gives Falstaff a home in
Arthur's bosom, calling in question not only Falstaff's damnation
but Hal's exclusive right to the legacy of this mythic Welsh
forefather. Moreover, here and in subsequent lines, Quickly's
language celebrates Falstaff's sensuality – his handling of women,
his love of sack, all of which seem in her jumbled speech to qualify
him for a holy death. In the language of this common woman the
sensual and the spiritual interpenetrate, as do the recording of sin
and the promise of salvation, carnivalizing, inverting, and mixing
categories elsewhere strictly hierarchized and held in separation.
This is very different from the speech and logic of Henry V, King
of England, who knows what makes a man an offender and has
no hesitation in ordering the death of his old friend Bardolph
because, as he says, "We would have all such offenders so cut off"
(III.vi.107–8). Quickly's presence in the play makes possible an
alternative understanding of what would constitute "justice."

Quickly's presence is important for yet another reason, having
this time to do with the presence of women in the audience
watching the play. As Andrew Gurr has made clear, women of all
classes went to the public theater (Gurr 1988: 59–64). In the Boar's
Head Tavern too, women are spectators to theatrical entertainment. When Hal and Falstaff undertake "The Arraignment of the
Prodigal Son," Quickly proves an avid and involved auditor. As

Falstaff prepares to take a turn at playing the king, Hal's father, she cries out, "O Jesu, this is excellent sport, i' faith!" and a moment later compliments Falstaff on his performance: "O Jesu, he doth it as like one of these harlotry players as ever I see!" (*Henry IV, I*: II.iv.390, 395–6). Quickly knows something of playing, at least enough to have a standard by which to compare Falstaff's performance.

Shakespeare's representation of Owen Glendower's daughter as an exotic, eroticized object of desire and anxiety is a projection of male fantasies, but it is tempting to imagine real-life counterparts for Doll and Quickly in the audience to the Henry IV plays; for, as the epilogue to *Henry IV, Part II* explicitly recognizes, that audience included women as well as men. However, the form that recognition takes – "All the gentlewomen here have forgiven me; if the gentlemen will not, then the gentlemen do not agree with the gentlewomen, which was never seen in such an assembly" (22–5) – makes all the women in the audience into "gentlewomen," thus distancing them from any imputation that they are Mistress Quicklys or Doll Tearsheets. The epilogue's acknowledgement of the women's presence is still significant, however, because it also constitutes an implicit acknowledgement that the theater constituted a "public" that consisted of more than the elite players of chronicle history. As Heywood was to argue in his *Apology for Actors*, the theater was one of the most noteworthy London institutions, an ornament to the city, a magnet for foreign visitors, a source of edification for England's people. That theater – communal, inclusive, and dedicated to the mutual pursuit of profit and play – bears more resemblances to Quickly's tavern than to the king's court. Officially denigrated as the seat of vice and disorder, the theater, like the tavern, let foolery thrive, situating the official discourses of chronicle history alongside the less decorous languages of swaggerer, prostitute, and tosspot. In the outrageous voice of Quickly – "Do me, do me, do me your offices" – is embodied the contradictions of this place, devoted to the pieties of dominant history and giving voice, simultaneously, to social forces which challenge that hegemony, among which we must include the entrepreneurial energies of the women in the tavern and the women in the theater audience.

12

HENRY V

At the beginning of *Henry V*, the Chorus acknowledges the inevitable distance that separates his heroic historical subject from its representation in the playhouse:[1]

> O for a Muse of fire . . .
> A kingdom for a stage, princes to act,
> And monarchs to behold the swelling scene!
> Then should the warlike Henry, like himself . . .
>
> (Prologue: 1–5)

One of the reasons Henry cannot be "like himself" is that the audience in the playhouse was not composed of monarchs. For although the subjects of Shakespeare's English histories were medieval kings and noblemen contending for the possession and defense of the crown, most members of the audiences for whom those plays were performed came from places considerably lower in the social hierarchy. Staging medieval history as the stories of successive monarchs constructed a historical precedent for the Tudor and Stuart project of extending monarchial power. Read in the order in which they appeared in the First Folio, the plays delineate a genealogical history of royal succession, interrupted by the deposition of Richard II, and finally restored in the accession of Henry VII and the birth of Elizabeth I. If the plays are read in the order in which they were first performed on the sixteenth-century stage, however, they tell a much more complicated story, shaped by the cultural pressures and contradictions of the changing world in which they were produced. The predicaments faced by Shakespeare's kings, and the steps they take to confront them, now appear to be shaped as much by the predicaments of the ordinary men in Shakespeare's audience as they were by the historical records that Shakespeare found in his chronicle sources.

As we have been arguing, although the plays of the second tetralogy deal with a historical time prior to the Wars of the Roses, the England they represent seems more like the early modern world in which they were produced. *Richard II* begins the sequence in nostalgia for an imagined medieval kingdom threatened by the degrading forces of modernity, but the England of Henry V looks much more like one of Benedict Anderson's "imagined communities," a nation conceived in strikingly modern terms. Here, unlike Shakespeare's earlier history plays, the trappings and ideology of chivalry and hereditary nobility are identified as French and gendered feminine, and the decisive Battle of Agincourt is represented as a communal enterprise, the triumph of a ragged band of Englishmen over a well-equipped French enemy obsessed with the accoutrements that mark their place in a hierarchical culture. As Anderson points out, "regardless of the actual inequality and exploitation that may prevail . . . the nation is always conceived as a deep, horizontal comradeship." "It is this fraternity," he continues, "that makes it possible, over the last two centuries, for so many millions of people, not so much to kill, as willingly to die for such limited imaginings" (1983: 15–16).

The characters of the kings, and of monarchy itself, are similarly transformed. Richard II derives his authority from hereditary right, but his loss of the throne is represented as the result of his personal deficiencies. The remainder of the tetralogy renegotiates the basis of royal authority, constructing a biography for Henry V that redefines the nature of monarchy and, at the same time, offers a royal model for emulation by early modern playgoers who needed to negotiate the cultural transition from a residual status system in which a man's identity was defined on the basis of patrilineal inheritance to an emergent culture of performative masculinity in which his wealth, status, and identity had to be secured by personal achievement. Despite the contradictions between the two models of masculine identity, both were available throughout Shakespeare's career, and both are present in all the plays. It is easy to miss the differences between them (indeed, the elision of those differences is one of the ideological projects of Shakespeare's narratives). Both models have rightly been described as patriarchal, and both required that women be kept in their place. But because the two versions of patriarchy were significantly different, so were the places of men and women within them. As we have seen in the Henry VI plays, the genealogical narratives that validated the older form of patriarchy centered on inter-generational relationships between fathers and sons. They tended to exclude female characters, or – because an adulterous woman at any point could make a mockery of the legitimating narrative of patrilineal inheritance – to represent women as dangerous, demonic others. The narratives of individual performance produced by the new version of patriarchy in plays like *Richard III* and *Richard II*, however, included idealized roles for women as the objects of sexual conquest and matrimonial possession that provide the final proof of the hero's manhood.

Despite the modernity of the Henry IV plays, they still include residual conceptions of women and sexuality. Here, as in the earlier plays, sexual continence is privileged as an expression of manly self-control, and lust is identified as a feminine, and effeminating, vice. Here too, there are female characters who resist domestication, and female sexuality still poses a threat to male authority. Falstaff's identification with the feminine is not mitigated but confirmed by his womanizing; Mortimer loses his manhood in heteroerotic sensuality, and Hal's association with "unrestrained loose companions" in the anachronistically modern Eastcheap stews makes him seem like an "effeminate boy" (*Richard II*: V.iii.7, 10); his manhood and royalty are revealed when he emulates Hotspur's chivalry at the Battle of Shrewsbury. Significantly, the first testimony to Hal's apotheosis comes in the form of a description of his "noble horsemanship" (*Henry IV, I*: IV.i.110). Like Falstaff's "uncolting" at Gadshill (II.ii.39), the celebration of Hal's horsemanship recalls the "chivalry" that distinguished the governed from the governing in medieval ideology.[2]

In the world of Henry IV, however, chivalry no longer suffices to make that distinction. The chivalric ideal is compromised, in fact, in the person of its leading exponent. Literalized in an obsession with horses, Hotspur's single-minded devotion to chival(*cheval*)ry makes him an ambivalent figure – the ideal of martial honor, but, because that ideal is outmoded in the modern world of Henry IV, an object of sophisticated ridicule as well.[3] To Douglas, he is the "king of honor" (*Henry IV, I*: IV.i.10), to his wife, the "light" by which "all the chevalry of England move[d]/ To do brave acts" (*Henry IV, II*: II.iii.19–21). On the other hand, his rude behavior at court, at home, and in Glendower's castle identifies him as a provincial boor. Shakespeare's Hotspur, like his historical prototype, is a great medieval nobleman, the son of the Earl of Northumberland and the brother-in-law of the lineal heir to the English throne, but he totally lacks the graces of a Renaissance courtier, which he despises as the tokens of effeminacy.

It is significant that Hotspur compares the effeminate courtier who infuriated him on the battlefield at Holmedon to a "bridegroom" (*Henry IV I*: I.iii.34). In Hotspur's view, the basis of male authority is not husbandry but horsemanship. His crop-eared "roan," he declares, "shall be my throne" (II.iii.70). Kate's playful threat to break his "little finger" (II.iii.87) comically echoes the threat of castration posed by the Welsh women; but Hotspur, unlike Mortimer, affirms his masculinity by rejecting his wife, and his only concession to her repeated demands for a declaration of love is a jocular promise that if she comes to see him ride, "when I am a' horseback, I will swear/ I love thee infinitely" (II.iii.101–2). For a modern audience, accustomed to hearing men brag about their sexual conquests, the promise sounds like a double entendre, but Kate complains that she has been "banish'd from [her husband's] bed" for a "fortnight" while he dreamed of "iron wars," murmuring in his sleep "of sallies and retires, of trenches, tents,/ Of palisadoes, frontiers, parapets,/ Of basilisks, of cannon, culverin,/ Of prisoners' ransom, and of soldiers slain" (II.iii.38–9, 48–54). The subjects of Hotspur's dreams are heroic battles rather than erotic conquests, but they come to Shakespeare's audience in the distinctly unheroic form of his wife's report of what she overheard when he talked in his sleep.

In the Eastcheap tavern, the sophisticated Londoner who actually stands to inherit the throne parodies Hotspur's exaggerated devotion to his horse and lack of regard for his wife when he imagines a conversation between the two:

> I am not yet of Percy's mind, the Hotspur of the north, he that kills me some six or seven dozen of Scots at a breakfast, washes his hands, and says to his wife, "Fie upon this quiet life! I want work." "O my sweet Harry," says she, "how many hast thou kill'd to-day?" "Give my roan horse a drench," says he, and answers, "Some fourteen," an hour after; "a trifle, a trifle."
>
> (*Henry IV, I*: II.iv.101–8)

Although Hotspur himself is represented as a distinctly single-minded character, his role in the play–like the place of the chivalric ideal he espouses – is ambivalent. In the Boar's Head Tavern, Hotspur is the subject of Hal's ridicule, but in his father's court and on the field at Shrewsbury, Hal acknowledges that he will have to appropriate Hotspur's honor in order to affirm his own right to the crown. He promises the king that he will make the "northern youth exchange/ His glorious deeds for my indignities" (III.ii.145–6) "and in the closing of some glorious day,/ Be bold to tell you that I am your son", thus "redeem[ing]" his "shame" "on Percy's head" (III.ii.132–4). At the battle of Shrewsbury, Hal declares his admiration for Hotspur and the old-fashioned chivalric ideal he represents:

> This present enterprise set off his head,
> I do not think a braver gentleman,
> More active, valiant, or more valiant, young,
> More daring or more bold, is now alive
> To grace this latter age with noble deeds.
> For my part, I may speak it to my shame,
> I have a truant been to chivalry.
>
> (V.i.88–94)

Challenging his rival to single combat, Hal does not dispute Hotspur's assertion that his "name in arms" is greater than Hal's; but he promises, "I'll make it greater ere I part from thee/ And all the budding honors on thy crest/ I'll crop to make a garland for my head" (V.iv.70–3).

At Shrewsbury, as in the tavern, Hal speaks for Hotspur and plays his role, but this time the speech is respectful and the role heroic. Hotspur's final speech ends in the middle of a sentence: "No, Percy, thou art dust,/ And food for –" Hal completes the sentence – "For worms, brave Percy" – and then proceeds, "And even in thy behalf I'll thank myself/ For doing these fair rites of tenderness" to Hotspur's corpse (V.iv.85–6, 97–8). He plays Hotspur's role again at the Battle of Agincourt in *Henry V*. His response to the news that the French outnumber his forces five to one – "the fewer men, the greater share of honor" (IV.iii.22) – recalls Hotspur's reaction to the news of Northumberland's absence at the Battle of Shrewsbury; and the self-characterization that follows – "if it be a sin to covet honor,/ I am the most offending soul alive" (IV.iii.28–9) – reminds anyone in the audience who has seen *Henry IV, Part I* that the role the king is now playing is Hotspur's. Always the chameleon player, Hal, unlike Hotspur, is capable of a variety of roles and voices: plebeian, regal, comic, heroic, Welsh, English, subversive, authoritative – the list is not complete. He plays the paragon of chivalry at Shrewsbury, killing Hotspur in single combat, paying courteous tribute to his rival's honor, and appropriating it for his own. A minute later he makes no protest when Falstaff dishonors Percy's corpse. He also allows Falstaff to claim credit for killing the valiant nobleman (a claim which, if believed, would dishonor Percy's memory)[4] and to take possession of the corpse, which he now refers to as "luggage" (*Henry IV, I*: V.iv.156). In each case, Hal adopts the role that will show him to best advantage. Like Bottom, who thought he could perform all the roles in Peter Quince's play, Hal claimed to have incorporated in himself "all humors that have show'd themselves humors since the old days of goodman Adam" (*Henry IV, I*: II.iv.92–4), but unlike Bottom, Hal appears to be successful: appropriating every possible subject position and every available form of authority, his performance projects as a personal achievement early modern absolutist fantasies of extended monarchial power. It is not surprising, therefore, that Henry V emulates Hotspur's chivalry to play the heroic role of a soldier king at Agincourt. What is surprising is that he also emulates Hotspur's behavior with his wife when he courts the French princess (Maguire 1992: 152):

> Marry, if you would put me to verses, or to dance for your sake, Kate, why, you undid me. . . . If I could win a lady at leap-frog, or by vaulting into my saddle with my armor on my back, under the correction of bragging be it spoken, I should quickly leap into a wife. Or if I might buffet for my love, or bound my horse for her favors, I could lay on like a butcher, and sit like a jack-an-apes, never off. . . . I speak to thee plain soldier.
>
> (*Henry V*: V.ii.132–49)

The sophisticated habitué of the London taverns, the king who is so much the master of eloquence that "when he speaks,/ The air, a charter'd libertine, is still,/ And the mute wonder lurketh in men's ears/ To steal his sweet and honeyed sentences" (I.i.47–50), speaks to his prospective wife as a "plain soldier" who compares vaulting into a saddle with leaping into a wife. Here again, however, he plays the role with a difference, for Henry's comparison, unlike Hotspur's, suggests that what *he* needs to validate his authority is a wife.

To a student of history, it would also be surprising that both women are called Kate. The historical wife of Hotspur was named Elizabeth, Hall gives her name as Elinor, and Holinshed writes it as Elianor (Maguire 1992: 131). Shakespeare's renaming of Hotspur's wife anticipates the English diminutive by which the victorious Henry V will domesticate the French princess Katherine, but it also recalls that most notable of all Shakespearean prototypes of a woman tamed, Katherine Minola. Already domesticated when we meet her, Hotspur's wife is never called anything but Kate; but in *The Taming of the Shrew*, as in *Henry V*, the appellation is specifically identified as an act of domestication, designed to reduce the self-willed woman "to a Kate/ Conformable as other household Kates" (*Taming of the Shrew*: II.i.277–8; Maguire: 132). Unwilling to be tamed, the object of Petruchio's rough courtship protests, "They call me Katherine that do talk of me." Petruchio replies,

> You lie, in faith, for you are call'd plain Kate,
> And bonny Kate, and sometimes Kate the curst;
> But Kate, the prettiest Kate in Christendom,
> Kate of Kate-Hall, my super-dainty Kate,
> For dainties are all Kates.
>
> (II.i.184–9)

The name, he explains, is proper because it has a homonym in the common noun "cates," meaning "dainty foods."

Talbot uses the same term at the end of his encounter with the Countess of Auvergne in *Henry VI, Part I*. Having easily thwarted the woman's attempt to capture him, he courteously forgives her, asking only that he and his soldiers may "taste of your wine and see what cates you have" (II.iii.79). Subdued to her proper domestic function, the lady who had attempted to emulate Tomyris, the warrior queen who killed Cyrus the Great in battle, becomes a hostess who will provide "cates" for English soldiers. In the second tetralogy, however, as in *The Taming of the Shrew*, the women themselves become cates, an identification that reduces them to the objects of male consumption. Hotspur uses the homonym for his wife's name when he denounces Glendower's hospitality (Maguire 1992: 138):

O, he is as tedious
As a tired horse, a railing wife,
Worse than a smoky house. I had rather live
With cheese and garlic in a windmill, far,
Than feed on cates and have him talk to me
In any summer house in Christendom.
                    (*Henry IV, I*: III.i.157–62)

Predictably, Hotspur is immune to the attractions of Glendower's entertainment. Equally predictably, his norms are derived from horses and wives: the first should be spirited, the second subdued. What is not so predictable, although it is characteristic of Hotspur in many scenes, is the homely colloquialism of his language and the vivid particularity of his references to a smoky house and the common food of cheese and garlic; for although Hotspur repeatedly insists on his noble status, the language in which he voices that insistence is frequently drawn from the register of common life. His instructions to Kate are typical:

Heart, you swear like a comfit-maker's wife . . . .
And givest such sarcenet surety for thy oaths
As if thou never walk'st further than Finsbury.
Swear me, Kate, like a lady as thou art,
A good mouth-filling oath, and leave "in sooth,"
And such protest of pepper-gingerbread,
To velvet guards and Sunday citizens.

                                    (III.i.247–56)

Hotspur's language here, like the language of Henry V in the wooing scene, identifies the subjugation of wives as a middle-class project. The prototype of that project, significantly, is the middleclass comedy of *The Taming of the Shrew*.[5] There is a telling difference, however, between Henry's conquest and that of his predecessors; for both Petruchio and Hotspur demonstrate their masculine superiority in the traditional terms of sexual restraint, while Henry's conquest of his Kate is inscribed within a distinctively modern erotic discourse. In classical and medieval gender ideology, unlike our own, women's natures were regarded as more appetitive than men's, and, as we have seen in the Henry VI plays and *Henry IV, Part I*, sensual self-indulgence was identified as a female – and effeminating – vice. A man's desire for a woman, now coded as a mark of masculinity, then constituted a double degradation, the enslavement of a man's higher reason by his base bodily appetites and the subjection of the superior sex to the inferior one. Hotspur likens the effeminate courtier to a bridegroom, and although his affection for his own wife is apparent, he never allows it to overwhelm him. He affirms his masculinity, in fact, by banishing his wife from his bed. Petruchio's courtship of Kate begins with sexual double entendres (see, e.g. II.i.210–17), and it ends with his invitation (or command), "Come, Kate, we'll to bed" (V.ii.184). On the night of their wedding, however, he entertains his dismayed bride in the bedchamber by "making a sermon of continency to her" (IV.i.182); his plans for the rest of the night are to tear up the bed, flinging pillow, bolster, coverlet and sheets in every direction (IV.i.200–2). For both Hotspur and Petruchio, erotic restraint is an expression of male dominance and male superiority. Henry V, by contrast, demonstrates his masculine authority by acts of domination that are represented in specifically erotic terms.

The residual gender ideology which identified sexual congress with women as potentially effeminating to men also construed male homoerotic desire as entirely consistent with honorable masculinity. Erotic passion between men was admired, as Alan Sinfield explains, as long as it was "sufficiently committed to masculine warrior values. . . . it is women and popinjays [like the effeminate courtier at Holmedon] that are the danger" (1992: 136). The most striking Shakespearean examples of the association between homoerotic desire and manliness occur in *Coriolanus*. Greeting his general on the battlefield, Coriolanus exclaims,

> O! let me clip ye
> In arms as sound as when I woo'd, in heart
> As merry as when our nuptial day was done
> And tapers burnt to bedward!
>
> (I.vi.29–32)

Aufidius's declaration of his passion for Coriolanus is even more explicitly erotic:

> Know thou first,
> I lov'd the maid I married; never man
> Sigh'd truer breath; but that I see thee here,
> Thou noble thing, more dances my rapt heart
> Than when I first my wedded mistress saw
> Bestride my threshold.
>
> . . . .

> . . .Thou hast beat me out
> Twelve several times, and I have nightly since
> Dreamt of encounters 'twixt thyself and me;
> We have been down together in my sleep,
> Unbuckling helms, fisting each other's throat,
> And wak'd half dead with nothing.
>
> (IV.v.113–26)

In *Henry V* the old association between homoerotic desire and martial valor is exemplified in the deaths of York and Suffolk on the battlefield at Agincourt:

> Suffolk first died, and York, all haggled over,
> Comes to him where in gore he lay insteeped,
> And takes him by the beard, kisses the gashes
> That bloodily did yawn upon his face.
> He cries aloud, "Tarry, my cousin Suffolk!
> My soul shall thine keep company to heaven;
> Tarry, sweet soul, for mine, then fly abreast,
> As in this glorious and well-foughten field
> We kept together in our chivalry!"

Finally, Exeter reports, York turned

> and over Suffolk's neck
> He threw his wounded arm, and kiss'd his lips,
> And so espous'd to death, with blood he seal'd
> A testament of noble-ending love.
>
> (IV.vi.11–19, 24–7)

Here, as in *Coriolanus*, the love between the two warriors is an expression of their nobility, but in *Henry V* it is identified with the dead chivalry of an older generation, and it carries the threat of effeminacy, at least for the younger men who are moved by it: "The pretty and sweet manner of it," Exeter admits, "forc'd/ Those waters from me which I would have stopp'd,/ But I had not so much of man in me,/ And all my mother came into mine eyes/ And gave me up to tears" (IV.vi.28–32). Equally sympathetic but more resolute in his manliness, the king responds, "I blame you not,/ For hearing this, I must perforce compound/ With [mistful] eyes, or they will issue too" (IV.vi.32–4).

We have seen how men in Shakespeare's earlier history plays are effeminated by heteroerotic passion – whether in marriage or

195

outside it. Mortimer's passion for his wife is the most striking example in the second tetralogy, but, as we argued in Part II, the first tetralogy contains many others. Suffolk declares that he would be happy to die in Margaret's lap, "As mild and gentle as the cradle-babe / Dying with mother's dug between its lips (*Henry VI, II*: III.ii.392–3). His passion for Margaret deprives him of his manhood, reducing him to the condition of a gentle, genderless infant. We saw the same conception of heterosexual passion as effeminating in the representation of Henry VI's uxorious infatuation with Margaret and Edward IV's lustful desire for Elizabeth Woodville as personal weaknesses that had devastating political consequences. Richmond's marriage to Elizabeth could ratify his royal authority because it was dictated by the legitimate motive of dynastic union: there is no suggestion that Richmond desires her. *Henry V* is the only Shakespearean history play where male authority is demonstrated in modern terms, by the hero's sexual conquest of a desirable woman; and it is not surprising that modern critics have admired the wooing scene as a final demonstration of Henry's "humanity."

The wooing scene in *Henry V* has proved popular with recent audiences; but, as Lance Wilcox has observed, Shakespeare's representation of Henry's courtship repeatedly identifies his conquest of Katherine as a kind of rape (Wilcox 1985). Unprecedented in Shakespeare's earlier plays, the identification of rape as a model of masculine dominance illuminates the dark underside of the emergent conception of marriage as the proof of manhood and the necessary basis for patriarchal authority – the production of rape as the gatekeeper for the gender hierarchy. For if the ideology of patrilineal inheritance made cuckoldry a dangerous crime, the ideology of masculine performance makes rape a necessary one. The first criminalized women as potential cuckold-makers, the second disempowers them as potential victims.

"Performative masculinity," the term we have used to designate the emergent conception of male identity, is adapted from an article by Susan Jeffords: "Performative Masculinities, or, 'After a Few Times You Won't be Afraid of Rape at All'." Jeffords' remarkably prophetic analysis was published in the Spring— Summer 1991 issue of *Discourse*, well before the eruption of the Tailhook scandal,[6] the furious public response to President Clinton's promise to end American military discrimination against gay and lesbian soldiers, and the widely publicized systematic rape of civilian women by soldiers in Bosnia. Jeffords' title comes from a 1986 film, *Opposing Force*, in which the setting is a mock prisoner of war camp established by the American Air Force to train pilots for survival in enemy captivity. The heroine, the first woman to be trained in the camp, is raped by a superior officer, who claims, in the words of Jeffords' title, that the rape is a necessary part of her training for military service. "You're frightened now," he explains. "But after a few more times you won't be afraid of rape at all."

Two of the many strengths of Jeffords' analysis are her insistence upon making distinctions between historically different versions of patriarchy and her focus upon war as the arena in which the terms of the gender hierarchy are renegotiated (see also Jeffords 1989). Situating her own analysis in the present, she documents both the widespread practice of raping civilian women in recent wars and the equally widespread exploitation of the threat of rape by modern governments as an excuse for excluding women from combat duty. She argues that in both cases biological sexual difference becomes the ground for re-establishing a gender hierarchy destabilized by the modern ideology of universal citizenship in civil society. "'Equal citizenship,'" she explains, "has come to be a part of the way that a dominant gender system presents itself in the US. But in tandem with this abstraction of equality is an insistence on what are viewed as the concrete differences of biology, drawing attention . . . to the body as the site of difference" (1991: 108–9).

Jeffords' analysis goes a long way towards explaining, not only the specific examples of sexual persecution we mentioned (Tailhook, Bosnia, gay-bashing) but also the current obsession with women's bodies, the increasingly pornographic representations of the relationships between men and women in popular culture and the preoccupation with bodies (reified as "the body") and sexuality in much contemporary literary scholarship. However, the beginnings of the process Jeffords describes can be traced at least as far back as Shakespeare's *Henry V*, a play that responds remarkably well to the sort of analysis she proposes, a fact which probably helps to explain both its popularity in recent productions and the attention it has received in recent feminist criticism.

More than any of Shakespeare's earlier English histories, *Henry V* defines the roles of men and women in terms that clearly prefigure the performative masculinity and embodied female vulnerability that Jeffords identifies as ideologically motivated responses to our own historical situation. Military conquest provides the arena and sexual conquest the warrant for establishing the male protagonist's authority, and female characters are defined primarily in terms of their sexuality. The logic of sexual difference in *Henry V* is now so familiar that it is easy to miss how innovative it was at the end of the sixteenth century. As Tania Modleski has observed, "contemporary [i.e. late twentieth-century] texts devoted to analyzing 'the enduring appeal of battle' tend to focus obsessively on the issue of sexuality – to the point indeed of excluding almost every other factor" (1991: 61). Although the re-enactment of historical battles is one of the chief attractions in Shakespeare's history plays, it is only in *Richard III* and *Henry V* that rape is associated with military invasion. Significantly, these are also the only Shakespearean histories in which marriage represents the desired conclusion of the action, and the only ones in which no woman appears, or is even mentioned as appearing, on the fields of battle. All these differences mark the emergence, at the ends of the two tetralogies, of a recognizably modern model of masculine identity and male dominance.

In the plays where the logic of patrilineal feudal succession is privileged, rape is never associated with military conquest or valorized as the "natural" instinct of men. Instead, it serves to separate "low" men from their betters. The only references to rape in the Henry VI plays are associated with Jack Cade's rebellion, where it is identified with the dangers of a world turned upside down. As we explained in Part II, the quarto version of the play contains an account of a rape committed by one of Cade's followers and Cade's enthusiastic approval of the act. Although this incident is absent from the folio text, Cade's own proposal that "There shall not a maid be married, but she shall pay to me her maidenhead ere they have it" (*Henry VI, II*: IV.vii.121–3) appears in both versions. In this inversion of *droit de seigneur*, the supposed right of a feudal lord to take the virginity of his vassal's bride (Hattaway 1991: 189n), as in the Gothic barbarians' rape of Lavinia in *Titus Andronicus* and Caliban's attempt to rape Miranda in *The Tempest*, the historical actuality of class and colonial oppression is displaced and denied. The function of rape as a means by which the powerful control the less powerful is elided; the would-be perpetrators are foreign barbarians and plebeian rebels. Prospero colonizes the island, but he never rapes a native woman.[7] The Romans capture Tamora, but they do not rape her. Cade's warning to his followers about the tyranny of the nobility, who "break your backs with burthens, take your houses over your heads, ravish your wives and daughters before your faces" (IV.viii.29–31) reflects the social reality of a world where female laborers were always vulnerable to sexual exploitation at the hands of their masters, but this is the only reference to that fact in all of Shakespeare's history plays.[8] In each case, a socially or racially inferior man is represented as attempting to deprive another man of his rightful property, and the desire to rape signals the bestiality of its perpetrator. Not only a dishonor to the victim and to the men to whom she rightfully "belongs," it also criminalizes the rapist.

A similar conception of rape persists in *Richard III*, the first play where rape is mentioned among the dangers of war. It is the villain who introduces the threat of rape, and the rapists are stigmatized not only as ignoble but also as unmanly. Their leader, according to Richard, is a "milksop" who has been "Long kept in Britain [i.e. Brittany] at our mother's cost" (V.iii.324–5). The potential rapists are beggars, bastards, and foreigners, all of which means that they are not real men:

> If we be conquered, let men conquer us,
> And not these bastard Britains [i.e. Bretons], whom our fathers
> Have in their own land beaten, bobb'd, and thump'd,
> .   .   .   .
> Shall these enjoy our lands? lie with our wives?
> Ravish our daughters?
>
> (*Richard III*: V.iii.332–7)

In *Henry V*, by contrast, the hierarchies of status and nation are supported rather than threatened by sexual violence. Not only masculinity but nationality and military prowess are now grounded in embodied sexual difference. Describing the departure of the English fleet "holding due course to Harflew" (III.Ch.17), the Chorus to Act III explains that England has been left

> Guarded with grandsires, babies, and old women,
> Either past or not arriv'd to pith and puissance;
> For who is he, whose chin is but enrich'd
> With one appearing hair, that will not follow
> These cull'd and choice-drawn cavaliers to France?
>
> (III.Ch.20–4)

Apparently, the only people who are qualified for membership in the English army are sexually mature men. Their qualifications are shown by the appearance of hair on their chins and proved by their ability to rape women – an ability which is specifically articulated at the gates of the French city which the Chorus identifies as the army's destination.[9] In this moment of threatened sexual violence, which is powerfully articulated in Branagh's updated film version of the play but already explicit in Shakespeare's text, it is the heroic English king who voices the threat of rape. Moreover, in this play, unlike *Richard III*, it is English soldiers who will do the raping and French women who will be the victims.

Like *Henry V*, *Richard III* represents a royal marriage as the desired conclusion of the historical action. Here, as in their association of rape with military conquest, both plays prefigure modern conceptions of masculine authority, and here too *Henry V* is significantly more modern than *Richard III*.[10] Although both plays end by announcing that victories won on the battlefield will be ratified in marriage and both marriages serve to insure the bridegroom's sovereignty, the bride-to-be in *Richard III* is a disembodied name, while the French princess in *Henry V* is brought on stage as a sexualized object of theatrical display and erotic desire. In this connection Richard Loncraine's recent film version of *Richard III*, starring Ian McKellen, offers an interesting parallel when it includes Elizabeth of York among the dramatis personae and also shows Richmond making love to her on the night before the Battle of Bosworth Field – in an interpolated scene which gives new meaning to Richmond's oversleeping on the morning of the battle and his declaration that he had "the sweetest sleep and fairest-boding dreams/ That ever ent'red in a drowsy head" (V.iii.227–8). In Shakespeare's script, Richmond dreams about the ghosts of Richard's victims, who exhort him to victory in the coming battle, and Elizabeth never appears on stage. *Henry V* is the only Shakespearean history play where male authority is demonstrated in modern terms, by the hero's sexual conquest of a desirable woman; and it is not surprising that modern critics have admired the wooing scene as a final demonstration of Henry's "humanity" or that Loncraine and McKellen found it necessary to embellish their version of the earlier play by showing how the founders of the House of Tudor consummated their marriage. In *Richard III*, the courtship of Lady Anne provided a remarkable display of Richard's masculine power, but Richard's power, unlike that of Richmond – and unlike that of Henry V – is never depicted as legitimate. In *Henry V*, for the first time in Shakespeare's English histories, male heterosexual dominance achieves its modern status as the "natural" basis of legitimate masculine authority.

Richard III and *Henry V* are also the only Shakespearean history plays in which battlefields are designated as exclusively male terrain, and here too both plays signal their modernity, for, as Jeffords (1991) points out, the sexual logic of performative masculinity requires the exclusion of women from military combat.[11] Women's exclusion from combat is not a universal practice, grounded in nature and ratified by immemorial custom; but the pressure of modern gender ideology tends to erase or minimize historical facts that threaten to contradict it, even for professional historians. Noting the "blindness of historians to women's military roles" Barton Hacker points out that "when military history emerged during the latter part of the nineteenth century, armies were not what they had been even a few decades earlier.... Women's absence from late nineteenth-century armies debarred them from military history in its formative stages, and ever since has obscured the meaning of their presence in other armies at other times" (Hacker 1981: 645; see Plates 8, 9, and 10). A history of women's roles in medieval and early modern armies has yet to be written, for just as military histories tend to ignore the roles of women, histories of women tend to ignore their roles as soldiers. Despite their absence from military history, women were present in large numbers as "a normal part of European armies . . . until well into the nineteenth century" (Hacker, 1981; 643). Many were noncombatants – wives, prostitutes, sutlers, and serving women who accompanied the soldiers (Hacker 1981, Contamine 1984: 241). But some of these women also fought, like the Frisian woman described by Froissart who "fought in the front rank and died pierced with arrows" in 1396 or the woman who carried the Flemish banner in a battle against Charles VI in 1382 (Contamine 1984: 242). For the most part, common women, like the common men in early armies, were nameless in historical records, but there were numerous accounts of aristocratic women warriors. As Philippe Contamine points out, "The participation of armed ladies . . . was considered, when everything is taken into account, as fairly normal, given the fact that many feudal customs gave them a formal right to succession" (1984: 241).

Plate 8 A striking image of Joan of Arc dressed for battle, illustrating a sixteenth-century French text, André Thévet's *Les vraies pourtraits et vies des hommes illustres* (1584).

Source: Reproduced by permission of the Rare Books and Manuscripts Division, The New York Public Library, Astor, Lenox and Tilden Foundations

202

Plate 9 Woodcut illustration of the ancient British queen, Boadicea, addressing her army. It appeared in the 1577 edition of Raphael Holinshed's *Chronicles of England, Scotland and Ireland*.
Source: Reproduced by permission of the Furness Collection, Department of Special Collections, Van Pelt-Dietrich Library, University of Pennsylvania

Plate 10 Woodcut illustration from the 1577 edition of Raphael Holinshed's *Chronicles of England, Scotland and Ireland*. On the right men and women go into battle together against, on the left, an array of men with firearms.
Source: Reproduced by permission of the Furness Collection, Department of Special Collections, Van Pelt-Dietrich Library, University of Pennsylvania

In the first tetralogy and *King John*, Shakespeare's representations of medieval battles exploit the historical fact of women's presence. In *King John*, as in history, Elinor of Aquitaine is a "soldier" (I.i.150) who leads her own forces in France.[12] In the Henry VI plays, Shakespeare follows his historical sources in making Margaret a better general than her husband and in representing Joan as leading the French army to repeated victories; and he improves on their accounts by having Joan defeat the Dolphin and fight the great Talbot to a draw in single combats spectacularly performed on stage. As many recent critics have been quick to notice, however, the figure of the woman warrior was already a source of anxiety when the Henry VI plays were first performed – a cultural contradiction expressed in numerous and conflicting references to Amazons in contemporary texts as well as the circulation of the story that Queen Elizabeth had appeared at Tilbury dressed in armor and explaining that although she had "the body of a weak and feeble woman," she had "the heart and stomach of a king, and of a king of England too." Shakespeare's representations of Joan and Margaret seem clearly designed to exploit the shock value of the appearance of a woman warrior (Jackson 1988: 54). In *Henry VI, Part III* the Duke of York tells Margaret that her warlike behavior is completely antithetical to women's nature: "Women are soft, mild, pitiful, and flexible," he explains, "Thou stern, obdurate, flinty, rough, remorseless." He also denounces Margaret as an "Amazonian trull," linking the masculinity of the female warrior with the sexual promiscuity of the harlot (I.iv.141–2, 114). The same associations color Shakespeare's characterization of Joan, who is both the leader of the Dolphin's army and his "trull" (*Henry VI, Part I*: II.ii.28).[13] However, although their behavior is clearly marked as sexually transgressive, neither of these warrior women is ever subjected to the danger – or even the threat – of rape. Margaret's charms are twice described as "ravishing" (*Henry VI, Part I*: V.v.15; *Henry VI, II*: I.i.32); but no one ever attempts – or contemplates attempting – to ravish Margaret. The notoriously sensationalized violence in *Henry VI, Part III* includes the abuse of a corpse, the flourishing of a decapitated head, and the murders of two children, all performed on stage, but it does not include any references to rape.

The conflation of military conquest with rape helps to produce a naturalized categorical difference between male and female. As York tries to explain, the violence of the battlefield should be a male monopoly. In the Henry VI plays and *King John* this is not yet the case. As we noted earlier, York speaks as the victim of Margaret's violence in one of the most brutal scenes in those plays, when she taunts him with a napkin stained in the blood of his murdered child and has him crowned with a paper crown. York responds with a long and eloquent denunciation of Margaret's brutality, explaining that women are not supposed to behave this way. At the end, it will be recalled, he breaks down in tears, and Northumberland, Margaret's henchman, also admits that he can "hardly ... check [his] eyes from tears" (*Henry VI, III*: I.iv.151). Margaret, however, is unmoved: she orders York killed, delivers the *coup de grâce* herself, and ends the scene with the grisly joke: "Off with his head, and set it on York gates,/ So York may overlook the town of York" (I.iv.179–80).

Like Joan's single combats with Talbot and the Dolphin, Margaret's murder of York is Shakespeare's invention; both appealed to a contemporary appetite for representations of Amazonian women. As York's complaint makes clear, the figure of the woman warrior was already a cultural anomaly, but, as Shakespeare's embellishments of his historical sources make equally clear, she was also an object of fascinated interest. The twentieth-century editor of the Arden edition of *Henry VI, Part III*, by contrast, seems oblivious to her attractions. Carefully noting that "Margaret is not present, according to the chronicles, in this scene," he seems to find the spectacle of female violence so intolerable that he attempts to obliterate the stage-Margaret's presence ("Margaret *is* not present") rather than simply recording the historical Margaret's absence (in which case he would, presumably, have written, "*was* not present").

Shakespeare's own erasure of the woman warrior is one of the projects of the later plays. In the second tetralogy, female soldiers no longer appear on stage, but in *Richard II*, we learn that "distaff-women manage rusty bills" [that is, pikes, or long spears] in arms against the king (III.ii.118); and *Henry IV, Part I* begins with the abbreviated account of the battlefield mutilation of the English soldiers' corpses by the Welsh women. In these plays, women's presence on the battlefield is briefly told rather than extensively shown, the distaff-women are not generals, the violence the Welshwomen commit is a gendered act of sexual mutilation, and, of course, they are foreigners. Mortimer's Welsh bride wants to "be a soldier too" and follow her husband "to the wars" (III.i.193), but Hotspur's English wife has no such unruly desires. By the time we get to *Henry V*, even the French women are safely contained at home. The gendered distinction between hearth and battlefield is now fully in place, and no woman appears – or is mentioned as appearing – in any army. Entirely confined to domestic settings and domestic roles, female characters serve only as the objects of male protection and the occasions for masculine competition.

Consider again the transformation of Mistress Quickly. The first thing we hear about her in *Henry V* is that she is now married to Pistol. In what looks very much like a parodic anticipation of a modern war movie, the quondam Quickly bids her new husband a fond farewell as he departs for France. "Prithee, honey-sweet husband," she implores, "let me bring thee to Staines "[i.e. to a town on the road to Southampton, where the army will embark for France]. He refuses, explaining that his "*manly* heart doth ern" (II.iii.1–3, italics added) and ordering his clinging bride to keep the home fires burning in terms which designate as his property the tavern that was hers in both parts of Henry IV. "My love, give me thy lips," he says. "Look to *my* chattels and *my* moveables" (II.iii.47–8, italics added).

Domesticated and dependent, the female characters in *Henry V* are both economically and sexually vulnerable. Pistol goes on to admonish his newly acquired wife, who has been running the tavern as long as we have known her, "the [word] is 'Pitch and pay';/ Trust none" (II.iii.49–50). Pistol is a lying braggart, but the economic dependency of women receives better testimony in Act IV, when the upright common soldier Williams admonishes his king (and Shakespeare's audience) that when soldiers die there will be "wives left poor behind them" and "children rawly left" (IV.i.139–41). The aristocratic women in the play are equally helpless. The French princess Katherine, her lady-in-waiting, and her mother the queen are all confined to the enclosed space of the palace, and their roles in the play are limited to the provision of sexual titillation for the audience and a bride for the soldier hero.

As we noted earlier, Quickly's domestication implies an effort to contain the threat represented by her economic independence – and that of her counterparts in Shakespeare's audience. What is also striking in *Henry V* is that the proto-bourgeois project of domestication is now universalized, and the forces of modernity are, for the first time, privileged. Beginning with the non-elite, entrepreneurial London woman in the anachronistically modern tavern, the new model of wifely dependence reaches across the English channel and up to the highest place in the social hierarchy to provide a precedent for the domestication of the future bride of Henry V, a woman who was also, by her later marriage to Owen Tudor, the great-great-grandmother of Elizabeth I. The gendered resemblances between the French princess and the English tavern-keeper are numerous, superseding social and national difference to affirm the universality of the sexualized difference between men and women. In the person of the princess, the entire French nation will assume the role of a married woman, the *feme covert* whose identity was legally subsumed in that of her husband and whose property became his possession.

Before Henry can assume the title of *Héritier de France*, however, the patrilineal right that authorizes the Dolphin's claim to that title must be discredited. In striking contrast to the earlier history plays, the vestigial ideology of chivalry and hereditary nobility is now identified with the French and gendered feminine, while the modern culture of personal achievement and national identity is now identified as masculine and English. In *Henry V* it is not the virile English king but the effete French Dolphin who inherits Hotspur's obsession with horses. A descendent of the effete courtier who infuriated Hotspur at the Battle of Holmedon, the Dolphin is also a descendent of Hotspur himself, for just as Henry takes on Hotspur's heroic honor, the Dolphin takes on his exaggerated devotion to his horse. In the Dolphin's declaration, "my horse is my mistress" (III.vii.44), in the inflated language in which he describes his infatuation, and in his revelation that he "once writ a sonnet in his praise" (III.vii.39), chivalry itself becomes the object of satire. Moreover, the Dolphin's identification of the horse as male provides a significant contrast to Hotspur's comparison of the effeminate courtier at Holmedon to a bridegroom. In *Henry V*, the status of a bridegroom provides the final proof of Henry's masculine authority, and the Dolphin's effeminating passion for his horse is associated with deviance from an emergent heterosexual norm.

The quarto version of *Henry V* assigns the Dolphin's part in the Agincourt scenes to the Duke of Bourbon. The folio attribution of these lines to the Dolphin helps to discredit the grounding of political authority in patrilineal right and thus to prepare for Henry's assumption of the Dolphin's hereditary title to the French throne. Whichever version is accepted, however, the satirical portrait of a Frenchman in love with his horse serves to discredit the feudal ideal of chivalry, and throughout the Agincourt scenes the culture of hereditary status distinctions is identified with the French and discredited. Before the battle, the French Constable contemptuously predicts, "our superfluous lackeys and our peasants,/ Who in unnecessary action swarm/ About our squares of battle, were enow/ To purge this field of such a hilding foe" (IV.ii.26–9). Moreover, the chief representative of the French at Agincourt is Montjoy, a proud French herald who comes to the English camp so often that his appearance becomes a kind of joke (IV.iii.128). After the battle of Agincourt, Montjoy returns again, "his eyes . . . humbler than they used to be," to beg permission (IV.vii.67)

> That we may wander o'er this bloody field
> To book our dead, and then to bury them;
> To sort our nobles from our common men.
> For many of our princes (woe the while!)
> Lie drown'd and soak'd in mercenary blood;
> So do our vulgar drench their peasant limbs
> In blood of princes, and [their] wounded steeds
> Fret fetlock deep in gore, and with wild rage
> Yerk out their armed heels at their dead masters,
> Killing them twice.
>
> (IV.vii.72–81)

What distresses the French herald is the failure of chivalry: the horses turn against their masters; the peasants are drenched in the blood of princes. Like this speech, the prominence given the French herald in the Agincourt scenes identifies the French with the culture of hereditary entitlement. The English herald, like his French counterpart, is associated with the books that recorded the names of the noble. The notes he gives his king after the battle list the names and titles of the noblemen killed in both the armies but only the number of the "other men" who died. However, his role in the scene is minimal; he himself is nameless, he has only one line to speak, and his only function is to provide the king with lists of the dead. The English cause at Agincourt is defined by the king himself, who associates it with the emergent values of manhood and personal achievement. Unlike the French herald, Henry declares that he wants his common subjects to mingle their blood with his:

For he to-day that sheds his blood with me
Shall be my brother; be he ne'er so vile,
This day shall gentle his condition;
And gentlemen in England, now a-bed,
Shall think themselves accurs'd they were not here;
And hold their manhoods cheap whiles any speaks
That fought with us upon Saint Crispin's Day.

(IV.iii.61–7)

A high moment in patriotic modern productions of the play, Henry's promise to his soldiers still helps to enforce the ideological regime it helped to produce: it denies social distinctions and relies on gender distinctions to identify England as the prototype of the modern nation state, a place where men are men and women are women, but all men are brothers. These are blatantly ideological claims whose "truth" is established only by enormous cultural effort. They are nonetheless claims that have come to underpin the modern nation state and its attendant gender ideologies.

Like Henry's speech at Agincourt, the fact that the common woman of the English tavern provides a prototype for the role of the French woman in the royal palace identifies the project of modernization with English imperialism. Just as the scenes in Quickly's tavern have already done in both parts of *Henry IV* and continue to do in *Henry V*, the scenes in Katherine's palace provide comic relief from the serious, masculine business of war. Both women bring considerable property to their new husbands – Pistol becomes the landlord of the tavern, Henry the lord of France – but here again Quickly does it first. Even Katherine's language – a mangled English that is riddled with inadvertent sexual double entendres – has a prototype in Quickly's malapropisms.

Although Henry's claim to France requires the erasure of national difference, it is also identified as a specifically English project: the national identity that must be obliterated is French; the language the French princess must learn to speak is English. Describing the full-blown imperialism of the nineteenth century, Benedict Anderson characterizes it as "a certain inventive legerdemain . . . required to ["affirm the identity of dynasty and nation"] and permit the empire to appear attractive in national drag" (1983: 83). Anderson's suggestively gendered language has a remarkable prototype in Shakespeare's play, for the contradictions implicit in Henry's proto-imperialist project can be resolved only by reference to the imagined body of the French princess, which mystifies territorial expansion and naturalizes dynastic marriage as heterosexual conquest. Here, as in later imperialist discourse, the territory to be conquered is imagined as the body of a woman, and the project of imperial expansion is conceived as a distinctively male activity. In learning English, the French princess is symbolically stripped of her clothing. The naked body which provides a "natural" basis for the differences between male and female roles in modern society is the subject of Katherine's language lesson, which is almost entirely devoted to words for the parts of her body. The only exception is "la robe," introduced at the end so both the French women can mispronounce its English translation. The English word *gown* becomes in the mouths of the Frenchwomen, "le count" (in the folio) or "le coune" (in the quarto), thus ending the scene with an uproarious sexual joke that unambiguously specifies the purpose of the entire exercise. The scene, moreover, is designed not only to name Katherine's body but also to exhibit it – in Shakespeare's own version of "national drag" – for the best way for the boy actor who played Katherine's part to make the French words comprehensible to an English audience would be to point, as he named each of the body parts, to the place on his own body where it was (or was imagined to be).

Both Katherine's language lesson and the scenes in the London tavern interrupt the historical narrative of Henry's French conquest, but in both cases the irrelevance of the comic interlude is only apparent. Act II begins with the Chorus's announcement that the English army is departing for France:

> The King is set from London, and the scene
> Is now transported, gentles, to Southampton;
> There is the playhouse now, there must you sit,
> And thence to France shall we convey you safe,
> And bring you back, charming the Narrow Seas
> To give you gentle pass; for if we may,
> We'll not offend one stomach with our play.
> (II.Cho.34–40)

That looks like the end of the Chorus, but another two lines, which sound like an afterthought, immediately follow: "But till the King come forth, and not till then,/ Unto Southampton do we shift our scene." Many editors have speculated that the Chorus's final couplet and the London scene it introduces were, in fact, revisions to an original playscript that did not include them; but whatever their respective dates of composition, the tavern scene seems clearly designed to follow, and provide an implicit comment on, the opening Chorus in its entirety.

"Now all the youth of England are on fire," the Chorus began, "and honor's thought/ Reigns solely in the breast of every man" (II.Cho.1–4). No sooner does the Chorus finish than Nym and Bardolph take the stage and we learn about another contest for masculine honor, this one centering on the possession of the hostess, whom Pistol has just married despite her previous betrothal to Nym. Both England and France have already been personified as women (I.ii.155–65, 227) and defined as the subjects of masculine competition; but Pistol reinforces the connection when he parodically echoes the imagery the Chorus has just used, declaring that his "cock is up,/ And flashing fire will follow" (II.i.52–3). He also names what is at stake in both contests when he agrees at the end of the scene to settle his quarrel with Nym by paying the money he owes him, but only "as manhood shall compound" (98). At the end of the play, Pistol loses his wife to venereal disease in the same scene where he loses his honor to Fluellen's cudgel (V.i). The name he uses for the disease that bespeaks his wife's sexual promiscuity – "malady of France" (82) – reiterates the association between the imperial dominance of the English nation and the domestic dominance of the English husband: a chaste wife would not have contracted the "French" disease.

Honor and manhood are also at stake in Henry's determination to conquer France, a conquest that he defines in a curiously gendered simile. "Or there we'll sit," he declares,

> Ruling in large and ample empery
> O'er France and all her almost kingly dukedoms,
> Or lay these bones in an unworthy urn,
> Tombless, with no remembrance over them.
> Either our history shall with full mouth
> Speak freely of our acts, or else our grave,
> Like Turkish mute, shall have a tongueless mouth,
> Not worshipp'd with a waxen epitaph.
>
> (I.ii.225–33)

Although this speech comes in Act I, before there has been any talk of marrying Katherine, Henry already thinks of France as a woman ("her") and defines his conquest as the necessary validation of his manhood. If he fails, he says, his grave, "like Turkish mute, shall have a tongueless mouth." This allusion to the bodily mutilation that deprives a eunuch in a seraglio of his manhood (Taylor 1984: 113n) also recalls Westmerland's description in *Henry IV, Part I* of the mutilation of the English soldiers following their defeat on a Welsh battlefield. The image of the waxen epitaph recalls the traditional textual basis of masculine authority but renders it ephemeral: the image of the Turkish mute implies a new, universal basis for that authority in embodied sexual difference but insists on its vulnerability. As the Turkish mute demonstrates, a body can be altered.

The victory Henry requires conflates military conquest with male sexual potency, and leads ineluctably, by the logic of performative masculinity, to the imagery and actuality of rape that Jeffords (1991) identifies as salient features of the modern discourse and modern practice of war. The exclusion of women from the battlefield and their relegation to the roles of civilian victims in *Henry V* looks ahead to the increasing cultural insistence that because men and women have different bodies they have different roles to play in life. The language lesson, with its sexualization of the imagined woman's body, hints at what was to become a dominant ideology of a gender hierarchy naturalized in embodied sexual difference.[14] The play also looks to the future when – in a connection unprecedented in Shakespeare's earlier history plays – military conquest is associated by the leaders of both the opposing armies with rape.

The association appears to be intentional, for the speech Henry delivers at the gates of Harfleur is Shakespeare's invention. Holinshed briefly describes the "distresse" the inhabitants of Harfleur suffered when the English took the city, but there is no reference to rape in his account (Holinshed 1587: 3: 73–4). In Shakespeare's version, however, Henry warns the besieged citizens that unless they surrender, "the flesh'd soldier, rough and hard of heart ... shall range/ With conscience wide as hell, mowing like grass/ Your fresh fair virgins and your flow'ring infants." He repeats the threat twice more: "your pure maidens," he warns, will "fall into the hand/ Of hot and forcing violation."

"Look to see/ The blind and bloody soldier with foul hand/ [Defile] the locks of your shrill-shriking daughters" (III.iii.11–14, 20–1, 33–5).[15]

The terms in which the victims are described, "*your* fresh fair virgins," "*your* pure maidens," and "*your* shrill-shriking daughters," clearly identify Henry's warning as a threat, through their property, to the *men* of Harfleur, an identification that is echoed later when Bourbon exhorts his fellow Frenchmen to return to battle.

> Shame and eternal shame, nothing but shame!
> Let us die! In once more! back again!
> And he that will not follow Bourbon now,
> Let him go hence, and with his cap in hand
> Like a base pander hold the chamber-door
> Whilst [by a] slave, no gentler than my dog,
> His fairest daughter is contaminated.
> (IV.v.10–16)

Although Bourbon's warning lacks the pornographic redundancy and vivid details of Henry's threats to the citizens of Harfleur, it belongs to the same discourse. In both cases, as in Pistol and Nym's fight for possession of the hostess, the contest for manhood and honor takes the form of a contest for the sexual possession of women.

In *Henry V*, in fact, the entire French kingdom is represented as a woman to be conquered by the masculine force of the English army, a conceit that is implied by the placement of Katherine's language lesson immediately after Henry's speech at Harfleur and literalized in the final scene when Henry claims the French princess for his bride (Wilcox 1985).[16] In terms that resonate with his threats at Harfleur, he jokes with the Duke of Burgundy that because "love is blind and enforces," he, being a blind lover, "cannot see many a French city for one fair French maid that stands in my way." The French king replies obligingly that "the cities [are] turn'd into a maid; for they are all girdled with maiden walls that war hath [never] ent'red" (V.ii.300–1, 317–19, 321–3). In what might appear to be, but is certainly not, a *non sequitur*, Henry replies with the blunt question, "Shall Kate be my wife?" and, having received the desired response, reiterates the connection one more time:

I am content, so the maiden cities you talk of may wait on her;
so the maid that stood in the way for my wish shall show me
the way to my will.

(324–8)

Branagh's film nicely captures the threat of sexual violence
overshadowing Henry's future bride, but although Henry describes his courtship in the language of rape and warfare, it is
important to emphasize that the marriage is not a rape. Burgundy's description of France in the final scene as an unhusbanded
garden that can be saved only by union with England implies a
necessary ideological distinction between the benevolent rule of a
husband and the destructive conquest of a rapist: both Katherine
and France, he implies, need to be husbanded by Henry (Hodgdon
1991: 201–3). It is, however, even more important to Henry that
the marriage take place, for it is only by legal possession of
Katherine that he can acquire legitimate authority over France
and, through it, over England.

From the beginning of the play Henry has defined the conquest
of France as the means by which he will secure the royal legitimacy
that he could not inherit from his usurping father. Lacking a
legitimate patrimonial title to the name of king, Henry secures it
by matrimonial conquest. "No king of England, if not king of
France" (II.ii.193): it is only by marrying Katherine that he can
legitimate both titles. The final concession Henry requires from
the French king is that he name him, in writing, in both French
and Latin, as his son and the heir to France. "Let that one article
rank with the rest," Henry demands, "And thereupon give me
your daughter" (V.ii.346–7).[17] The contract by which Henry finally
acquires the royal father who can legitimate his identity as king
has all the familiar attributes of what Gayle Rubin has identified
as the traffic in women; but Katherine also has all the traditional
attributes of a rape victim. Sexualized from the moment of her first
appearance on stage, her destiny is already inevitable – it has
already been described, in fact, in the immediately preceding
scene when Henry told the citizens of Harfleur what would
happen to their daughters when his soldiers conquered the city
(Wilcox 1985: 66). The courtship scene at the end of the play comes
as close as it can to enacting the predicted rape. First characterized
in language that associates her with the conquered cities of France,
Katherine is then subjected to a symbolic rape when Henry forces

214

her to endure his kiss. From that moment on, she has not another word to say. Silenced, like Philomel and like Shakespeare's own Lavinia, Katherine provides the proof of Henry's manhood as well as the legitimation of his identity as king. The modernity of this conflation probably helps to explain the emphasis that the Harfleur speech, the language lesson, and the wooing scene have received in recent criticism. It also helps to explain the effectiveness and accessibility of Kenneth Branagh's *Henry V*, a film which reveals how thoroughly Shakespeare's play anticipates the terms in which we have come to think out sexuality and its relationship to male and female identities. Shakespeare and his audiences did not, however, take the sex–gender arrangements of *Henry V* for granted. They had to travel a long way to get there.

In Shakespeare's earlier history plays, where masculine authority is still conceived as the product of patrilineal succession, royal marriages never turn out well. The marriage of Henry VI, for instance, is repeatedly characterized as a "fatal" mistake, the reason for his loss, first, of manhood and royal authority and finally of the crown he inherited from his father. In fact, the narratives in the earlier plays can never reach their desired conclusions until female characters are banished from the stage of history. But once personal performance displaces patrilineal genealogy as the basis for male authority, the narrative reaches its desired conclusion when the hero acquires a wife. At the end of *Henry VI, Part I*, Joan is hustled off the stage to be burned at the stake. In *Henry V* Shakespeare literalizes the Pauline injunction, "It is better to marry than to burn" (I Corinthians 7.9) when another French woman is hustled on to the stage to provide a bride for the conquering English hero and a focus for the sexual fantasies of the audience.

Naturalized in the discourse of biological sexual difference, the supposedly instinctive desire of men to rape and the assumed physical vulnerability of women to be raped have provided a remarkably durable rationale for male heterosexual privilege. The images of rape that characterize Henry's acquisition of a wife establish, almost at the moment of its conception, the connection between the nascent bourgeois ideal of heterosexual marriage and the savage fantasies of rape that attend it.[18]

NOTES

1 THOROUGHLY MODERN HENRY

1 All quotations from Shakespeare's plays refer to Evans, G. B. *et al.* (1974).
2 Shakespeare's theater company, The Lord Chamberlain's Men, moved to their new venue, the Globe, in the summer of 1599. It is possible that *Henry V* was one of the first plays they performed there, but some theater historians believe it may have opened at The Curtain (Gurr 1992: 236).

2 THE HISTORY PLAY IN SHAKESPEARE'S TIME

1 When first printed in quarto form, the play now called *Henry VI, Part II* was titled *The First Part of the Contention betwixt the two famous Houses of York and Lancaster* and *Henry VI, Part III* was titled *The True Tragedy of Richard Duke of Yorke*. It is quite possible that these two works were actually composed before *Henry VI, Part I*.
2 At the end of his career, probably in 1613, a final history play bearing Shakespeare's name and based on the reign of Henry VIII was performed at the Globe Theatre, the home of Shakespeare's acting company. Distant in time of composition from the earlier histories and regarded by many scholars as a product of authorial collaboration, it is also distinct from them in form and style – a distinction which has prompted the editorial decision to include it in the volume in this series devoted to Shakespeare's late romances.
3 Many early modern books lacked page numbers or, if page numbers were supplied, they were sometimes inaccurate. Much more important were the combinations of letters and numbers, called "signatures," provided by printers to indicate to a book binder how the printed sheets sent to him were to be folded and bound. For example, four sheets of paper printed on both sides and folded once down the middle would, when bound together in any one "gathering" of a book, produce eight leaves or sixteen pages. Many of the leaves in any one gathering would be marked by the same capital letter. In an

opened book, the first right-hand page following the title page and any other prefatory material usually would be marked "A" at its bottom (we would read it as "A1"). This page was the "recto," or front, of the leaf. Its back – the page on the left, when you turned this first leaf over – was called the "verso." A superscript "r" (for recto) or "v" (for verso) indicates whether one is referring to the front or the back of a particular leaf. The next right-hand page of this gathering would be marked, at its bottom, "A2"; the next after that, "A3" and so forth. But final leaves in a gathering were often left unsigned. For example, if there were 8 leaves or 16 pages in a particular gathering, leaf 8 (the right-hand half of the sheet whose first half formed leaf A1) might bear no signature. In that case, the recto of that leaf would be cited as [sig. A8^r], the brackets indicating that the reader has added the signature. The leaves in successive gatherings would be marked B1, B2, B3, etc. Hence, a quotation cited as coming from "sig. C4^v" would mean that the quotation could be found on the back side of leaf four in the "C" gathering of the book in question.

3 FEMINISM, WOMEN, AND THE SHAKESPEAREAN HISTORY PLAY

1 Kolin's bibliography gives the following statistics for 1975–88:

14 items	*Richard III*
12 items	*1 Henry VI*
11 items	*2 Henry VI*
9 items each	*3 Henry VI, King John,* and *Henry VIII*
8 items each	*1 Henry IV, Henry V*
3 items each	*Richard II, 2 Henry IV*

The *MLA Bibliography* for the same years gives the following:

153 items for	*Richard II*
139 for	*Henry V*
132 for	*1 Henry IV*
123 for	*Richard III*
89 for	*2 Henry IV*
74 for	*King John*
52 for	*Henry VIII*
23 each for	*2 Henry VI* and *3 Henry VI*
17 for	*1 Henry VI*

2 This was a comedy called *Wise Man of West Chester* (Harbage 1941: 49).
3 Here are the percentages of words spoken by female characters in Shakespeare's English history plays, compiled from Spevack (1968):

Richard III	22.059
Henry VIII	16.238
King John	14.636
2 Henry VI	14.501

3 *Henry VI*	12.516
1 *Henry VI*	12.497
Richard II	9.778
2 *Henry IV*	9.584
Henry V	4.499
1 *Henry IV*	3.468

4 As Urkowitz (1988a) demonstrates, Margaret is even stronger and more aggressive in the folio versions of *Henry VI, Part II* and *Part III* than she is in the earlier published "bad quartos" of those plays. Of course, no one knows who was responsible for these changes, or even which texts were actually written first, but it is interesting that the folio versions record a preference for a dominant Margaret.

5 The strongest characters in those earlier plays are often women. In *Henry VI, Part I*, for instance, the most vividly conceived and memorable character is not any of the men, but Joan La Pucelle. Moreover, the only character who appears in all four plays of the first tetralogy is Margaret. She develops during the course of those plays from a beautiful young girl, captured by Suffolk and the object of both his and the king's romantic infatuation, to the prophetic crone of *Richard III* who provides the only significant opposition to the villainous protagonist throughout most of the play. Significantly, however, no major critical studies have based their analysis of the plays' progression on her development. The second tetralogy, by contrast, is frequently designated in recent criticism as "The Henriad," an epic series that tells a connected story of the maturation and triumph of a single figure, the heroic king, first mentioned in *Richard II*, who provides the link between the four plays.

5 HENRY VI, PART I

1 As Catherine Belsey has observed, female characters who transgress "the system of differences which gives meaning to social relations ... are defined as extra-human, demonic," a demonization which "places them beyond meaning, beyond the limits of what is intelligible" (Belsey 1985b: 184, 85).

2 Frye (1992) casts doubt upon the accounts of Queen Elizabeth's appearance at Tilbury and the speech she is said to have delivered there, but whether or not these accounts were true, their circulation illustrates the importance of the cultural functions they served.

3 Marcus 1988: 66. See also Chapter 2, "Elizabeth," *passim*. Among many illuminating observations about the connections between Joan and Elizabeth, Marcus points out that the two Frenchmen Joan claims to have been her lovers – the Duke of Alençon and the Duke of Anjou – have the same names as the Frenchmen Elizabeth "had come closest to marrying" in the previous decades (68).

4 The advent of colonialism required the institution of another category of difference – that of race – in order to distinguish European settlers and merchants from the native inhabitants of the lands they conquered and with which they traded. The transition from nativity (place of birth and

residence) to racial inheritance as the ground of identity can be seen in Renaissance discourse on blackness. Karen Newman (1991: 78) quotes an example from the *Discourse* (1578) of the English traveler George Best:

> I my selfe have sene an Ethiopian as blacke as a cole brought into England, who taking a faire English woman to wife, begat a sonne in all respects as blacke as the father was, although England were his native countrey, and an English woman his mother: whereby it seemeth this blacknes proceedeth rather of some natural infection of that man, which was so strong, that neither the nature of the Clime, neither the good complexion of the mother concurring, could any thing alter.

Othello's inability, despite his prodigious military achievements and his acquisition of a fair Venetian wife, to transcend his racial otherness derives from this emergent conception of nationality and identity as grounded in race. Within Shakespeare's English histories, however, the essential categories of difference are social status, gender and nativity.

5 See Orgel 1989: 9 and 28, n. 2. We are also indebted here to a fine unpublished paper by Frances K. Barasch, "The Lady's not for Spurning: An Investigation of Italian Actresses and their Roles in Commedia dell' Arte as Shakespeare's Inspiration." Barasch makes the intriguing suggestion that Shakespeare's witty, independent female characters may have been inspired in part by the performances of Italian actresses, who, because they worked from scenarios rather than from scripts, were in some measure the authors of their own theatrical selves.

6 It is tempting to speculate that a similar attempt at containment lies behind the dialogue between Joan and Lucy, for Lucy's glorious language, unlike Joan's fictitious speech, takes its authority from an enduring historical monument, Talbot's tomb at Rouen, where they were inscribed (Sanders 1981: 220). Reciting the words of the inscription, Lucy invokes a historical authority that might have been regarded as more permanent and less mediated than the narratives of Shakespeare's chronicle sources. And although Lucy is barely mentioned in those sources, he himself possesses a similar authority, for a real man named Sir William Lucy did in fact live in Shakespeare's neighborhood at the time of Henry VI, and it has been suggested that Shakespeare knew of him from local oral tradition (Shaaber 1940: 639–40; Halliday 1958: 292; Sanders 1981: 214). If these speculations are correct, then Lucy represents Shakespeare's attempt to invoke a historical authority beyond historiographic mediation in order to refute Joan's subversive appeal to physical presence.

7 It is interesting that even in Margaret's own time, she was associated with Joan. Patricia-Ann Lee (1986: 198–9) quotes from *The Commentaries of Pius II* both a speech in which Margaret is reported to have enjoined her French captains, "You who once followed a peasant girl, follow now a queen," and a report that those who heard the speech "said that the spirit of the Maid, who had raised Charles to the throne, was renewed in the queen." Although Lee questions the veracity of Pius's account, what is significant, we believe, is that his fiction draws the same connection between Joan and Margaret that Shakespeare's does.

6 HENRY VI, PART II

1 The date of composition is also uncertain. While it is generally agreed that *Part I* had to have been written by summer of 1592, it is much less clear when *Part II* was composed. Dates as early as 1589 and 1591 have been suggested (Wells and Taylor 1987: 111).

2 This is one of several places where the quarto and folio versions of the play differ significantly. In the quarto version Gloucester is murdered on stage; in the folio his death occurs offstage, and the audience simply sees his murderers fleeing the scene.

3 By 1620 the relationship between unmanly men and mannish women had become such a commonplace that two tracts, *Hic Mulier* and *Haec Vir*, were published celebrating and bewailing this gender confusion. While the manly woman in *Haec Vir* at first insists that she has every right to act in a manly fashion, she ends the tract with a plea that men be more manly so that women can reassume their proper gender roles. "Cast then from you our ornaments and put on your own armor; be men in shape, men in show, men in words, men in actions, men in counsel, men in example; then will we love and serve you; then will we hear and obey you; then will we like rich Jewels hang at your ears to take our Instructions, like true friends follow you through all dangers, and like careful leeches pour oil in your wounds" (quoted in Henderson and McManus 1985: 288).

4 Ann Jones and Peter Stallybrass (Parker *et al.* 1992: 157–71) discuss the ways the Irish in the sixteenth century were distinguished from the English by their shaggy mantles or cloaks and by the long hair, or glibs, with which they hid their countenances.

7 HENRY VI, PART III

1 The quarto text reverses the order, having Richard and Somerset's battle occur *before* York's fight with Clifford. The quarto arrangement places maximum emphasis on York's triumph over Old Clifford, King Henry's chief champion, but it dilutes the folio's emphasis on the son's actions as an echo of the father's.

2 In another reading of this speech, Janet Adelman suggests that Richard's anger is directed against the maternal body in which his deformity had its origins and that his turn against his brothers is an attempt to separate himself from all the issue of that mother's body (1992: 2–3). In contrast to this psychoanalytic reading of the scene, we focus on the representational force of the deformed body as a mark, rather than a cause, of Richard's separation from other men, including his kin, and on the way the appearance of a female figure is repeatedly the catalyst in this text for fracturing male bonds.

8 RICHARD III

1 Gosson's charge that tragedy would incite womanly passions in its auditors had an ancient and respectable precedent in Book X of Plato's

Republic, where Socrates condemned the sympathetic raptures stirred up by the tragedian as "the part of a woman" (Plato *c.* 373 BC, in Adams 1992: 36). For a perceptive discussion of the effeminacy of the tyrant figure and the effeminating effects of his representation in tragedy, see Bushnell 1990.

2 In addition to the repeated use of similar description in antitheatrical invective, it is noteworthy that Burbage himself, the actor who first played Richard's role, was compared in admiring contemporary descriptions to Proteus, the shape-shifter. For a good summary of Elizabethan descriptions of actors, including Burbage, see Montrose 1980: 55–7. On the image of Proteus as applied to actors, see Barish 1981: 99–107.

3 For arguments that emphasize the differences between Richard and later tragic heroes, see Belsey 1985b: 37–9 and Adelman 1992: 9. In Belsey's view Richard's isolation and self-assertion declare his alignment with the Vice "rather than defining an emerging interiority." To Adelman "the effect" in Richard's final soliloquy "is less of a psyche than of diverse roles confronting themselves across the void where a self should be." She sees Richard as possessing a "powerful subjectivity" in *Henry VI, Part III,* which is emptied out in *Richard III,* as Richard remakes himself "in the shape of the perfect actor who has no being except in the roles he plays" (8–9). For a discussion that emphasizes Richard's status as prototype for the modern tragic hero, see Weimann 1978: 159–60. In his view, Richard "marks the point of departure for modern tragedy . . . the *Charakterdrama* of an individual passion and a self-willed personality" who combines the self-expressive theatrical energy of the traditional Vice with the "mimetic requirements of a *locus*-oriented royal personage." Weimann concedes that *"Richard III,* of course, only points the way," but he also insists that "the pattern seems clear."

4 Many writers have made this point, but see especially Williamson 1986: chapter 3 and Schochet 1975.

5 As Pearl Hogrefe explains, "When a woman married in Tudor England (and later and earlier also) her property came immediately under the control of her husband. . . . By law she was under his guardianship, becoming a feme covert, a sheltered, protected woman" (Hogrefe 1975: 12).

6 On the exclusion of female characters from the *platea,* see Helms 1992: 554–65. Helms associates the male monopoly of the *platea* in public theater plays with the fact that men's roles were played by adult shareholders in the companies, while women's roles were played by boy apprentices. Cf. Forse 1993: 71–99 for an argument that female parts were also played by adult shareholders, including William Shakespeare, who, he speculates, played the role of Margaret.

10 RICHARD II

1 The indeterminacy often worries modern readers, but it may have been less important to Shakespeare's original audience because sexual lust was regarded as effeminating to men, regardless of the gender of the sexual partner. In this case, it is not clear whether the dissolute courtiers

introduced other women into the king's bed or were themselves involved in sexual dalliance with him.

2 As Carol Pateman argues, the erosion of classical patriarchal ideology based on father right did not mean that patriarchy disappeared from political thought: it simply took a new form. Fraternal patriarchy and the emergent ideology of the civil subject required that "women must be subject to men because they are naturally subversive of men's political order" (Pateman 1988: 96).

3 Many critics have discussed Elizabethan anxieties and ambivalence about the queen's authority, but see especially Montrose (1983) and Ferris (1981). Ferris also provides an excellent analysis of the many ways in which Richard is gendered feminine.

4 Cf. the allusion in *Macbeth*, III.iv.64–5 to "a woman's story at a winter's fire,/ Authoriz'd by her grandam."

5 Both the Duchess of Gloucester's description of Edward's seven sons as "seven fair branches springing from one root" (I.ii.13) and the queen's description of Richard as "my fair rose" (V.i.8) seem to recall the title page of Hall's *Union*, with its representation of Henry VIII and his dynastic forebears as roses growing on a bush (see Plate 4). The image of the rose associates Richard with a stereotypical emblem of feminine beauty (Ferris 1981: 13), but it also naturalizes his patrilineal authority as a true branch of the royal tree.

11 THE HENRY IV PLAYS

1 Cf. Manley's description of the second half of John Stow's *Survey of London*: Conducting a "street-by-street perambulation of the wards, a technique he seems to have borrowed from William Lambarde's 1572 *Perambulation of Kent*," the prototypical chorography, Stow "transformed what was ... essentially a blazon or at best a triumphal procession of the city's attributes into an extended *voie* or exploration of the landscape" (Manley 1983: 363).

2 A suggestive gloss to the marking of Eastcheap as a feminine space is provided by Lawrence Manley's observation that cities were gendered feminine. He cites examples ranging from "the book of Revelation's contrast between Jerusalem, the bride of Christ, and Rome, the whore of Babylon" (Manley 1983: 355) to "the feminine personages who mark the towns on the maps in Michael Drayton's *Polyolbion*" (371, n. 37). He points out that "London was almost invariably personified as a woman in the city's annual mayoral pageants" and that when Ben Jonson, in his text for the coronation pageant of James I represented the Genius of the City as a man, Jonson's collaborator, Dekker, felt obliged to object (371 n. 37).

3 It is generally agreed that Falstaff was originally named Sir John Oldcastle. A historical figure who lived during the reign of Henry IV, Oldcastle was often viewed as an early Protestant martyr. His descendents included the powerful Brooke family, who may have objected to the fact that Shakespeare's dissolute knight had been given this name, with the

result that "Oldcastle" was changed to "Falstaff" in the quarto texts of *Henry IV, Part I* published in 1598, although there remains a reference to Falstaff as "my old lad of the castle" (I.ii.41–2). In the epilogue to *Henry IV, Part II*, however, Shakespeare is at pains to declare, "Oldcastle died [a] martyr, and this is not the man" (Epi.32).

4 Effeminated by sexual passion, Mortimer nonetheless remains a frightening figure. Long before Mortimer appears on stage, we witness the king's agitated response to Hotspur's demand that he be ransomed and brought home (I.iii), but the threat of an alternative royal line with a better claim to the throne is also dramatized in Mortimer's association with the dangerously seductive Welsh woman. By her sex and by her nationality, she both represents and threatens the true legitimacy that the Tudor sovereigns, as well as their male subjects, always needed to claim but could never truly have.

5 The threefold association of female power, foreignness, and atrocity appears to be a persistent feature of early modern colonialist discourse. Ralegh's *Discoverie of Guiana* (1596) reports that Amazons "are said to be very cruel and bloodthirsty" (quoted in Montrose 1991: 26). Even more suggestive is a late sixteenth-century travel narrative quoted by Stephen Greenblatt, which reports that "near the mountains of the moon there is a queen, an empress of all these Amazons, a witch and a cannibal who daily feeds on the flesh of boys. She ever remains unmarried, but she has intercourse with a great number of men by whom she begets offspring. The kingdom, however, remains hereditary to the daughters, not to the sons" (Greenblatt 1980: 181). What is especially interesting for our argument is that this account, like Fleming's account of the female atrocities in Wales, comes to its readers doubly mediated. It is recorded in the diary of Richard Madox, an English traveler in Sierra Leone, but Madox claims that he heard the story from a Portuguese trader. Carroll Smith-Rosenberg has found still another account of female savagery, most closely resembling Fleming's in *The Columbian Magazine and Monthly Miscellany* I (Philadelphia, 1787), p. 549. This account is also represented as doubly mediated (told to the writer by an unnamed "gentleman" met "near Alexandria, in Virginia, in 1782"). In this report, a surveyor named Colonel Crawford, captured by Indians, "was delivered over to *the women*, and being fastened to a stake, in the centre of a circle, formed by the savages and their allies, the female furies, after the preamble of a war song, began by tearing out the nails of his toes and fingers, then proceeded, at considerable intervals, to cut off his nose and ears; after which they stuck his lacerated body full of pitch pines, large pieces of which they inserted (horrid to relate!) into his private parts; to all of which they set fire, and which continued burning, amidst the inconceivable tortures of the unhappy man, for a considerable time. After thus glutting their revenge, by arts of barbarity, the success of which was repeatedly applauded by the surrounding demons, they cut off his genitals, and rushing in upon him, finished his misery with their tomohawks, and hacked his body limb from limb."

6 Mullaney points out that although Henry VIII had outlawed Welsh in

1535, the alien language ("nothing like, nor consonant to the natural Mother Tongue within this realm") consistently defied English efforts "to control or outlaw it." Resisting repeated "pressures of assimilation and suppression ... Welsh remained a strange tongue, a discomfiting reminder that Wales continued to be a foreign and hostile colony, ruled and to an extent subjected but never quite controlled by Tudor power" (Mullaney 1988: 77; 162, n.47).

7 Cf. Stephen Greenblatt's exposition of the ways the allurements of the Bower of Bliss threaten the "civilization – which for Spenser is achieved only through renunciation and the constant exercise of power" and the analogies he draws between European responses to the natives of Africa and North America and English colonial struggles in Ireland (Greenblatt 1980: 173–4, 179–92). In these accounts, as in the story from the *Columbian Magazine* cited in note 5 above, contact with native people results in a loss of masculinity.

12 HENRY V

1 Our discussion of *Henry V* is based on the folio text of the play, not on the much shorter quarto version published in 1600. The status of the quarto text is uncertain. Traditionally it has been regarded as a memorial reconstruction of the folio text or as a version shortened for performance; recent editors have suggested that it may record some authorial revisions or cuts made for political, rather than theatrical, reasons (Patterson 1989: 71–92). In the quarto all the lines spoken by the Chorus are missing, including the prologue and epilogue; also missing are the first scene between Canterbury and Ely; much of the dialogue involving Jamy and Macmorris; Henry's speech in III.i, "Once more into the breach"; much of Henry's speech threatening the sack of Harfleur; much of the action in the French camp; much of the final wooing scene; and a number of other passages too numerous to list. The Dolphin's part is reduced throughout. As in the historical sources, he does not appear at Agincourt (although he does in the folio), and his praise of his horse in III.vii is assigned to Bourbon. Most modern editors use the folio text as the basis for their editions, and in what follows we use it as the basis for our analysis, largely because it is the fullest version of the text and the one that over time has had the broadest cultural impact.

2 For another Shakespearean example of the traditional analogy that associated a rider's control of his horse, a governor's control of the state, and a man's control of his passions, see *Measure for Measure*, I.ii.159–62, when Claudio speculates that "the body public be/ A horse whereon the governor doth ride,/ Who, newly in the seat, that it may know/ He can command, lets it straight feel the spur," and II.iv.159–60, when Angelo, having yielded to his lust for Isabella, says, "I have begun,/ And now I give my sensual race the rein."

3 By the time Beaumont wrote *The Knight of the Burning Pestle* – no earlier than 1607, according to Rabkin (1976: 2: 518) – Hotspur's devotion to chivalric honor was apparently sufficiently well established as an object

of ridicule that Beaumont could have Rafe recite Hotspur's lines from I.iii.201 ff. ("By heaven, methinks it were an easy leap . . .") as an example of a "huffing part" and an attempt to get a laugh from the theater audience. See Beaumont 1613: Induction, 84–8.

4 As Stephen Greenblatt points out, "A heroic encounter is a struggle for honor and must conform to the code which requires that the combatants be of roughly equal station. . . . the symbolic economics of appropriation suggested by the Church of England hymn: 'Conquering Kings their titles take/ From the foes they captive make'" (Greenblatt 1983: 10).

5 Maguire (1992) identifies numerous resemblances between the three Kates. In addition to the ones I have already cited, she notes that both Katherine Minola and Hotspur's wife are described as hanging on their husbands' necks (*Shrew*: II.i.308–9; *Henry IV, II*: II.iii.44) and that Henry V claims that the French language "will hang upon [his] tongue like a new-married wife about her husband's neck, hardly to be shook off" (V.ii.179–81). She also points out that all three husbands "view women as adjuncts to their relationships with their horses" and that "both Petruchio and Henry V demand that their brides kiss them in public, a request which is initially resisted as being contrary to custom" (138).

6 The Tailhook scandal resulted from an attempted cover-up at the highest levels of the American navy of sexual assaults upon women by naval officers at their 1991 convention in Las Vegas, Nevada.

7 Native men had far fewer opportunities to rape European women than European male colonizers had to rape native women. Moreover, the North American woodland tribes that English settlers encountered in Virginia and New England, unlike their European colonizers, did not have a rape culture. Mary Rowlandson's account of her four-month captivity by Indians is a vivid case in point. Rowlandson's insistence that although she was starved and beaten, she was never sexually threatened by her captors reveals a profound difference between her own culture and that of the Indians: Rowlandson had assumed, and she knew that her readers would assume, that she would "naturally" be raped by her captors (Rowlandson 1682: 360–1).

8 A comparison between Shakespeare's text and its source at this point is instructive. Shakespeare's account of Jack Cade's rebellion draws heavily on accounts of the even earlier Peasants' Revolt in the time of Richard II. Cade's fleeting reference to the sexual oppressions of the nobility is the only trace of a detailed account that Holinshed supplies as a possible explanation for the beginnings of the rebellion: Parliament having passed a levy on every man and woman above the age of sixteen, a tax gatherer came to the house of John Tiler, the man who, as leader of the revolt, was to assume the name of Jack Straw. Tiler had a "a faire young maid to his daughter," but Tiler's wife informed the officer that the girl was not yet of age to be taxed. Holinshed notes that the tax "monie was in common speech said to be due for all those that were undergrowne, bicause that yoong persons as well of the man as of the womankind, comming to the age of fourteene or fifteene yeares, have commonlie haire growing foorth about those privie parts, which for honesties sake nature hath taught us to cover and keepe secret. The officer therefore not satisfied with the

mothers excuse, said he would feele whether hir daughter were of lawfull age or not, and therewith began to misuse the maid, and search further than honestie would have permitted." The cries of the outraged mother bring her husband home, whereupon he kills the officer and the rebellion begins. An alternative explanation, also supplied by Holinshed, states that the rebellion was started by "one Thomas Baker" after "one of the kings servants named John Leg, with three of his fellowes, practiced to feele young maids whether they were undergrowne" (Holinshed 1587: 2: 735–6).

The only vestige of these accounts in Shakespeare's text is the fleeting reference to sexual oppression in the list of unsubstantiated charges against the nobility that Cade uses to stir the mob to rebellion. The anonymous play *The Life and Death of Jacke Strawe* (1593), by contrast, opens with a confrontation between Strawe and the tax collector over the very incident that Holinshed describes. Strawe denounces the collector for his "abuse [of] the poore people of the Countrie./ But chiefest of all vilde villaine as thou art,/ To play so unmanly and beastly a part,/ As to search my daughter thus in my presence" (*Life* 1593: I.i.25–8).

9 Wolfthal (1993) shows that "Northern European [pictorial] images of rape undergo a change in tone and content over the course of the fifteenth and early sixteenth centuries. Early renderings more clearly condemn the rapist" (57). In later paintings, "the 'victim' is shown as a willing, in fact, an eager partner," and the rape is shown "simply as an amorous affair, with no hint of violence." "[B]eginning in the late fifteenth century," women "in Northern European art ... are increasingly depicted as seductresses. Even models of chastity become temptresses. For example the heroine Tomyris, traditionally represented fully clothed, is by the turn of the century shown nude" (60). Moreover, while earlier representations of rapes tend to focus on the victims, "the rapist is now the focus" (62).

10 *Henry V* is also more modern in its focus on the king's character. Richmond's character is not an issue in *Richard III*, but the issue of Henry's character is foregrounded in both parts of Henry IV as well as *Henry V*, and it is represented in prototypically modern terms. Both the dispute with Williams in IV.i. and its resolution in IV.viii, for instance, are based on the public/private binary, which divides "Henry the king" from "Henry the man." The modernity of this issue is attested by the fact that the enigma of Henry's characterization has dominated modern critical discussions of the plays.

11 The same restrictions apply, of course, to theatrical representations. On March 18, 1993, the *Philadelphia Inquirer* reported a lawsuit to force the American National Park Service to permit women to participate in re-enactments of Civil War battlefields. The plaintiff in the suit was able to produce documentation on about 125 women who actually enlisted during the war under male aliases, but the officials of the Park services told her, "We don't allow women in uniform here" and informed her that she could only participate if she removed the uniform and took the part of one of the "local farm women or visiting ladies seeking loved ones."

12 Like many other women, the historical Elinor also fought in the Crusades (Contamine 1984: 241; Salmonson 1992: 79; Kelly 1957: 45).

13 As Simon Shepherd points out (1981: 16), "the connection of Amazons with lust has a long history." See also Loomba (1989: 47) and Shapiro (1987).

14 As Thomas Laqueur has argued, the dominant gender ideology at the time this play was written was not yet grounded in embodied sexual difference, for the Galenic conception of male and female bodies as essentially homologous meant that biological sex did not yet "provide a solid foundation for the cultural category of gender but constantly threatens to subvert it" (1990: 124).

15 Here too Shakespeare anticipates some of the modern narratives of performative masculinity described by Jeffords (1991). In the 1986 film *Opposing Force* she points out that "As viewers we are asked to watch the performance of rape from the point of view of the man who is not raping, the 'friend'" (113), but the enemy–friend binary is, by the logic of performative masculinity, constantly subject to redefinition as benevolent male figures become rapists and rapists reform (111–15).

16 The same trope is suggested in the representation of England in I.ii.158 as a "mourning widow," subject to invasion by the Scot "with . . . fullness of his force" (150), but it is much less fully and consistently developed. Lines 155 and 158 use feminine pronouns for England, but the "her" in line 163 did not appear until the eighteenth century. The folio has "their," and the quartos have "your."

17 This transaction transforms the crown into private property that the king can leave to Henry even though the Dolphin is his son (Hodgdon 1991: 203). This is in sharp contrast to the negative representations in earlier plays, such as *Richard II* and *Henry VI, Part III*, of royal attempts to interrupt the line of patrimonial succession by bequeathing the crown to usurpers.

18 For many other examples of this coupling, see Wofford (1992), who demonstrates that "the representation of scenes of violence against women" as wedding entertainment or on wedding gifts "is attested to rather widely in early modern culture" (194 *et passim*). Especially striking is her description of the popularity of rape scenes as decorations on the wedding chests (*cassoni*) used in fifteenth-century Florentine marriages. Catherine Belsey has found an interesting counterpart to the *cassoni* in a needlework panel representing Tereus and Procne which dates from the end of the sixteenth century (private communication).

BIBLIOGRAPHY

Adams, H. (ed.) (1992) *Critical Theory Since Plato*, New York: Harcourt.

Adelman, J. (1992) *Suffocating Mothers: Fantasies of Maternal Origin in Shakespeare's Plays, Hamlet to The Tempest*, London: Routledge.

Amin, S. (1989) *Eurocentrism*, trans. Russell Moore, New York: Monthly Review Press.

Anderson, B. (1983) *Imagined Communities: Reflections on the Origin and Spread of Nationalism*, London: Verso.

Anderson, P. (1974) *Lineages of the Absolutist State*, London: New Left Books.

Aristotle (*c*. 330 BC) *Poetics*, trans. S. H. Butcher, in Adams (1992): 50–66.

Austern, L. (1989) '"Sing Againe Syren': Female Musicians and Sexual Enchantment in Elizabethan Life and Literature," *Renaissance Quarterly* 42: 420–48.

Balibar, E. and Wallerstein, I. (1991) *Race, Nation, Class: Ambiguous Identities*, London: Verso.

Barasch, F. (no date) "The Lady's not for Spurning: An Investigation of Italian Actresses and their Roles in Commedia dell' Arte as Shakespeare's Inspiration," unpublished paper.

Barish, J. (1981) *The Antitheatrical Prejudice*, Berkeley: University of California Press.

Barnes, C. (1995) "Troupe's 'Henry VI' Fit for a King," *New York Post*, March 8.

Beaumont, F. (1607) *The Knight of the Burning Pestle*, in Fraser and Rabkin (1986) 2: 517–48.

Belsey, C. (1985a) "Disrupting Sexual Difference: Meaning and Gender in the Comedies," in *Alternative Shakespeares*, ed. John Drakakis, London: Methuen: 166–90.

—— (1985b) *The Subject of Tragedy: Identity and Difference in Renaissance Drama*, London: Methuen.

Berkowitz, G. (1996) "Richard II," *Shakespeare Bulletin: A Journal of Performance Criticism and Scholarship* 14: 9.

Berman, R. (1962) "Fathers and Sons in the *Henry VI* Plays," *Shakespeare Quarterly* 13: 487–97.

Bevington, D. (1966) "The Domineering Female in 1 *Henry VI*," *Shakespeare Studies* 2: 51–8.

Black, J. (1979) *"Henry IV*: A World of Figures There," in *Shakespeare: The Theatrical Dimension*, ed. P. C. McGuire and D. A. Samuelson, New York: AMS Press: 165–83.

Bray, A. (1988) *Homosexuality in Renaissance England*, 2nd edn, London: Gay Men's Press.

Bredbeck, G. (1991) *Sodomy and Interpretation: Marlowe to Milton*, Ithaca: Cornell University Press.

Brenner, R. (1993) *Merchants and Revolution: Commercial Change, Political Conflict, and London's Overseas Traders, 1550–1653*, Princeton: Princeton University Press.

Brooke, N. (1984) "Reflecting Gems and Dead Bones: Tragedy Versus History in *Richard III*," in *Shakespeare's Wide and Universal Stage*, ed. C. B. Cox and D. J. Palmer, Manchester: Manchester University Press: 104–16.

Burckhardt, S. (1968) "'I am but Shadow of Myself': Ceremony and Design in *1 Henry VI*," in *Shakespearean Meanings*, Princeton: Princeton University Press: 47–77.

Bushnell, R. W. (1990) *Tragedies of Tyrants: Political Thought and Theater in the English Renaissance*, Ithaca: Cornell University Press.

Cairncross, A. S. (ed.) (1957) *The Second Part of King Henry VI*, London: Methuen.

—— (ed.) (1962) *The First Part of King Henry VI*, London: Methuen.

—— (ed.) (1964) *The Third Part of King Henry VI*, London: Methuen.

Calderwood, J. (1971) *Shakespearean Metadrama*, Minneapolis: University of Minnesota Press.

Callaghan, D. (1989) *Woman and Gender in Renaissance Tragedy*, Atlantic Highlands, N. J.: Humanities Press International.

Cartelli, T. (1994) "Jack Cade in the Garden: Class Consciousness and Class Conflict in *2 Henry VI*," in *Enclosure Acts: Sexuality, Property and Culture in Early Modern England*, ed. Richard Burt and John Michael Archer, Ithaca: Cornell University Press: 48–67.

Castiglione, B. (1561) *The Book of the Courtier*, trans. T. Hoby, London.

Cavendish, M. (1664) *Sociable Letters*: CCXI, in *The Riverside Shakespeare*, ed. Evans *et al.* (1974): 1847.

Chambers, E. K. (1923) *The Elizabethan Stage*, 4 vols, Oxford: Clarendon Press.

Churchill, W. (1940) Speech to the House of Commons, and radio broadcast.

Clark A. (1919) *Working Life of Women in the Seventeenth Century*; (1992) reprint, London: Routledge.

Contamine, P. (1984) *War in the Middle Ages*, trans. Michael Jones, Oxford: Basil Blackwell.

Cook, A. J. (1977) "'Bargaines of Incontinencie': Bawdy Behavior in the Playhouses," *Shakespeare Studies* 10: 271–90.

Corbet, R. (1618–21) *Iter Boreale* in *The Poems of Richard Corbet, Late Bishop of Oxford and of Norwich (1807)*, ed. Octavius Gilchrist, London: Longman, Hurst, Rees, and Orme.

Curren-Aquino, D. T. (ed.) (1989) *King John: New Perspectives*, Newark: University of Delaware Press.

Dash, I. (1981) *Wooing Wedding and Power: Women in Shakespeare's Plays*, New York: Columbia University Press.

Dean, P. (1990) "Forms of Time: Some Elizabethan Two-Part History Plays," *Renaissance Studies* 4: 410–30.

Disch, T. M. (1995) "Regarding 'Henry' – Highly," *New York Daily News*, March 7.

Dolan, F. E. (1994) *Dangerous Familiars: Representations of Domestic Crime in England 1550–1700*, Ithaca: Cornell University Press.

Donaldson, P. (1991) "Taking on Shakespeare: Kenneth Branagh's *Henry V*," *Shakespeare Quarterly* 42: 60–71.

Drayton, M. (1961) *The Works of Michael Drayton*, vol. 2, ed. J. W. Hebel, Oxford: Basil Blackwell.

Dusinberre, J. (1990) "*King John* and Embarrassing Women," *Shakespeare Survey* 42: 37–52.

E., T. (1632) *The Lawes Resolutions of Womens Rights*.

Eggert, K. (1994) "Nostalgia and the Not Yet Late Queen: Refusing Female Rule in *Henry V*", *English Literary History* 61: 523–55.

Evans, G. B. *et al.* (eds) (1974) *The Riverside Shakespeare*, Boston: Houghton Mifflin.

Ferris, D. (1981) "Elizabeth I and *Richard II*: Portraits in 'Masculine' and 'Feminine' Princes," *International Journal of Women's Studies* 4: 10–18.

Fleming, J. (1989) "*The French Garden*: An Introduction to Women's French," *English Literary History* 56: 19–51.

Foucault, M. (1979) "What is an Author?" in *Textual Strategies: Perspectives in Post-Structuralist Criticism*, ed. J. V. Harari, Ithaca: Cornell University Press:141–60.

Forse, J. H. (1993) "Why Boys for (wo)Men's Roles? or Pardon the Delay, 'the Queen was Shaving,'" *Selected Papers from the West Virginia Shakespeare and Renaissance Association*, 15: 6–27.

Fraser, A., and Rabkin N. (eds) (1986) *Drama of the English Renaissance*, 2 vols, New York: Macmillan.

Frye, S. (1992) "The Myth of Elizabeth at Tilbury," *The Sixteenth Century Journal* 23: 95–114.

Furness, H. H., Jr (ed.) (1908) The Variorum edition of Shakespeare's *Richard III*, Philadelphia: Lippincott.

Geoffrey of Monmouth (*c.* 1136) *Historia Regum Britanniae*, translated as *The History of the Kings of Britain* (1966), trans. L. Thorpe, Harmondsworth: Penguin Books.

Gifford, G. (1587) *A Discourse of the subtill Practices of Devilles by Witches and Sorcerers*, London.

Gilbert, A. (ed.) (1962) *Literary Criticism: Plato to Dryden*, Detroit: Wayne State University Press.

Girouard, M. (1978) *Life in the English Country House: A Social and Architectural History*, New Haven: Yale University Press.

Goldberg, J. (1992) *Sodometries: Renaissance Texts, Modern Sexualities*, Stanford: Stanford University Press.

Gosson, S. (1579) *The Schoole of Abuse*, London.

—— (1582) *Playes Confuted in five Actions*, in Chambers (1923) 3: 213–19.

Greenblatt, S. (1980) *Renaissance Self-Fashioning: From More to Shakespeare*, Chicago: University of Chicago Press.
—— (1983) "Murdering Peasants: Status, Genre, and the Representation of Rebellion," *Representations* 1: 1–29.
Greene, R. (1592) *Greene's Groatsworth of Wit*, in Chambers (1923) 4: 240–2.
Greenfeld, L. (1992) *Nationalism: Five Roads to Modernity*, Cambridge, Mass.: Harvard University Press.
Gurr, A. (ed.) (1984) *King Richard II*, Cambridge: Cambridge University Press.
—— (1988) *Playgoing in Shakespeare's London*, New York: Cambridge University Press.
—— (1992) *The Shakespearean Stage 1574–1642*, 3rd edn, Cambridge: Cambridge University Press.
Hacker, B. C. (1981) "Women and Military Institutions in Early Modern Europe: A Reconnaissance," *Signs* 6: 643–71.
Hall, E. (1548) *The Union of the Two Noble and Illustre Famelies of Lancastre &Yorke*; (1809) reprint, London: J. Johnson *et al.*
Hall, K. F. (1996) *Things of Darkness; Economies of Race and Gender in Early Modern England*, Ithaca: Cornell University Press.
Haller, W. and M. (1941–2) "The Puritan Art of Love," *The Huntington Library Quarterly* 5: 235–72.
Halliday, F. E. (1958) *Shakespeare and His Critics*; (1963) reprint, New York: Schocken Books.
—— (1964) *A Shakespeare Companion 1564–1964*, Baltimore: Penguin Books.
Halpern, R. (1991) *The Poetics of Primitive Accumulation: English Renaissance Culture and the Genealogy of Capital*, Ithaca: Cornell University Press.
Hammond, A. (ed.) (1981) *King Richard III*, Arden edition, London: Methuen.
Hampton, W. (1995) "3 into 2: History Plays Rearranged," *New York Times*, March 7.
Harbage, A. (1941) *Shakespeare's Audience*, New York: Columbia University Press.
Harington, Sir J. (1591) *A Preface, or rather a Briefe Apologie of Poetrie*, in Smith (1904) 2: 194–222.
Harrison, W. (1587) *The Description of England*; (1994) reprint, ed. Georges Edelen, Washington, D.C. and New York: The Folger Shakespeare Library and Dover Publications.
Hattaway, M. (ed.) (1990) *The First Part of King Henry VI*, Cambridge: Cambridge University Press.
—— (ed.) (1991) *The Second Part of King Henry VI*, Cambridge: Cambridge University Press.
—— (ed.) (1993) *The Third Part of King Henry VI*, Cambridge: Cambridge University Press.
Hawkes, T. (1986) *That Shakespeherian Rag: Essays on a Critical Process*, London: Methuen.
Helgerson, R. (1992) *Forms of Nationhood: The Elizabethan Writing of England*, Chicago: University of Chicago Press.

Helms, L. (1992) '"The High Roman Fashion': Sacrifice, Suicide, and the Shakespearean Stage," *PMLA* 97: 554–65.

Hemingway, S. B. (ed.) (1936) *A New Variorum Edition of Henry the Fourth Part I*, Philadelphia, Lippincott.

Henderson, K. and McManus, B. (eds) (1985) *Half Humankind: Contexts and Texts of the Controversy about Women in England, 1540–1640*, Urbana: University of Illinois Press.

Hendricks, M. and Parker, P. (eds) (1994) *Women, 'Race,' and Writing in the Early Modern Period*, London: Routledge.

Hennessy, R. (1993) *Materialist Feminism and the Politics of Discourse*, London: Routledge.

Heywood, T. (1612) *An Apology for Actors*, London.

Highley, C. (1990) "Wales, Ireland, and *1 Henry IV*," *Renaissance Drama* new series, 21: 91–114.

Hobday, C. C. (1979) "Clouted Shoon and Leather Aprons: Shakespeare and the Egalitarian Tradition," *Renaissance and Modern Studies* 23: 63–78.

Hodgdon, B. (1991) *The End Crowns All: Closure and Contradiction in Shakespeare's History*, Princeton: Princeton University Press.

Hogrefe, P. (1975) *Tudor Women: Commoners and Queens*, Ames, Iowa: Iowa State University Press.

Holderness, G. (1985) *Shakespeare's History*, New York: St. Martin's Press.

Holinshed, R. (1587) *Chronicles of England, Scotland and Ireland*, 6 vols, 2nd edn; (1808) reprint, London: J. Johnson *et al.*

Honigmann, E. A. J. (ed.) (1967) *King John*, Arden edition, London: Methuen.

Howard, J. E. (1994) *The Stage and Social Struggle in Early Modern England*, London: Routledge.

—— (forthcoming) "Other Englands: The View from the Heywood History Play," in *Other Voices, Other Views: Expanding the Canon in English Renaissance Studies*, ed. Helen Ostovich and Graham Roebuck.

Howard, J. E. and O'Connor, M. F. (eds) (1987) *Shakespeare Reproduced: The Text in History and Ideology*, London: Methuen.

Howell, M. (1986) *Women, Production, and Patriarchy in Late Medieval Cities*, Chicago: University of Chicago Press.

Humphreys, A. (ed.) (1966) *King Henry IV, Part II*, Arden edition, London: Methuen.

Hyde, T. (1985) "Boccaccio: The Genealogies of Myth," *PMLA* 100: 737–45.

Jackson, G. B. (1988) "Topical Ideology: Witches, Amazons, and Shakespeare's Joan of Arc," *English Literary Renaissance* 18: 40–65.

Jeffords, S. (1989) *The Remasculinization of America: Gender and the Vietnam War*, Bloomington: Indiana University Press.

—— (1991) "Performative Masculinities, or, 'After a Few Times You Won't Be Afraid of Rape at All'," *Discourse* 13: 102–18.

Jones, A. and Stallybrass, P. (1992) "Dismantling Irena: The Sexualizing of Ireland in Early Modern England," in Parker *et al.* (1992): 157–71.

Jones, E. (1961) "Stuart Cymbeline," *Essays in Criticism* 11: 84–99.

Kahn, C. (1981) *Man's Estate: Masculine Identity in Shakespeare*, Berkeley: University of California Press.

Kastan, D. S. (1982) "Shakespeare and 'The Way of Womenkind'," *Daedalus* 111: 115–30.

—— (1986) "Proud Majesty Made a Subject: Shakespeare and the Spectacle of Rule," *Shakespeare Quarterly* 37: 459–75.

Kelly, A. (1957) *Eleanor of Aquitaine and the Four Kings*, New York: Vintage.

Kolin, P. C. (1991) *Shakespeare and Feminist Criticism: An Annotated Bibliography and Commentary*, New York and London: Garland Publishing.

Korda, N. (1995) "Household Property, Stage Property: Henslowe as Pawnbroker," unpublished paper.

Laqueur, T. (1990) *Making Sex: Body and Gender from the Greeks to Freud*, Cambridge, Mass.: Harvard University Press.

Lee, P. (1986) "Reflections of Power: Margaret of Anjou and the Dark Side of Queenship," *Renaissance Quarterly* 39: 183–217.

Leggatt, A. (1988) *Shakespeare's Political Drama: The History Plays and the Roman Plays*, London: Routledge.

Levin, R. (1989) "Women in the Renaissance Theatre Audience," *Shakespeare Quarterly* 40: 165–74.

Levine, L. (1994) *Men in Women's Clothing: Anti-theatricality and Effeminization 1579–1642*, Cambridge: Cambridge University Press.

Levy, F. J. (1967) *Tudor Historical Thought*, San Marino, Calif.: Huntington Library.

—— (1990) Review of Stanley Mendyk, *Speculum Britanniae: Regional Study, Antiquarianism and Science in Britain to 1700*, in *Renaissance Quarterly* 43: 869–70.

The Life and Death of Jacke Straw (1595) London: John Danter.

Lindenberger, H. (1975) *Historical Drama: The Relation of Literature and Reality*, Chicago: University of Chicago Press.

Loomba, A. (1989) *Gender, Race, Renaissance Drama*, New York: St. Martin's Press.

McLuskie, K. (1985) "The Patriarchal Bard: Feminist Criticism and Shakespeare: *King Lear* and *Measure for Measure*," in *Political Shakespeare: New Essays in Cultural Materialism*, ed. J. Dollimore and A. Sinfield, Ithaca: Cornell University Press: 88–108.

—— (1989) *Renaissance Dramatists*, Atlantic Highlands, N.J.: Humanities Press International.

McMillin, S. (1984) "Shakespeare's *Richard II*: Eyes of Sorrow, Eyes of Desire," *Shakespeare Quarterly* 35: 40–52.

Maguire, L. E. (1992) "'Household Kates': Chez Petruchio, Percy and Plantagenet," in *Gloriana's Face: Women, Public and Private, in the English Renaissance*, ed. S. P. Cerasano and M. Wynne-Davies, Detroit: Wayne State University Press: 129–65.

Manley, L. (1983) "From Matron to Monster: Tudor–Stuart London and the Languages of Urban Description," in *The Historical Renaissance: New Essays on Tudor and Stuart Literature and Culture*, ed. H. Dubrow and R. Strier, Chicago: University of Chicago Press: 347–74.

Manning, R. (1988) *Village Revolts: Social Protest and Popular Disturbances in England 1509–1640*, Oxford: Clarendon Press.

Marcus, L. (1988) *Puzzling Shakespeare: Local Reading and its Discontents*, Berkeley: University of California Press.

Meres, F. (1598) *Palladis Tamia, Wits Treasury*, in Smith (1904) 2: 309–24.

MLA International Bibliography of Books and Articles on the Modern Languages and Literatures, online version (1994), New York: Modern Language Association of America.

Modleski, T. (1991) *Feminism without Women: Culture and Criticism in a "Postfeminist" Age*, New York and London: Routledge.

Montrose, L. A. (1980) "The Purpose of Playing: Reflections on a Shakespearean Anthropology," *Helios*, new series 7(2): 51–74.

—— (1983) "'Shaping Fantasies': Figurations of Gender and Power in Elizabethan Culture," *Representations* 1: 61–94.

—— (1991) "The Work of Gender in the Discourse of Discovery," *Representations* 33: 1–41.

Mullaney, S. (1988) *The Place of the Stage: License, Play and Power in Renaissance England*, Chicago: University of Chicago Press.

Nashe, T. (1592) *Pierce Penilesse his Supplication to the Divell*, in Chambers (1923) 4: 238–40.

Neale, J. (1934) *Queen Elizabeth I*; (1967) reprint, London: Jonathan Cape.

Neill, M. (1994) "Broken English and Broken Irish: Nation, Language, and the Optic of Power in Shakespeare's Histories," *Shakespeare Quarterly* 45: 1–32.

Newman, K. (1991) *Fashioning Femininity and English Renaissance Drama*, Chicago: University of Chicago Press.

Orgel, S. (1989) "Nobody's Perfect: Or Why Did the English Stage Take Boys for Women?" *South Atlantic Quarterly* 88: 7–29.

Orlin, L. (1994) *Private Matters and Public Culture in Post-Reformation England*, Ithaca: Cornell University Press.

Ornstein, R. (1972) *A Kingdom for a Stage: The Achievement of Shakespeare's History Plays*, Cambridge: Harvard University Press.

Osborne, L. E. (1985) "Crisis of Degree in Shakespeare's *Henriad*," *Studies in English Literature 1500–1900* 25: 337–59.

—— (1991) "Female Audiences and Female Authority in *The Knight of the Burning Pestle*," *Exemplaria: A Journal of Theory in Medieval and Renaissance Studies* 3: 491–517.

Parker, A., Russo, M., Sommer, D., and Yaeger, P. (eds) (1992) *Nationalisms and Sexualities*, New York: Routledge.

Paster, G. K. (1993) *The Body Embarrassed: Drama and the Disciplines of Shame in Early Modern England*, Ithaca: Cornell University Press.

Pateman, C. (1988) *The Sexual Contract*, Stanford: Stanford University Press.

Patterson, A. (1989) *Shakespeare and the Popular Voice*, Oxford: Basil Blackwell.

—— (1993) "Rethinking Tudor Historiography," *South Atlantic Quarterly* 92: 185–208.

—— (1994) *Reading Holinshed's Chronicles*, Chicago: University of Chicago Press.

Plato, (c. 373 BC) *Republic*, trans. Benjamin Jowett, in Adams (1992): 18–38.

Pugliatti, P. (1992) "'More than History can Pattern': The Jack Cade Rebellion in Shakespeare's *Henry VI, 2*," *Journal of Medieval and Renaissance Studies* 22: 451–78.

Rabkin, N. and Fraser, R. (eds) (1976) *Drama of the English Renaissance*, 2 vols, New York: Macmillan.

Rackin, P. (1987) "Androgyny, Mimesis, and the Marriage of the Boy Heroine on the English Renaissance Stage," *PMLA* 102: 29–41.

—— (1990) *Stages of History: Shakespeare's English Chronicles*, Ithaca: Cornell University Press.

—— (1992) "Historical Difference/Sexual Difference" in *Privileging Gender in Early Modern Britain*, ed. J. Brink, Kirksville, Mo.: Sixteenth-Century Journal Publishers: 37–63.

Riggs, D. (1971) *Shakespeare's Heroical Histories: Henry VI and Its Literary Tradition*, Cambridge, Mass.: Harvard University Press.

Rose, M. B. (1988) *The Expense of Spirit: Love and Sexuality in English Renaissance Drama*, Ithaca: Cornell University Press.

Rowlandson, M. (1682) *A Narrative of the Captivity and Restauration of Mrs. Mary Rowlandson*, in *So Dreadful a Judgment: Puritan Responses to King Philip's War* (1978) ed. R. Slotkin and J. K. Folsom, Middleton, Conn.: Wesleyan University Press: 315–69.

Rubin, G. (1975) "The Traffic in Women: Notes on the 'Political Economy' of Sex," in *Towards an Anthropology of Women*, ed. R. Reiter, New York: Monthly Review Press: 157–210.

Ryan, L. (ed.) (1989) *Henry VI, Parts I, II, III*, rev. edn, New York: New American Library.

Saccio, P. (1977) *Shakespeare's English Kings: History, Chronicle, and Drama*, New York: Oxford University Press.

Salmonson, J. A. (1992) *The Encyclopedia of Amazons: Women Warriors from Antiquity to the Modern Era*, New York: Doubleday.

Sanders, N. (ed.) (1981) *The First Part of King Henry the Sixth*, Harmondsworth: Penguin Books.

Schochet, G. (1975) *Patriarchalism in Political Thought: The Authoritarian Family and Political Speculation and Attitudes Especially in Seventeenth-Century England*, Oxford: Basil Blackwell.

Schoenbaum, S. (1978) *William Shakespeare: A Compact Documentary Life*, Oxford: Oxford University Press.

Scot, R. (1584) *The Discoverie of Witchcraft*, London.

Sen Gupta, S. (1964) *Shakespeare's Historical Plays*, New York: Oxford University Press.

Shaaber, M. A. (ed.) (1940) *A New Variorum Edition of The Second Part of Henry the Fourth*, Philadelphia and London: Lippincott.

Shapiro, S. C. (1987) "Amazons, Hermaphrodites, and Plain Monsters: The 'Masculine' Woman in English Satire and Social Criticism from 1580–1640," *Atlantis* 13: 65–76.

Shepherd, S. (1981) *Amazons and Warrior Women: Varieties of Feminism in Seventeenth-Century Drama*, Brighton: Harvester.

Sidney, Sir P. (1595) *An Apologie for Poetrie*, in Smith (1904) 1: 148–207.

Sinfield, A. (1992) *Faultlines: Cultural Materialism and the Politics of Dissident Reading*, Berkeley: University of California Press.

Smith, A. G. R. (1984) *The Emergence of a Nation State: The Commonwealth of England, 1529–1660*, London and New York: Longman.

Smith, G. C. (ed.) (1904) *Elizabethan Critical Essays*, 2 vols, Oxford: Oxford University Press.

Spevack, M. (1968) *A Complete and Systematic Concordance to the Works of Shakespeare*, vol. 2, Hildesheim: Georg Olms.

Stallybrass, P. (1982) "*Macbeth* and Witchcraft" in *Focus on Macbeth*, ed. J. R. Brown, London: Routledge and Kegan Paul.

Stokes, J. (1993) "Women and Mimesis in Medieval and Renaissance Somerset (and Beyond)," *Comparative Drama* 27: 176–96.

Stone, L. (1966) "Social Mobility in England, 1500–1700," *Past and Present* 33: 15–55.

—— (1977) *The Family, Sex and Marriage in England, 1500–1800*, New York: Harper and Row.

Taylor, G. (ed.) (1984) *Henry V*, Oxford: Oxford University Press.

—— (1995) "Shakespeare and Others: The Authorship of *Henry the Sixth, Part I*," *Medieval and Renaissance Drama in England* 7 (1995): 145–205.

Thirsk, J. (1995) "England's Provinces: Did they Serve or Drive Material London?" unpublished paper.

Thompson, A. (1988) "'The Warrant of Womanhood': Shakespeare and Feminist Criticism," in *The Shakespeare Myth*, ed. Graham Holderness, Manchester: Manchester University Press: 74–88.

Tillyard, E. (1944) *Shakespeare's History Plays*, London: Chatto and Windus.

Traub, V. (1992) *Desire and Anxiety: Circulations of Sexuality in Shakespearean Drama*, London: Routledge.

The Troublesome Raigne of John, King of England (1591), London: Sampson Clarke.

The True Tragedy of Richard III (1594), London: Thomas Creede; (1929) reprint, Oxford: Malone Society.

Underdown, D. E. (1985) "The Taming of the Scold: The Enforcement of Patriarchal Authority in Early Modern England," in *Order and Disorder in Early Modern England*, ed. A. Fletcher and J. Stevenson, Cambridge: Cambridge University Press: 116–36.

Ure, P. (ed.) (1961) *Richard II*, Arden edition, London: Methuen.

Urkowitz, S. (1988a) "Five Women Eleven Ways: Changing Images of Shakespearean Characters in the Earliest Texts," in *Images of Shakespeare: Proceedings of the Third Congress of the International Shakespeare Association, 1986*, ed. W. Habicht, D. J. Palmer, and R. Pringle, Cranberry, N.J.: Associated University Presses: 292–304.

—— (1988b) "'If I Mistake in those Foundations which I Build Upon': Peter Alexander's Textual Analysis of *Henry VI Parts 2 and 3*," *English Literary Renaissance* 18: 230–56.

Vaughan, V. M. (1989) "*King John*: A Study in Subversion and Containment," in Curren-Aquino (1989): 62–75.

Vega, L. de (1609) *The New Art of Making Comedies*, trans. Olga Marx Perlzweig, in Gilbert (1962): 541–48.

A Warning for Fair Women: A Critical Edition, ed. Charles Dale Cannon (1975), The Hague: Mouton.

Watson, D. G. (1990) *Shakespeare's Early History Plays: Politics at Play on the Elizabethan Stage*, Athens: University of Georgia Press.

Wayne, V. (ed.) (1991) *The Matter of Difference: Materialist Feminist Criticism of Shakespeare*, Ithaca: Cornell University Press.

Webbe, W. (1586) *A Discourse of English Poetrie*, in Smith (1904) 1: 226–302.

Weimann, R. (1978; paper 1987) *Shakespeare and the Popular Tradition in the Theater: Studies in the Social Dimension of Dramatic Form and Function*, ed. Robert Schwartz, Baltimore: The Johns Hopkins University Press.

—— (1988) "Bifold Authority in Shakespeare's Theatre," *Shakespeare Quarterly* 39: 401–17.

Weisner, M. (1993) *Women and Gender in Early Modern Europe*, Cambridge: Cambridge University Press.

Wells, S., and Taylor, G. (1987) *William Shakespeare: A Textual Companion*, Oxford: Clarendon Press.

Wikander, M. (1986) *The Play of Truth and State: Historical Drama from Shakespeare to Brecht*, Baltimore: The Johns Hopkins University Press.

Wilcox, L. (1985) "Katherine of France as Victim and Bride," *Shakespeare Studies* 17: 61–76.

Williamson, M. (1986) *The Patriarchy of Shakespeare's Comedies*, Detroit: Wayne State University Press.

Willis, D. (1995) *Malevolent Nurture: Witch-Hunting and Maternal Power in Early Modern England*, Ithaca: Cornell University Press.

Wilson, R. (1993) *Will Power: Essays on Shakespearean Authority*, Detroit: Wayne State University Press.

Wofford, S. L. (1992) "The Social Aesthetics of Rape: Closural Violence in Boccacio and Botticelli," in *Creative Imitation: New Essays on Renaissance Literature in Honor of Thomas M. Greene* (Medieval and Renaissance Texts and Studies 95), ed. D. Quint, M. M. Ferguson, G. W. Pigman III, and W. A. Rebhorn, Binghamton, N.Y.: State University of New York Press: 189–238.

Wolfthal, D. (1993) "'A Hue and a Cry': Medieval Rape Imagery and its Transformation," *Art Bulletin* 75: 39–64.

Womack, P. (1992) "Imagining Communities: Theatres and the English Nation in the Sixteenth Century," in *Culture and History 1350–1600: Essays on English Communities, Identities, and Writing*, ed. David Aers, Detroit: Wayne State University Press.

Yates, F. (1975) *Majesty and Magic in Shakespeare's Last Plays*, Boulder, Col.: Shambhala.

INDEX

actors 25–6; early modern professional 31–2, terms used to describe 60, 64, 110–11, 155, 221n.2, female 32, 167, 219n.5; medieval 11, 31 (*see also* names of individual actors)

Adelman, J. 220n.2, 221n.3

adultery 62–5, 68, 69, 72–3, 107, 121, 130–3, 138–9; 188 (*see also* bastardy)

Africans 13, 219n.4, 223n.5, 224n.7

Agincourt, Battle of 3 (*see also* Henry V)

Alanson, Duke of (in *Henry VI, Part I*) 59, 218n.3

Alençon, Duke of (historical figure) 218

Amazons 35–6, 94, 204, 223n. 5, 227n.13

Amin, S. 13

anachronisms 39, 161, 164, 175,

Anderson, B. 12, 187, 209

Anne, Lady (in *Richard III*) 109–12, 200

antitheatrical charges 32, 101, 154, 164–5, 173–4, 183

Antony and Cleopatra 104, 173

An Apology for Actors 18, 185

Arden of Faversham 20

aristocracy, Elizabethan 143 (*see also* courtiers, nobles)

Aristotle 101

armies: women in 201–6, 226n.12 (*see also* women warriors)

Arthur, King 46, 168, 184

Arthur, Prince (in *King John*) 124, 127, 130, 132

Asherson, R. 9

atrocities committed by women 223n.5; Margaret's 94–95; Welsh women's 45, 137, 168–72

audience (*see* playgoers)

Austern, L. 172

authority: dynastic 26, 47–9, 158–9, 162; female 45–6; genealogical 46, 56, 90, 114–15, 162 (*see also* genealogy, legitimacy); historical 219n.6; masculine, based on achievement 47, 114, 142, 187, 198, 207–8 (*see also* performative masculinity); monarchial 12, 29–30, 37–8, 87, 114–15, 132, 147–57, 159–64, 168, 187, 214–15; patriarchal 5–6, 120, 131, 158–9, 187–8, 222n.2; Shakespeare's (*see* Shakespeare)

authorship (*see* collaborative authorship)

Auvergne, Countess of (Shakespearean character) 55, 57, 59–60, 63, 120, 192

Baker, T. 226n.8

Balibar, E. 13

Barasch, F. 219n.5

Bardolph 179, 181, 184

Barish, J. 32, 221n.2

Barnes, C. 23

238